MAR 2 0 2021

Magnolia Library

About Island Press

Since 1984, the nonprofit organization Island Press has been stimulating, shaping, and communicating ideas that are essential for solving environmental problems worldwide. With more than 1,000 titles in print and some 30 new releases each year, we are the nation's leading publisher on environmental issues. We identify innovative thinkers and emerging trends in the environmental field. We work with world-renowned experts and authors to develop cross-disciplinary solutions to environmental challenges.

Island Press designs and executes educational campaigns, in conjunction with our authors, to communicate their critical messages in print, in person, and online using the latest technologies, innovative programs, and the media. Our goal is to reach targeted audiences—scientists, policy makers, environmental advocates, urban planners, the media, and concerned citizens—with information that can be used to create the framework for long-term ecological health and human well-being.

Island Press gratefully acknowledges major support from The Bobolink Foundation, Caldera Foundation, The Curtis and Edith Munson Foundation, The Forrest C. and Frances H. Lattner Foundation, The JPB Foundation, The Kresge Foundation, The Summit Charitable Foundation, Inc., and many other generous organizations and individuals.

Generous support for this publication was provided by Katie Dolan.

The opinions expressed in this book are those of the author(s) and do not necessarily reflect the views of our supporters.

Unnatural Companions

Unnatural Companions

RETHINKING OUR LOVE OF PETS IN AN AGE OF WILDLIFE EXTINCTION

Peter Christie

ISLANDPRESS | Washington | Covelo

Copyright © 2020 Peter Christie

All rights reserved under International and Pan-American Copyright Conventions. No part of this book may be reproduced in any form or by any means without permission in writing from the publisher: Island Press, 2000 M Street, NW, Suite 650, Washington, DC 20036

ISLAND PRESS is a trademark of the Center for Resource Economics.

Library of Congress Control Number: 2019952209

All Island Press books are printed on environmentally responsible materials.

Manufactured in the United States of America
10 9 8 7 6 5 4 3 2 1

Keywords: Island Press, pets, conservation, biodiversity, biophilia, extinction, wildlife, cats, dogs, birds, exotic pets, Edward O. Wilson, sustainability, invasive species, wildlife disease, pet trade, pet food, pet industry, pet therapy, pet effect, nature deficit disorder, wildlife trapping, conservation dog, animal smuggling, parrot, axolotl, salamander, frog, snake, lizard , turtle, mammal, amphibian, reptile, fish, tropical fish, forage fish, Everglades, Burmese python, songbird, seabird, Xochimilco, Children's Hospital of Eastern Ontario, Cornwall, Ontario, Mexico City, Montana, Alberta, Florida, lion, wild dog, black-footed ferret, guardian dog, cockatoo

For Hannah and Laura, as always.

Humanity is exalted not because we are so far above other living creatures, but because knowing them elevates the very concept of life.
—E. O. Wilson, *Biophilia*

Whether society prefers to have wolves or dogs remains to be seen.
—1989 editorial, *Science* magazine

Contents

Prologue

My dog is watching. Lying not far from where I work, she's studying me. Around us, the morning is quiet; the sun is in the window, and the kids are at school. This is our habit: I type and glance at the dog; she lifts her head and returns my gaze. Her expression seems unmistakable: she wants to know what I'm thinking—I think. Day after day, often a couple of times in an hour, Maggie and I repeat this workspace ritual. I look, and she looks back. Her head tilts, and her ears cock. They are brief moments, but they're important. They're reassuring; our curiosity about one another, revisited again and again, is comforting. We share mutual incomprehension the way close friends swap stories. Something visceral and abiding and possibly essential is in it. (At least, for me; I can only guess for her.) It is—or so I imagine—the tensile filament that connects us.

Maggie is the family dog and my latest pet. I've lived with many others over the years: turtles, geese, lizards, fish, salamanders, hamsters, canaries, a gray squirrel. The list is long. Each time, I find myself believing the solitudes of our separate species are joined by some inscrutable link. When I was a teen, our family raised an orphaned raccoon. He would accompany me to a nearby pond after school where we'd climb the same waterside willow to watch beavers swim beneath. For a time, during university, I was a falconer. Learning mostly from books—like T. H. White, author of *The Goshawk*, who (clumsily) taught himself hawking out of his personal longing to "revert to a feral state"—I trained and flew a delightfully aerobatic European kestrel for years. I kept a noisy merlin for a time—an unfortunate "imprint" raised to think she was a person—and a prairie falcon named Mary after other falconers passed them into my care. The practice is ancient, and it felt that way. Sharing with these birds the exhilaration of flight, casting falcons from a fist to witness them knife through the air, is a tradition that goes back 4,000 years—to a time before the first Egyptians when the last of the woolly mammoths still roamed the land.[1]

Pet keeping is much older still. Its true origins, like many origins, are murky. One day around 30,000 to 40,000 years ago, the wolves joined our camp. A pup, lying somewhere in a dense Southeast Asian thicket, was happened upon by one of our ancestors who decided (remarkably) to scoop it up and raise it. Or maybe this was in northern Eurasia or in the Middle East or Europe. Maybe, according to a more recent suggestion, the wolves came willingly: A pregnant she-wolf—conditioned by millennia of mutually beneficial contact between our two hunting species—made her den next door. Her young habituated to their two-legged neighbors, and an unprecedented partnership was born. The wolves came home, and everything changed. Evolution—for both species—was forever transformed. The animals shrank and became less menacing. Their faces squared, and their teeth became smaller. Their ears drooped. They accepted our affection. They tuned in to our peculiar wants and mysteries. They became pets. They became Maggie.[2]

Why we humans wanted or agreed to this arrangement is far from obvious. The benefits of a domesticated wolf in our midst—as a hunting companion, a warning system, and protector—became clear quite quickly; wolf-pets soon gave their human minders an evolutionary leg up. Some say they helped launch our trajectory as future remodelers of the planet. But that came later. In the beginning, before the animal could be tamed, trained, or do anything beneficial, there was only a helpless, mewling whelp that required our care. And we were busy enough. The prospect of future utility could hardly justify the rash act of playing nanny to another species; there was too much front-end work. Consider today. Most pets stopped being essential to our survival centuries ago, but we keep more of them around than ever: pets in the United States now outnumber people. Nothing about their usefulness can explain this lopsided fact. The birth of pet keeping—the first impulse to raise creatures as companions—was undoubtedly about more than a shrewd recruiting strategy to help us get ahead. Some other inclination must have had a hand in it too. Quite possibly we were simply fascinated first.[3]

Four decades ago, the Pulitzer Prize–winning Harvard biologist Edward O. Wilson explained this kind of fascination: "Biophilia," he wrote, is our "innate tendency to focus on life and lifelike processes." We're intrigued by animals and other living things quite naturally, Wilson argued. Evolution may well have wired us that way. By paying close attention to creatures and plants, our hunter-gatherer forebears learned the secrets they needed to hunt, forage, and survive. Over thousands of millennia, natural selection fixed the tendency into our DNA. It's fundamental to who we are. Wilson recognized the idea as profound. He also saw it as profoundly hopeful. Now in his tenth decade, the eminent biologist remains one of the world's most impassioned voices for wildlife conservation. Years of fieldwork in distant jungles made him a horrified witness to the accelerating spectacle of plant and animal extinctions worldwide. Humans are transforming the planet in a way no other creature has before us. The earth's living tapestry is being unstrung, and the loss of species threatens the natural systems upon which all of us—wild organisms and people alike—depend. Biophilia, he reasoned, could be a key to our salvation. Acknowledging and encouraging our innate love of other life might help curb our ecological recklessness: "In other words," he wrote, "instinct in this rare instance is aligned with reason. The conclusion I draw is optimistic: to the degree that we come to understand other organisms, we will place a greater value on them, and on ourselves."[4]

This is the story of how biophilia went wrong. It's about what we can do to fix it. Our love of pets is at its heart: while Wilson hoped our innate fascination with other organisms would inspire us to end the extinction of wildlife, our connection to creatures is increasingly expressed not through our relationship with nature but through our companionship with pets. From the day we began coaxing wolves to become dogs, our urge to link our lives to other species has been transformed and subverted by our insistence that they live by our terms and by our side. With the human population exceeding 7.7 billion, the number of owned and captive dogs, cats, birds, fish, turtles, lizards, and other beasts around the world has soared like never before. Now, as the chapters of this book describe, our animals at home are profoundly affecting the survival of their remaining brethren in the wild. The stories I tell reflect just some of those I encountered combining journalistic purpose and chance, but similar examples are all around us: biophilia—expressed as an ancient and apparently visceral desire to keep creatures for company—has spawned a multibillion-dollar pet and pet products industry that's paradoxically contributing to a global conservation crisis. It's threatening the very diversity of life that—according to Wilson's hypothesis—we're evolutionarily programmed to cherish. Almost without notice and certainly without intent, Maggie has become a menace.

Or, not necessarily. My pet, like yours, doesn't have to be the problem. On the contrary, creature companionship can transform our relationship with other life. My intention in this book is to create awareness about the ways in which pet keeping—often without our knowledge—is threatening the variety of life so vital to this planet and to human society. But there's more: my hope is that these pages will help those of us who keep pets to recognize ourselves as essential to turning the tide of vanishing wildlife. Pet owners—the legions of us who intuitively understand our inner devotion to nonhuman creatures—are vital to this critical time in nature conservation. Our animal companions can draw our insulated, increasingly urban species closer to the wild world beyond us. They can catalyze awareness and understanding and even help save beleaguered species. They can inspire in us an urge to champion life, to step up for nature.

The aim of this book is not to cause pet keepers to recoil or feel guilt. It is, instead, a call to action. None are more aware than pet owners of the mystery and satisfaction behind our ties to other species. None are more intuitively familiar with the urging of biophilia. Pet practices can change direction when we know where they've strayed off course. Pet owners can do the steering. This vast pet-owning community of the world's greatest animal lovers—my community—is essential to solving these problems. My wish is for this book's readers to finally recognize our place as pet keepers and animal lovers as the best hope for a new conservation nation. In times of extraordinary environmental change and with a wild world more delicate than ever, nature—the nature to which our pets and other animals belong—needs us.

CHAPTER 1
The Biophilia Paradox

Xochimilco Ecological Park in southern Mexico City is incongruously calm. The city around it, teeming with some 21 million people, is one of the most populated metropolitan centers in the Western Hemisphere. It's a Latin American megalopolis, and it roils and churns. Twisting freeways and tumbling barrios stretch from one side of the Valley of Mexico to the other. Some two million cars and trucks choke the streets. (Municipal driving restrictions haven't helped the city's air quality, considered among the worst in the Americas.) Historic plazas are filled with restaurants and music. Businesspeople and vendors jostle. It's a restless and relentless place, pressed inward on all sides by the ragged peaks of volcanic mountains.

Xochimilco park, meanwhile, is a near-silent sanctuary in the thick of it. The roughly two-square-kilometer (0.8 square mile) nature reserve is flanked on all sides by the insistent city, but its watery, green paradise seems quietly unfazed. Equable. Tranquil canals pass lush, artificial islands—known as "floating gardens," or *chinampas*—created by pre-Columbian farmers centuries ago. Willows line the banks, while egrets and gallinules wait in the reeds. Brazilian water lilies float by.

Xochimilco somehow resists even the sound of the clamoring city that surrounds it. As the urban hurricane of Mexico's capital howls, the park is like the storm's weirdly tranquil eye. A sense of pause is here, as if besieged nature itself is holding its breath.

Alejandro Martinez moves our flat-bottomed boat through one of the park's lush channels, pushing us silently with a long, thin pole. "It's pretty chill here," he says, dryly.

Martinez is my guide to this national protected area (and World Heritage Site). He's a relaxed, lanky post-Millennial in sagging jeans and a black Brooklyn Nets ball cap. It's the uniform of a young man more at home at a dance club, out in the energized urban world beyond this sleepy scene. But Martinez grew up here on the edge of the park, and his affection for it is deep. He fished its canals as a boy and even farmed flowers with his uncle on a traditional *chinampa* for a time. The peacefulness, he admits, can be downright coma inducing, and—compared with the lively seven years he spent working, playing, and learning English in North Carolina—the pace of the refuge takes some getting used to. Nevertheless, he says, Xochimilco is where he's most comfortable: the wildlife, the sense of old Mexico, and the feel of lost time make Martinez charmingly protective of the place. Xochimilco's famous endangered salamanders, for example, matter to him.

The salamanders are called axolotls, and they're almost completely gone from here. Beneath us, under the still surface of this inky water, the last few hundred of the strange, rubbery, and entirely aquatic amphibians face a final struggle against total annihilation in the wild. That's because the roughly 170 kilometers (106 miles) of canals crisscrossing Xochimilco comprise the beleaguered creature's only natural home. The channels are all that remain of a system of lakes where the salamander—also known as the Mexican walking fish—once thrived and where it once wriggled its way into the cultural consciousness of Mexico's early Mesoamerican history.

Centuries ago, for instance, the powerhouse Aztec empire built its flourishing capital of Tenochtitlán on these waters not far from where we're floating, and its people revered the salamander as a god. Axolotl—according to the story—was the crafty twin brother to one of the most supreme of Aztec deities, Quetzalcoatl. Faced with the threat of being sacrificed to the sun, Axolotl slipped away, eventually disguising himself as a salamander to hide in the greasy mud. For centuries of Mexican life since, axolotls have remained a powerful, symbolic presence—even as the lakes were drained away and Mexico's modern capital crowded around them. They've been a food delicacy. They've been medicine. They've been a significant symbol of the nation's identity. Today, the Mexican senate is considering a national "Day of the Axolotl" to celebrate the famous creature—even if the honor may come too late.[1]

"I give them two more years," says Martinez, matter-of-factly. Martinez has witnessed the staggering free fall of the salamander's population firsthand. Not many years ago, he says, catching axolotls was as easy as the simple toss of a throw net. You wouldn't wait long, watching for the telltale dimple on the surface when the salamanders rise to gulp air. Not anymore. The dimples and the salamanders are all but gone, he says.

Scientific surveys bear him out: A first thorough census of the axolotls in 1998 estimated about 6,000 axolotls could be found per square kilometer (0.4 square mile) in Xochimilco's waterways. A follow-up study a few years later revealed the number had dropped to 1,000. By 2008, it was down to a hundred. More recently, estimates for the species—declared critically endangered in 2006—suggest a mere 35 of the animals per square kilometer remain. And even that may be optimistic: for a while in 2015, scientists were certain the wild axolotls had blinked out of existence for good—but happily one showed up a few weeks later.[2]

Martinez poles us over to a bamboo shack beside the canal, a stone's throw from his childhood home. Here, he shows me a living display of the cast of characters in the axolotl's recent tragic drama. A painted sign announces "El Ajolotario," and in the dim, otherwise-barren hut, a local fisherman has arranged a rickety bank of aquariums for tourists to view. Many are filled with mottled brown or pale axolotls—motionless and blank eyed, with great, gummy grins. Other tanks hold Nile tilapia and carp. These are among the chief villains in the axolotl story. The nonnative fish were introduced to Xochimilco's waterways by the government in the 1970s and 1980s to encourage local fish farming. The numbers, however, soon got out of control. Now, while legions of carp vacuum axolotl eggs and larvae from the bottom, the voracious tilapia gobble them as they swim. Pollution from the surrounding city, meanwhile, means the salamander's watery home is not only infested with introduced predators, it's often too salty, alkaline, and contaminated with chemicals for the animals to thrive.[3]

Martinez stands beside me, peering at the tanks. "It's not easy for them, man," he says. "It's like they don't stand a chance."

There's a profound irony in the axolotl story: while the wild salamanders of Xochimilco teeter at oblivion's edge, tens of thousands of these animals are nevertheless alive and well and living in home aquariums around the world. No other amphibian, perhaps, is more globally popular as an endearing fish-tank pet.

And none, perhaps, is better suited to the role. Axolotls, unlike most other salamanders, never grow up. They're "Peter Pan" animals, stuck in their underwater larval phase never to emerge in an adult form on land. (To scientists, animals that keep juvenile characteristics throughout life are called "neotenic.") The axolotls grow, but they never really change. Their heads remain broad and flat with black-dot eyes. Their external gills stay perched on their heads like cartoon antlers. Their look is oddly infantile, and it's a big hit with enthusiastic aquarists around the world. Online peddlers—with names like BuyAxolotls.com and The Axolotl

Factory—ship them by air via the US postal service. And the axolotls, for their part, seem perfectly content. Resting drowsily at the bottom of their well-lit tanks, rising occasionally to gulp down commercially available bloodworms, pet axolotls are living the dog's life—almost literally.

"This is the challenge," biologist Luis Zambrano tells me when we meet in his office at the National Autonomous University of Mexico, some 15 kilometers (9 miles) from Xochimilco's quiet oasis. "Pet axolotls are everywhere."

Zambrano is sitting forward in his chair, pressing his short salt-and-pepper beard into his fist. He has the look of a man who has trouble keeping still, and his bleary-eyed energy is infectious. Zambrano is on a mission: he's been trying to save Mexico's wild axolotls—and their troubled Xochimilco ecosystem—since he was first asked to count the animals almost 20 years ago. "They knew there was a problem," Zambrano recalls, "but they didn't know how big." The biologist and his team documented the first evidence of the salamander's calamitous crash, and they've been working since to engage governments, international groups, and, importantly, the local *chimpaneros*—farmers who still work the *chinampa* island plots—to save them. Their focus is the salamander but also its beleaguered habitat, a last remnant of Mexico City's wetlands and a key piece in mitigating the local impacts of climate change. The axolotl is a so-called umbrella species: their continued presence signals a healthy ecosystem; their sudden absence, on the other hand, means something else. "If we lose the axolotl, we will lose Xochimilco," says Zambrano, "and Xochimilco is highly important."

Zambrano's work—including efforts to improve the water, cordon off sections of canal from the invading fish, and reintroduce captive-bred, wild-stock axolotls—isn't easy. Engaging farmers is essential, but many of them require convincing. It's a race, explains Zambrano, that pits time-demanding ecological restoration against the scientific near certainty that—all things being equal—the salamanders will be extinct by 2025. The biologist pauses to correct his last phrase: "Extinct in the *wild*," he says.

Pet axolotls aren't going anywhere. Most of these pets—as well as the many axolotls living in research laboratories worldwide—are the lucky descendants of just 34 ancestors taken from Xochimilco and shipped to Paris more than 160 years ago. Scientists at the time were fascinated by the strange creature's unusual life cycle and its remarkable ability to regrow severed toes, legs, and tails. A bonus was the fact that the salamanders were easy to keep and not shy about breeding in captivity any time of year. The Paris axolotls soon became scientific celebrities, and thousands of their offspring were subsequently distributed to eager biologists throughout Europe. Much of our basic understanding about early developmental biology emerged from these labs. Today, the salamander is still widely used in laboratory studies. Scientists explore mechanisms behind tissue and nerve regeneration—often in the hunt for better treatment for people with spinal cord injuries, severed limbs, or brain damage.[4]

The University of Kentucky's Ambystoma Genetic Stock Center is an axolotl breeding facility that supplies thousands of salamanders to labs throughout North America and elsewhere. Yet, the pedigree of even these animals—beginning with a group shipped from Krakow, Poland—traces back to the original Paris colony. Despite periodic efforts to stir the genetic pot with wild specimens or by hybridizing axolotls with tiger salamanders, the laboratory population is highly inbred. Malformations, such as too many toes, are becoming more common. Not long ago, the center itself experienced a mysterious massive die-off. The same genetic bottleneck faces the domestic population of pet axolotls. While these salamanders may look comfortable in their home aquariums and laboratory tanks, researchers worry the loss of genetic diversity risks epidemics. It also raises the possibility that the salamanders in captivity may be simply missing some of the key characteristics that make their wild Xochimilco counterparts unique. In truth, they may not be the same anymore.[5]

More than that, argues Zambrano, they're not wild: the idea that thriving pet populations somehow make the salamander's disappearance from its native home more palatable misses an essential point. Only wild axolotls represent the critical ecology of Mexico City's most famous refuge, he says. The wild salamanders alone can be considered the same animals central to Mexico's collective imagination and culture for 500 years. Only the remaining axolotls swimming free in Xochimilco's dark water survive as what Zambrano describes as "the most important species in Mexico." The pet axolotls around the world are something else entirely.

"I use polar bears [as an example], because everybody knows polar bears," he says. "We could say, 'Okay, let's save polar bears. Let's buy a huge fridge and put them all in there.' But it's not the same. The importance of the polar bear is that it lives in the North Pole and the North Pole is melting down. It's the same with the axolotls. We could have all the axolotls in all the tanks in all the world—we have it, actually; there's no problem about that—but the problem is that these are *not* the axolotls that live in the wild in Xochimilco. And that's the difference."

Unfortunately, it's a difference most people seem unable—or unwilling—to see.

For the majority, especially the billions of us who live in cities, pets are what we think of first when we think of animals. They're what we're familiar with. Encountering dogs or cats or even caged canaries is both likely and frequent in the lives we lead. For many of us, a pet may even greet us at the door or watch us from an aquarium. Meeting wild animals where they live, on the other hand, is far less likely (city park squirrels and starlings excepted). Most wildlife is out of sight and out of mind, pets have our attention. In a simple Google search, for instance, cat videos outnumber wildlife videos by an order of magnitude (2.9 billion compared with 275 million).

In some cases, even when we think of wild creatures, we discover more of them in our tamed, domestic environment than beyond it. A glimpse of the nearly extinct-in-the-wild axolotl, for example, is more assuredly accomplished at a local pet shop than in Mexico. Seeing an iconic tiger—another disappearing and endangered species on the International Union for Conservation of Nature's Red List—is now far more likely in the backyards of American pet owners than in any of its native habitats around the globe. Several troubled bird species—Indonesia's critically endangered black-winged mynahs, for example—are also more common in the cages of bird fanciers than they are in treetops. Père David's deer from China and the scimitar-horned oryx of North Africa were absent from the wild for years. They were extinct from their natural homes, surviving only in enclosures kept and protected by human caregivers until recent reintroduction efforts began.[6]

Increasingly, pets *are* the animals of our world. In 2018, about 393.3 million pet dogs, cats, fish, birds, reptiles, and other small animals were at home in more than two-thirds (84.6 million) of American households. Today, companion animals in the United States significantly outnumber their human owners (by as much as 66.1 million in 2018, according to the American Pet Products Association). Canada, too, is plump with pets. At last count, about 41 percent of Canadian households are home to about 7.6 million dogs, and 37 percent housed 8.8 million cats. Almost half of people in the United Kingdom keep, in total, about 51 million pets, and it's not much different in a lot of other nations around the world. Brazil, for example, holds the top spot as a keeper of caged birds (more than 190 million of them).[7]

Pets are the creatures we see and the creatures we know. They're also the creatures we feel attached to—often very deeply. Nine of every 10 pet owners, for instance, consider their pet to be a member of their family. In 2018, for instance, Americans spent about $72.6 billion on their pets, according to the American Pet Products Association, more than double the spending from just 15 years earlier. The gross domestic product of any of the majority of countries around the world is billions less. It's a lot, but why not? We love our pets. For many of us, the magnitude of this attachment can be downright disorienting. In an American Animal Hospital Association poll a few years ago, for example, half of US and Canadian pet owners said they'd pick a dog or a cat to be their sole companion on a deserted island compared with 47 percent who said they'd choose another person. More than 9 of every 10 respondents also told pollsters they were "very likely" or "somewhat likely" to risk their life for the sake of their pet. Small wonder, then, that pets have become the regular subject of heated custody battles in the bitter-but-common world of divorce.[8]

There's something about pets; our response to them is visceral, familiar, and occasionally fearsome. It's almost as if they are people too. But not quite. Common denominators exist, say researchers, but most of us don't generally seem to think and feel that our relationships with pets and those with people are interchangeable. How we see pets—and we see a lot of them—is separate, and the feelings they evoke, strong as they are, are not the same ones arising from our interactions with people. It more closely compares with our human response to animals more generally: creatures—all creatures, the ones at home or otherwise—fascinate us.[9]

Animals command our attention in a way that other inanimate, non-living things simply don't. We can't take our eyes off them. We track birds coursing the sky and recoil at climbing spiders. If an animal is in a scene, our attention flies to it like an arrow. We can't help ourselves. For children, especially, creatures are magnetic and irresistibly so. The inclination seems to begin at birth. Our wonder at animals, including pets, may not be the same as our fundamental need for other human company, but it's probably no less primal or ingrained. It is, very likely, a modern relative of a distant, original, and ancestral human fact—we're simply enthralled by other life.

Forty years ago, Harvard scientist Edward O. Wilson came up with a name for this enchantment: "Biophilia," as he calls it, "is the innately emotional affiliation of human beings to other living organisms."[10]

After decades of pondering the ways people see and react to nature, Wilson theorized that our urge to affiliate with other living beings is no mere personal preference; it's more likely a biological imperative. It's probably rooted in our DNA. The fundamental tendency to distinguish life from nonlife and to "move toward it like moths to a porch light" seems to be an urge passed down through generations. While most of us can hardly cast our minds back to a time before cell phones, more than 99 percent of human history exists before any technology at all, before we settled into farms or towns, back when our ancestors lived crude and often-desperate lives as roaming hunter-gatherers. That's when most of the genetic blueprint for our species evolved to distinguish us from other apes. That's when natural selection—the perpetuation of genetic changes through improved survival and a better chance at leaving descendants—was busily shaping our bodies and honing our behavior. Our approach to learning about the world was molded at the time as well.[11]

Biophilia, argues Wilson, makes evolutionary sense. Since the earliest emergence of our genus, *Homo*, our intimate understanding of life around us has been crucial. Paying attention to wildlife and natural history, for instance, would have been necessary for a successful hunt; to kill an animal, as any hunter will tell you, you have to know how and where it lives. Basic botany is needed to find seasonal fruit in the right place at the right time. Meanwhile, failing to notice the approach of a lion or misidentifying a toxic plant could be fatal. Our forebears—the ones who came out ahead in the evolutionary race—were those whose brains and intelligence naturally latched onto and learned the ways of wildlife. It may seem foreign and distant to those of us in cities today, but hundreds of thousands of years ago, if you didn't notice nature, you didn't last long.

Think of snakes. They're the best-known example, and Wilson returns to them a few times to make the biophilia case. Venomous snakes with neurotoxins potent enough to paralyze or kill large animals, including apes, were around long before humans came on the scene. Early evolution would have done well to program our species to learn to avoid them— and that appears to be exactly what happened. In human societies around the world, serpents are a kind of malignant common denominator. People everywhere hold snakes in a strange sort of awe that readily gives way to fear. In ancient Egypt, for example, spitting cobras were a symbol of fearsome sovereignty and divine authority. The Aztecs of Mesoamerica, meanwhile, gave all their wrathful gods snakelike qualities, including their supreme deity, Quetzalcoatl (meaning "feathered serpent"). Today, in the United States, more than 38,000 people are killed by guns every year while only about 5 die from snakebites, yet modern Americans are far more likely to shrink from a legless reptile than from a firearm.[12]

When psychologists first wondered about this aversion to snakes, experiments with rhesus monkeys pointed to clues. Researchers discovered lab-reared monkeys with no exposure to snakes weren't inherently afraid of them, but they readily learned the fear after seeing wild monkeys react in terror. The horror itself didn't seem to be hardwired; it was learned. Yet, when scientists used video trickery to suggest that the wild monkey mentors were also frightened by a flower, the naive lab monkeys didn't fear flowers as a result. That kind of fear couldn't be taught. In other words, some sort of innate pattern of learning was at work: the monkeys weren't born with a fear of snakes, but they readily took ophidiophobia lessons to heart. More recent research involving humans reveals something similar. Scientists found both adults and babies could detect images of snakes among a variety of nonthreatening objects more quickly than they could spot flowers, frogs, or caterpillars. Another study showed infants as young as six months dilated their pupils—a sign of stress—when faced with a picture of a snake compared with images of flowers and fish.[13]

Our seemingly innate focus on living nature, says Wilson, is really a set of rules for learning. Our attention is naturally drawn to the wild world because we're inherently primed for the lessons it offers. Our insistent need to know about the life around us has been so influential in our evolutionary history that our brains naturally veer in that direction—even as we try to technologically distance ourselves from it. Our appetite for knowledge wants biological food first. Our imaginations can't survive without it. Animals, plants, and vast, untrammeled landscapes are fuel for our powers of metaphor and myth, connection, and understanding. Human curiosity was formed in a grassy, leafy, living place. Our sense of wonder, suggests Wilson, dwells there still.

Wilson is arguably one of the world's greatest living biologists. His nine decades of inquisitive life, all of them spent pondering this teeming planet, make him uniquely qualified to make the biophilia claim. For the better part of a century, he's been the world's leading authority on ants, a cofounder of the theory of island biogeography (understanding the evolutionary consequences of geographic isolation), the father of sociobiology (the controversial science of genetically based social behavior in animals and people), an advocate for ideas of gene-culture coevolution, and a two-time Pulitzer Prize–winning author. He is a tall, slender, stately man with a great lick of parted gray hair and a warm, thoughtful face. He is also a rare figure in the field of biology: a passionate conservationist who, even after witnessing firsthand many wildlife and wilderness losses across this beleaguered globe, remains resolutely hopeful. His notion of biophilia comes from there: "The conclusion I draw is optimistic," he writes in his book-length exploration of the idea published in 1984. "[T]o the degree that we come to understand other organisms, we will place a greater value on them, and on ourselves."[14]

In a swelling, rapturous, nineteenth-century fashion, Wilson champions biophilia as a way to marry his evolutionary thinking with his extraordinary emotional response to biology and to the transcendent grandeur of life. The science behind the hypothesis, consequently, has been pretty hard to test. Research into human psychology and animal behavior continues to support the natural (and seemingly universal) affinity to notice and avoid snakes and, similarly, spiders (another group with deadly members). Other studies, meanwhile, suggest people may prefer—and sometimes create—landscapes that look and feel similar to the open, grassy, African savannah where our ancestors long-ago evolved. These days, biophilia turns up most often in designing cities and buildings, making spaces and places more amenable to our thirst for the natural.[15]

When Wilson first proposed his idea, however, his aim was elsewhere: he hoped his biophilia hypothesis would become the rationale for a new conservation ethic—inspiration not only to spare nature and nonhuman species but to save the human spirit from consequently losing its way. To the legendary biologist, the living world beyond us is essential to both the ecological processes we depend on and the intellectual and imaginative world within us. Nature is our endless well of mysteries and the only place our thirst for knowledge can properly find a drink. The human-made world just doesn't cut it. In a world surrounded by artifacts of our making, our gene-driven preference is still for the natural, living elements that typified our existence millennia ago. In nature, each mystery explained gives rise to new ones, and our appetite for knowing moves from one to the next; our attraction to the great variety and complexity of life is central to this search. This restlessness, says Wilson, best characterizes who we are as humans. It moves us forward and gives us meaning. If we allow other species to disappear, our pathways to inquiry and understanding—or even to aesthetic satisfaction and creativity—will disappear with them. Without new life and new places to urge us on, we will be stuck and listless. Dullness would settle like dust. "Without beauty and mystery beyond itself," Wilson explains, "the mind by definition is deprived of its bearings and will drift to simpler and cruder configurations."[16]

If people knew what our genes know, if we realized how essential other life is to our inherent yearning to understand it, if we acknowledged the imperative of our inbuilt biophilia, we would, of course, make wildlife a priority. We would work harder to save it—and to protect the vanishing world for which our mind and spirit were fashioned by evolution. It only makes sense. When Wilson initially outlined his theory, such a sunny outcome seemed obvious: "I suggest," he writes, "that as biological knowledge grows the ethic will shift fundamentally so that everywhere, for reasons that have to do with the very fiber of the brain, the fauna and flora of a country will be thought part of the national heritage as important as its art, its language, and that astonishing blend of achievement and farce that has always defined our species."[17]

It hasn't turned out that way.

Ecologist Gerardo Ceballos was 11 when he first realized the world's wildlife was in trouble. Ceballos grew up in the countryside west of Mexico's capital and, as a boy, happily searched for snakes and salamanders in the fields, woods, and marshlands surrounding his home. He was also an avid reader. That year, the young naturalist got his hands on a condensed Reader's Digest version of Fred Bodsworth's 1954 novel, *Last of the Curlews*, in Spanish. The story, a classic in nature writing, follows the imagined migration and vain search for a mate by a solitary male shorebird that's the last of its kind. The tale is fiction, but it presaged the real-life annihilation of the Eskimo curlew, a once immensely common species that migrated the length of the world but was eventually wiped out by hunters. Much of the book takes place in the Arctic—a barely comprehensible place for a boy in central Mexico—but the end of the novel, says Ceballos, left him deeply affected.

"I remember it said, 'the last of the dying species, he flies alone' or something like that. That really got me," he remembers, thoughtfully. "So, I decided then what I wanted to do is to try to save species from extinction."

Today, almost 50 years later—and four decades after Edward O. Wilson first proposed his buoyant notion of biophilia—Ceballos is still trying. And he's still waiting for the tide of disappearing wildlife to turn: "We're really in a massive extinction crisis," Ceballos tells me. His words have the sound of a plea. "Just for animals, to stop the extinction crisis, what we do in the next 20 to 30 years will define what's left on earth. . . . The sense of urgency is huge. We need to do something. We need to do something fast."

Ceballos's office at the National Autonomous University of Mexico's Institute of Ecology is next door and just down the hill from the biology building where Luis Zambrano works with his axolotls. Like Zambrano, Ceballos is a deeply passionate man. His features are heavy and brooding, and his dark eyes have the wistful, melancholic look of a Spanish poet. As a scientist, he is top-notch, even as he wears his worry on his sleeve. Here, at the Institute of Ecology, he is something of an academic superstar. In his more than two decades researching mammalian ecology and conservation, he's racked up multiple international scientific awards, including a Guggenheim Fellowship, and published thousands of academic and popular articles as well as more than two dozen books. His conservation work across his country has helped convince the government to preserve vast tracts of Mexican wildland as nature preserves.

These days, his main aim is to warn the world that today's pace of wildlife loss is both exceptional and exceptionally worrying. Working frequently with celebrated Stanford University biologist and writer Paul Ehrlich—best known for his decades of dire warnings about human population growth—Ceballos is on a mission as conservation's Cassandra. The immensity of the current biodiversity crisis still hasn't penetrated the global consciousness, he says. It needs to. Only five other times in the billions of years of life's history has the planet witnessed the die-off of global species this sudden and this massive. Those events were brought about by natural catastrophes—such as a giant meteor crash that wiped out dinosaurs and three-quarters of all species some 65 million years ago. That was the fifth and most recent mass extinction event before now. Today, the speed and scale at which creatures and plants are disappearing are too similar to those past events to ignore. For Ceballos—and many other conservation biologists—the evidence is clear: our current period of extraordinary wildlife loss has reached number six on the calamity hit list. "We are in the sixth mass extinction," he explains. One notable difference stands out, however: this time the cause of the biodiversity crisis isn't some freak occurrence in the natural world. This time we humans are to blame. The cause of the catastrophe is us. "In the last paper, we call it biological annihilation," says Ceballos, "because we're looking at the systematic annihilation of everything, you know."

That research, published in the *Proceedings of the National Academy of Sciences* in 2017, looks beyond the loss of species to the staggering decline in sheer numbers of animals: populations for one-third of the 27,600 vertebrate species examined by Ceballos and his colleagues are shrinking. Many of them dramatically. As days go by, fewer mammals, birds, reptiles, and amphibians are living in fewer places around the planet. In the past few centuries, hundreds of thousands to as many as a billion individual populations of all these species have disappeared altogether. For mammals, including wild cats, rodents, deer, and others, almost half have seen the ranges they once roamed reduced by more than 80 percent since 1900. Even thousands of abundant and sometimes ubiquitous species are among those whose numbers are dwindling. This last troubling fact—the decline of common species—is one that's often missed when studies focus on only extinctions or animals at risk and adds a new, rattling dimension to the scale of the crisis. In 2019, for example, falling numbers of some of the most common bird species over the past 50 years—including the ubiquitous European starling—were reported in the journal *Science* to have contributed to a loss of almost one-third of all of this continent's feathered creatures since 1970. These days, you don't have to be rare (yet) to be in trouble. Our destruction of habitat, our overexploitation, our ferrying of invasive creatures to places they don't belong, our pollution, and our contributions to climate change are equal-opportunity threats.[18]

And the problem is getting worse—fast. A couple of years ago, Ceballos led another team to see just how quickly life's great variety is racing toward oblivion. Using what we know from animal fossils, the scientists estimated the "background" rate for extinctions—before humans had a chance to really mess things up—was about two species of mammals lost for every 10,000 species every 100 years. Since 1500, however, the change has accelerated, and in the past two centuries—following the Industrial Revolution—extinction rates have soared. In the last 120 years alone, almost 500 species of mammals, birds, reptiles, amphibians, and fish have likely vanished forever. It's a tally that would have taken perhaps 10,000 years to disappear at the background rate before humans got here. Even this new extinction-rate calculation, says Ceballos, is likely conservative. "We're underestimating," he says.[19]

In 2019, an independent international science group—the Intergovernmental Science-Policy Platform on Biodiversity and Ecosystem Services—announced that as many as one million species around the world are currently threatened with extinction. The number, based on a consensus by hundreds of experts and other researchers from 50 countries, made headlines around the world when it was included in the group's global assessment of biodiversity. One in every five backboned species we know of is at risk of being erased from the earth, and each year, say scientists, about 52 different mammals, birds, and amphibians move one species-at-risk category closer to oblivion. Many biologists believe countless other species are vanishing even before science—so far familiar with about 1.7 million of the planet's billions of living species—knows they exist. Take insects, for example. Estimates suggest four out of every five insect species remain to be discovered, but the panel report suggests about half a million of these species are at risk of disappearing. In 2017, a German study made news around the world—a favored headline was "Insect Armageddon"—when it found the abundance of flying insects in German nature reserves had fallen to just a quarter of what it was just 27 years ago, as measured by weight.[20]

It's no small matter. Some warn of what they call an "extinction cascade," whereby the loss of one species, such as a butterfly or a bee, leads to the secondary extinction of a plant it pollinates, which, in turn, means the end of a specialist plant-eating animal and so on. As more and more of the living pieces in an ecosystem go missing, the system itself risks breaking down. Try removing the parts of your car one by one while still expecting it to get you somewhere. To Ceballos's way of thinking, our general and seemingly growing disregard for the sanctity of life's variety is like that. If we fail to stop more creatures from vanishing, the natural ecological functions of the world—the ones that keep our air and water clean and our food supply healthy—will most certainly falter. Some scientists warn that our mounting environmental insults may soon take us to a worldwide ecological "tipping point." Wildlife may be feeling the worst of it now, says Ceballos, but the reckoning for our own species is probably not far off.[21]

"Many scientists in many different fields feel there may be a collapse in civilization if this trend continues in the next 20 to 30 years," Ceballos tells me. His matter-of-factness is chilling.

Sometime in the mid-to-late 1800s—when Charles Dickens was chronicling the crowded squalor of London and Charles Darwin was championing his queer notion of "descent with modification"—the size of humanity's great mass eclipsed that of all the wild land mammals on earth.

The human population, according to one remarkable estimate, had grown until there were more of us *by weight* than the combined mass of all our wild mammal brethren. In the race to become the world's greatest life force, we had finally streaked past nature. Soon, we would leave it behind in our dust. By 1900, we weighed one-third more than wild mammals, and by the end of the following century—after the total weight of mammalian wildlife plummeted by half and the mass of people quadrupled—we became 10 times more abundant (by weight). Now, 7.7 billion of us dwell on this busy planet, and by midcentury, the number could be more like 10 billion. We have arrived at a point at which we absolutely dwarf the wild world. Like the proverbial bull in a china shop, we can scarcely move without breaking something.[22]

Unfortunately, we're a fidgety species. More than three-quarters of the earth's land surface (not including Antarctica) and almost 90 percent of oceans have been directly affected by what we've done so far. Between 1993 and 2009 alone, the total wilderness flattened to build new farms, towns, and mines around the world equaled an area larger than India. Where the wild lands go, so goes the wildlife; many consider our changes to the global landscape—for agriculture and development—amount to the single greatest threat to life's diversity in millions of years. But there are others. Our surging population now means excessive hunting, fishing, and harvesting (that is, taking more wildlife than can replenish itself) threaten more than 70 percent of the species facing extinction around the world. Climate change isn't helping. A fifth of the world's land surface is expected to see large-scale shifts in climate by the end of the century, thanks to the greenhouse gas consequences from our fondness for oil. Plants and animals that can't stand the heat will be forced to move or perish. Meanwhile, our penchant for polluting and spreading invasive species and disease only seems to gather steam.[23]

People, after all, will be people. And people—the growing billions of us—will keep pets.

There's the rub. In his inimitably hopeful way, Edward O. Wilson imagined a growing awareness of our innate biophilia would make our species—even in our clumsy, outsized dominance of the world—more caring about the nonhuman life around us. Our hardwired wonder for other beings was supposed to add delicacy to the way we manage our shared planet. Instead, biophilia may have found another outlet: pets. While one recent estimate suggests the total numbers of wild backboned creatures on earth have been cut by more than half in the last 50 years, the population of pets (at least, dogs and cats in the United States) has more than doubled during the same period. There's no sign the trend is slowing. Thirty million puppies and kittens are born in the United States each year—a ratio of seven pets born for every human birth. More pet birds, lizards, and other exotic beasts are bred or brought from the jungle. We may finally be acknowledging our genetic need for and attachment to animals—as Wilson wished—but not in the wild; we've brought them into our homes instead. Our soaring numbers of pets have become, as author and University of Bristol professor John Bradshaw suggests, our wildlife on demand.[24]

Our relationship with the natural world, meanwhile, is growing more estranged. More than half of the world's population already dwells in cities, and by midcentury, two out of every three of us will be leading urban lives. The proportion of people who will ever set foot in a wilderness is growing smaller. Those who've met a moose on a trail or watched a heron over an evening marsh are a smaller and smaller percentage of us. For the growing majority—among our swelling numbers in cities around the world—dogs, cats, and other pets are our chief experience and familiarity with animals. It's the pets we meet—and the pets we keep—that have our attention now. We're drawn to them in the way we've always been drawn to other living creatures. And, as Wilson predicted, the urge remains seemingly ancient, deep-seated, and stirring. The only difference is that the animals we're focused on aren't wild; they live with us. Increasingly, we seem to prefer having animals in *our* lives to visiting them in theirs.[25]

That's not all. Pets and the pet industry are not only replacing the role of nature in our human experience, they're devastating wildlife directly. In myriad ways, pets pose a clear threat to the wonderful, wild splendor of the rest of life on earth: cats and dogs stalk wildlife as human-subsidized killers; jungles are robbed of animals to satisfy the pet trade; diseases deadly to wild creatures are spread by globe-trotting pets; released pets in nonnative habitats (such as pythons in the Everglades) eat every wild animal in sight or squeeze them out as indomitable competitors; and the pet food business, with its insatiable demand, drains our oceans of vital forage fish.[26] The impacts are considerable. Over the past five centuries, pets have been among the leading culprits in clobbering literally hundreds of species of threatened and extinct birds, mammals, reptiles, and amphibians around the globe. Domestic cats alone have helped obliterate more than 60 species in that period—including the Stephens Island wren of New Zealand and the Hawaiian crow—creatures lost forever from the rich variety of our living planet. Dogs have been linked to the extinction of 11. Other pets, and the pet industry that supports them, have been linked to other dwindling wildlife populations around the world.[27]

Our biophilia has become fraught. Our love of pets is contributing to what is arguably the greatest environmental crisis faced by global ecosystems. The irony is that pet people are the same animal people the wild world needs to help get it back on its feet. Pet owners care more about animals; they're more likely to watch birds or to become enthralled by nature documentaries. The only problem is our affection for the animals we hold close at home is obscuring our view of those out of reach in nature. We're fond of our pets. They're part of our families. But the wild creatures of the world are vital too. They're the machinery of natural systems and hold the keys to our survival. They're part of our evolutionary history and essential to how we think. They're wild and, unlike pets, remain aloof from our pedestrian lives and human routine: untamed, their mystery survives, complex, inscrutable, and tangled in nature's vast, delicate web.[28]

In Xochimilco, it's late afternoon. The great egrets have settled to wait out the heat, and Alejandro Martinez levers his pole to steer us free of the lily pads. With a sweeping push, he maneuvers our boat clear, into the canal's open water, and back toward the dock. The drifting flowers slip by. "The other day," Martinez tells me, "a guy tried to sell me an axolotl for 2,000 pesos [US$100]." He smiles with incredulity. "Just for one, man."

The plight of Mexico's axolotls has made them famous. The story of their imminent extinction in the wild has made international headlines and newscasts in Mexico and across North America. Inadvertently, the attention has also made them something of a local commodity. While fishing for axolotls is a long tradition, many of Xochimilco's farmers who once caught the creatures for food ended the practice when they became scarce and eventually declared endangered. Nowadays, however, as Mexico's most famous salamander becomes increasingly rare, some unscrupulous locals have returned to netting them out of their native canals. They've discovered, as Martinez explains, they can command a good price selling the creatures not as food—but as pets.

"They catch them, man," says Martinez, "because it's easy money."

CHAPTER 2
Creature Comfort

The Children's Hospital of Eastern Ontario is a low, sprawling building in a leafy corner of Canada's capital, Ottawa. Not far away, the narrow, winding Rideau River makes its way north. The hospital is one of only a handful of wholly pediatric acute-care hospitals across the country, and its size speaks to its importance. A labyrinth of corridors penetrates the building's broad center, radiating this way and that into clinical care wings and offices. Sick and injured children from a large region of central and northern Canada arrive here when their cases become too much for local medical services to manage. Half a million kids are admitted every year. Almost 3,000 doctors, nurses, and other staff hustle through the hallways, busily and sometimes frantically doing what they can to help. It is—as all hospitals are—an unavoidably intense, worrying place, but splashes of color and artwork are settling reminders that it's a place for kids first. Most people call it simply CHEO. The acronym—far more cheerful than the austere original—helps soften the institutional edge.

Ann Lambert and her 14-year-old golden retriever, Chara, know the hospital well. Lambert has been bringing her dogs to CHEO's pet therapy program since it began more than 15 years ago. Chara's experience is hardly less extensive. When I meet Lambert and Chara in one of the hospital's multipurpose rehabilitation rooms, Michèle Taché is there to introduce us. Taché is a "child-life specialist" at the hospital. She helped launch the pet program in 2003. For Taché, this is a typical afternoon. Her work, she says, is to help young patients and their families cope with the tensions and trauma that come with being seriously ill and confined to an institution like this: her job involves "trying to reduce stress and anxiety, but also promoting growth for these kids, whether it's therapy or education," she says. The visiting pets play a big role. Kids, their parents, and sometimes even staff meet with the visiting dogs to try to dial down the anxiousness endemic to these places. Seeing, petting, and holding the pets seems to offer a measure of relief from the upset and nervousness of hospital life. Some say it even helps with recovery. Occasionally, greeting the therapy animals elicits a first-time smile or helps with other important emotional and therapeutic milestones. "Powerful magic, I call it," says Taché.

Lambert, listening, agrees. Chara, sitting nearby, offers no comment. The slender elegance of the dog and her handler is oddly similar. Lambert is a poised, retired elementary school teacher (and a grandmother) with short, gray hair and a kindly face. Chara is trim and groomed with gentle eyes and a stately white snout. The pair is one of eight teams that regularly visit CHEO from the volunteer-based, not-for-profit group called Ottawa Therapy Dogs. The organization dispatches volunteers to care facilities, schools, and social services across the city and surrounding region, offering, as the group's Web site says, "to provide the healing benefits of animal-assisted therapy to those in need," especially people with physical and mental health problems. "Humans and animals share a powerful bond," the site explains. "That bond can be a source of comfort, peace and relief for those who suffer from physical or emotional pain. . . . Therapy dogs can sometimes achieve results when other therapies have failed." The dogs are selected and trained to remain calm and approachable in strange, noisy circumstances. Ditto for the handlers. Lambert and Chara fit the bill perfectly; the retriever and owner alike are models of imperturbable patience.

Right now, for example, Chara is waiting stoically for four-year-old Xavier to pay her some attention. Xavier has a dog at home that he hasn't seen since he arrived here months ago, stricken and suddenly hospitalized by a devastating disease of the spinal cord known as transverse myelitis. He went to bed one Friday night feeling fluish and awoke the next morning unable to move. The doctors at the hospital saved him through fast work and transfusions, but the road back has been long. Xavier is still confined to a wheelchair, and he's been moody and morose for months. He won't let his mother, Rachel, out of his sight. This is his first dog encounter since he arrived here, and he's not so sure. For now, he's flipping through photos of Chara and her last litter of puppies in an album. His mom watches from a couch. After a time, Lambert gently urges Chara, the real-life dog, a little closer. Xavier looks up. A tail wags. A child's grin broadens.

"When you see a reaction, a positive reaction, when you see for yourself, you just keep going," Chara's owner tells me, laughing lightly. Her eyes flash with pride.

Lambert and Taché have little doubt: pets—generously affectionate and unconditionally caring—are healers. Once mere hunting partners or mice exterminators, dogs, cats, and other companion animals have become modern medicine to a lot of people. Stories of their curative powers—or, at any rate, their ability to make people feel less sick—have become regular features in popular media. In news stories and on the Internet, the restorative touch of companion animals can seem almost shamanic. Their therapeutic influence is everywhere: nursing homes, hospitals, psychotherapy clinics, schools, vaccination sites, workplaces, and waiting rooms. Owning or even visiting with pets is touted as effective treatment for heart conditions, depression, post-traumatic stress, Alzheimer's disease, and autism. Animal contact, say believers, can increase well-being, help children in their development, and ensure healthy aging.

There's even a new word for these pet-induced health benefits: "zoo-eyia," from the Greek words for animal (*zoion*) and the goddess of health (*Hygeia*). But a better-known phrase is "the pet effect." Adherents of the idea—from medical professionals to regular pet owners—can be quite insistent. Recently, major American airlines began tightening rules for passengers traveling with "emotional support animals." The creatures—riding for free in the cabins of commercial flights, ostensibly as an antidote to air-travel anxiety—numbered more than 750,000 in 2017, almost double from a year earlier. Meanwhile, reports have surfaced of other passengers being mauled and of companion pigs using the plane as a lavatory. In January 2018, a woman bringing her "emotional support peacock" to a United Airlines flight from Newark was turned away at the gate.[1]

The zeal isn't limited to jet-setting travelers. Recently, the for-profit National Service Animal Registry—it sells official-looking pet-therapy vests and certificates for owners—said it had 200,000 service and emotional support animals in its registry, including everything from insects to alligators. It's almost a hundredfold increase from 2011. In 2019, the *New York Times* reported that more than two dozen states have new laws to crack down on "support-animal" fraud. Even so, most US family doctors (97 percent, according to a recent survey) believe pets are generally good for you. Most said they'd seen patients improve after interactions with animals. Three out of four also declared that they would "prescribe a pet to improve overall health if the medical evidence supported it."[2]

Trouble is, the evidence generally doesn't: "It's not Rx a cat," says Alan Beck, wryly. "We're just not at that stage."[3]

Beck is director of the Center for the Human–Animal Bond at Purdue University's College of Veterinary Medicine. He has studied the interactions of people and their pets for decades. Beck is a lively, likeable man with short, curled white hair and a trim beard. His happy Brooklyn accent—he grew up there—complements his easy enthusiasm. While most of his intrigue is directed at animals, it wasn't always that way; they had little to do with his very urban boyhood (unless you count hikes to the Jamaica Bay dump to watch the scrambling rats). He had no pets. After teaching high school for a time, Beck decided on graduate school at Johns Hopkins University. He planned to study wolves, but his soon-to-be doctoral supervisor had a different idea: if Beck studied something more practical and applied—that is, if he researched instead the overabundant stray dogs around Baltimore "and pretended that they're wolves"—his science could get funding from the National Institutes of Health.

"My whole life changed," he remembers. Not long after, Beck found himself at the frontier of an entirely new field of science—the study of human–animal interactions, a research arena now commonly called "anthrozoology." He's written a number of books on the subject, including *Between Pets and People: The Importance of Animal Companionship*, which he coauthored with his longtime collaborator, psychiatrist Aaron Katcher of the University of Pennsylvania.

"Starting in the late seventies and early eighties," he explains, "people really started developing this idea that our relationship with animals has health implications." The idea had long been popular with pet lovers, but for years, researchers were stubbornly skeptical. Pioneering pet-psychotherapist Boris Levinson, for example, was derided at an early 1960s scientific conference when he claimed his dog, Jingles, was an invaluable therapeutic assistant, particularly adept at overcoming patient–doctor therapeutic barriers. ("I think it was probably an exaggeration to say he was laughed off the stage," says Beck, "but there was certainly stunned silence.") At the time, many other therapists were actually using pets in their practice (even Sigmund Freud apparently took his chow chow, named Jofi, to client sessions), but there was an almost-entrenched wariness about conferring scientific legitimacy to the notion.

In 1980, that changed. Researchers at the University of Pennsylvania were looking at links between lifestyle and survival rates for heart-attack patients when they noticed something startling in the data: among people who weren't soon killed by the severity of their disease, 94 percent of those with pets were still going strong after one year compared with just 40 percent with no pets at home. The paper was a sensation. Studies into the pet effect suddenly surged. The hunt was on to uncover the connection: What was going on? How did pets do it? Researchers from fields as diverse as medicine and psychiatry to veterinary science and animal behavior joined in. A new scientific journal was born— *Anthrozoös*—devoted to these uncanny powers as well as other human– animal interactions. Popular media took up the discovery, too, and it has yet to let it go. "The health benefits of animals became an official thing," explains Beck.[4]

The giddy news, however, glossed over some details: For instance, pet owners in the Pennsylvania study—which involved a relatively small sample—were generally younger. Older heart-attack survivors may be simply more likely to die within a year, regardless of their coincidental petlessness. When researchers repeated the study a few years later with more patients, the findings were more nuanced: dog-owning heart patients had higher survival rates, but owning cats showed almost no impact at all. Skeptics wondered whether even the dog benefits were artifacts: unhealthier people may choose nondog pets because dog walking is a strain. Disentangling cause and effect is more difficult than imagined.[5]

"As a research field, it has some really built-in problems," Beck says. Controlled experiments—similar to those that compare the impact of a drug with the effect of an unsuspected placebo, for example—are often impossible. Separating factors at play when people bond with their pets can be difficult too; reasons for keeping pets may be as tangled as our complex ties to other humans in our lives—and just as difficult to pin down. "We know there's a special way people have being with their pets," Beck offers, shrugging.

More recent papers seem to add to the pet effect's murkiness. One Australian study—two decades after the celebrated University of Pennsylvania paper—appears to contradict the findings of the original. Overall, "pet owners were *more* likely to experience a death or readmission" to hospital within a year of experiencing heart trouble, according to the authors. In particular, cat ownership—far from being good for you— was linked to a significantly *higher* risk of dying or relapse for these patients. Life with kitty, it seems, can be a killer.[6]

For Beck, the sobriety of the more recent research isn't surprising. The exuberance that greeted early pet-effect science looked a little overly optimistic to him even then: "Aaron [Katcher] and I did an article pointing out that, yes, things are changing, but we shouldn't go too far the other way," Beck explains. "As Aaron used to say, there are people who think animals can cure everything from psoriasis to cancer."

In many respects, it's nothing new. From the beginning, people have looked to living things to find relief from pain. Plants, fungi, insects, and even the venom and skin of snakes were early sources of the potions and mixtures made to make us feel better. The first medicines—the ones we discovered that didn't kill us first—were likely balms to soothe the skin of desert dwellers or fibrous herbs for the constipated. Plants or animals known for their healing powers acquired mystical significance. The transcendental, pain-obliterating effect of opium poppies, for example, has been known for thousands of years. While many salubrious compounds evolved as plant defenses or as poisons for killing prey, magic and religion often got the credit.[7]

Some think that similar nature-based mysticism may have helped launch pet keeping too. Indigenous peoples from around the world, for example, tell stories of close and ultimately spiritual relationships with wild canines living near them. The tales describe humans, down on their own hunting luck, gratefully scavenging from kills made by wolves. Then, during times of hunting success, the people would repay the helpful creatures with scraps of their own. The wolves, in some cases, became known as magical beings and religious creation figures. Domestication of these revered animals may have been a next natural step.

Some writers and researchers suggest the wolves may have had an influence on us, too. In their recent book, *The First Domestication: How Wolves and Humans Coevolved*, Raymond Pierotti and Brandy Fogg argue that exposure to wolf behavior and its mystical thrall may have added new ways of cooperating and sociability to the human repertoire as well—a kind of "lupification" of how people act around each other.[8]

The burial of dogs in Paleolithic human graves—beginning some 14,000 years ago—suggests the early importance and beliefs attached to animals. These pets-to-the-dead, say researchers, may have been sacrificed for their religious significance or as personal and intimate companions. Hieroglyphs on gravestones accompanying buried dogs in ancient Egypt, for example, give them human names—the Egyptian equivalent of Rover, Butch, or Maggie. Cats, meanwhile, began hunting in and around settlements of the first farmers in the Fertile Crescent 10,000 years ago. Some 6,500 years later, they were—as Egyptian artwork suggests—fully, obsessively celebrated pets and figures of religion. Their strange, dissonant capacity for both tenderness and cruelty made them obvious suspects behind the act of creation; only cats could dream up a world so oddly wonderful and starkly terrible at the same time. Several ancient Egyptian goddesses—including Bastet, a celebrated deity of fertility, motherhood, and protection—are represented as cats or catlike.[9]

Until the eighteenth and nineteenth centuries, only the powerful and the rich could afford to keep creatures simply to make themselves feel better or to get closer to god: for most rural poor, dogs worked the farm and cats managed the mice. In the sixteenth century, the English word "pet" first appeared as a term for companion animals, but another 200 years or so passed before anyone but the very wealthy experienced what it meant in a spiritual or emotional sense. Finally, following the Industrial Revolution, Europe's middle classes swelled, and pet keeping became more widespread. (Interestingly, the most common pets of this period weren't domesticated cats and dogs but exotic wildlife, such as tamed monkeys, squirrels, tortoises, and caged songbirds.) Farm dogs moved indoors, curling by the fire. Pets became valued as company but increasingly unhelpful. Pet owners, perhaps self-conscious about their odd, cross-species dependency, began looking once again for reasons to justify their companion animals: they must be more substantially good for us somehow.[10]

"People just love their animals," says Beck. "So, finding uses sort of gives them a sense of purpose or less embarrassment that they have this pet because 'oh, I like it, but they're really actually good for you.' You know, it allows us an excuse to do something we enjoy anyway."

Much has been made, for example, of the bewitching changes pets induce in our brains. A number of studies have linked our bond with pets to higher levels of the so-called love hormone, oxytocin (and its close relative, vasopressin). Oxytocin is considered a kind of neuroendocrine puppet master that makes mothers act motherly and the rest of us behave affectionately toward other people. We normally produce the stuff in the presence of our babies or other loved ones, but surges of the hormone are also triggered by our pets. Research by Azabu University researcher Miho Nagasawa and colleagues discovered that not only did oxytocin levels rise in pet owners after exchanging fond looks with their dogs, but the dog's oxytocin levels climbed too. It's Maggie and me in the office.[11]

Magnetic resonance imaging techniques, which light up a mother's brain activity when viewing photos of her children, show activity in the same brain area when she sees pictures of her pet. Pet love, in other words, has some of the same characteristics—including, perhaps, the same irrational headiness—of human love. It's far from an exact match, but pets seem to tap into our very natural inclination to want to attach ourselves to others. "It's not like it's a dog that's changing our physiology," explains Beck. "These are behaviors and actions that are part of our life anyway."[12]

Children, in particular, are drawn to pets, a fact that's widely seen as a good thing. Many believe young people become more empathetic—more humane and understanding, even less prone to violence—if they grow up with a household animal. Some families will buy a dog or a cat for that reason alone. Yet, empathy toward creatures and empathy toward people are actually distinct: life with a dog may make little Johnny more inclined to understand the emotional life of his particular pet or even of animals in general, but nothing about the experience is sure to make him feel differently about other kids or adults. Better evidence exists to suggest that pets make some people feel more generally at ease. Controlled experiments are rare, but in one, people randomly selected to stroke a rabbit or a turtle were significantly less anxious than those provided a toy rabbit, a toy turtle, or nothing at all. Other studies suggest people with pets have a lower resting heart rate and blood pressure than those without pets when subjected to the stress of a difficult, mentally demanding test. Research also shows most kids with autism become less stressed, smile and laugh more, and are more inclined to talk to other people when pets are in the room.[13]

Nevertheless, writes author and researcher John Bradshaw in his remarkable recent book *The Animals among Us: How Pets Make Us Human*, the jury is still out when it comes to the curative power of pets. While published pet therapy studies are generally positive, he explains, few take into account the possible placebo effect—the widespread publicity enjoyed by therapeutic animals may simply make people around them want to feel better. Further, other factors linked to pet ownership are often at play: pet owners tend to be more affluent, and consequently healthier, than those without pets. Studies that show *no* pet effect, meanwhile, may simply not make it into print. Negative research results are, after all, so uninterestingly *negative*. Some do get published, however. Not long ago, for instance, a large and long-term study of elderly people in Britain challenged the long-standing belief that pets can slow the effects of aging. Instead, older pet owners were found to be no better than similarly aged, petless people when tested for walking speed, breathing, grip strength, memory, symptoms of depression, and several other well-known signs of advanced years. More recently, researchers found no effect of pet ownership on suicide risk.[14]

"I sometimes have to remind my pet friends," says Beck, "that just because 55 to 60 percent of US households have a pet doesn't mean the other 40 percent is where all the sick and bad people come from." He laughs. "Those people somehow manage to survive."

So what is it? Could it be that our fondness for pets—along with any healing magic—has more to do with finding relief in living things and in nature more generally? Visiting parks, wilderness, and other green space has long been credited with a vital and perhaps evolutionary role in boosting our well-being. Perhaps we enjoy pets—as animals—because they link us to the natural world. Pets, in other words, may be an important, comforting reminder that for most of our evolutionary history, we lived in the outdoors, side by side with other beasts. From the beginning until only very recently, wildlands and wildlife shaped us. Our species learned to be attentive to our natural surroundings to survive. Our interest in other animals evolved to make us better hunters or to save us from being hunted ourselves. Nature makes us feel better because it—not our contemporary environment of parking lots, concrete, and glass—is our native human habitat, the leafy place in which we evolved to feel at home. "When people ask does everybody have a need for pets, I say, no," explains Beck. "However, I think the need for just having some contact with nature is universal."

American journalist Richard Louv coined the phrase "nature deficit disorder" in 2005. Our increasingly urbanized and technological lives are creating an existential crisis, the writer argues, by driving humanity's accelerating "alienation from nature," especially among children. The consequences are a "diminished use of the senses, attention difficulties and higher rates of physical and emotional illnesses." Like the pet effect, the nature deficit idea was immediately popular. It touched a nerve with worried parents and became a rallying cry for conservationists. Also like the pet effect, the concept was celebrated before it found much solid experimental support. Nature deficit remains, for example, not generally recognized as either a real medical diagnosis or a pressing public health issue. Nevertheless, several recent studies have linked exposure to nature with better health, particularly in the context of childhood obesity and immune disorders, as well as with lower disease prevalence and longer life. The bulk of the research also suggests more green is better, and any kind of exposure—from a walk in the park to deep woodland camping—is helpful. Mental health may be especially affected.[15]

"I think part of our relationship with life—with understanding nature especially—is so we don't get eaten or so we don't eat what we shouldn't eat, and it's been a strategy for survival from the very beginning," explains Beck. "One major strategy was our relationship with each other. Obviously, none of us could survive as isolated people. . . . We started domesticating [companion] animals merely to entertain us. And, it turns out, it's just another little tool or strategy. They're just part of the same appreciation of living things beyond merely ourselves."

In 2016, more than half of the world's 7.5 billion people dwelled in cities, and by 2030, almost two out of every three of us will be living urban lives. Memories of our earlier, wilderness human existence are dimming. Our connection to nature is fraying, and the gap is widening. Pets may be a convenient way across. Cats and dogs, products of millennia of domestication, are far from natural, in a true sense, but they may be all we need to quell our insistent and now seemingly pointless yearning for the wild. Perhaps nothing more is needed. When it comes down to it, pets may just make the natural world quaintly unnecessary and wearingly old-fashioned. With pets for company, why bother with other vanishing species at all?[16]

Why care about life's diversity has been a question at the heart of Bradley Cardinale's work for decades. Curiously, his interest in why we should care began with his very singular conviction that we shouldn't. At least, not so much.

These days, Cardinale is a professor at the University of Michigan's School for Environment and Sustainability in Ann Arbor and one of the world's leading ecologists. Despite his success, he's unassuming and comfortable to talk to. His face is cherubic with an easy smile. He doesn't look the part of the crazed, driven scientist. But more than two decades ago—back when he was an energetic doctoral student studying caddis fly larvae in Appalachia's burbling streams—Cardinale was on a mission. He wanted to join one of the great ecological debates of the age as a brash, young contrarian. "I thought that many of the claims being made about biodiversity and its importance were not well supported or substantiated," he tells me. Cardinale is sitting at his office desk in Michigan, grinning at his youthful audacity. "It certainly wasn't what I was seeing in my own individual research."

Years before, at the 1992 Rio "Earth Summit," nations of the world turned their attention to the tide of disappearing wildlife. Extinctions, they agreed, were gathering momentum, but few had any idea what it meant for humanity. Scientists were spurred to find an answer, and soon they had one: biodiversity, in many respects, actually runs the show. Quite apart from soft claims that nature makes people feel better or otherwise has some cultural or spiritual value, the world's grand variety of animals, plants, and other organisms are key to keeping the planet— and us—alive. A series of studies and theoretical papers throughout the 1990s claimed researchers had evidence. Among the leaders in this work was a prominent American ecologist named David Tilman.

The articles argued that natural ecosystems with more different species were more productive, stable, and resistant to pests and diseases than those with few. Forests with more species of trees, for example, reliably generate more wood. Greater production, in particular, is vital; it means more plants turn more of the sun's energy into living tissue, and more animals and other life forms use the plants to accumulate energy. It's this energy that keeps us all going. Meanwhile, greater production also sucks a lot of carbon dioxide out of the air, regulating the climate, and filters water, thereby cleaning it. "David [Tilman]," explains Cardinale, "was basically saying that all of the things people care about and get from ecosystems are controlled by biodiversity."

But not everyone was buying it. Toward the end of the decade, a group of other researchers began raising questions. Cardinale's early doctoral research, for example, convinced him that the creatures and plants in his streams could be coaxed to nab more nutrients, capture the sun's energy, and clean more water without help from additional species. Not that Cardinale had anything against biodiversity. On the contrary, his fondest boyhood memories include watching wildlife in the arid wildlands of Arizona while on surreptitious hunting and fishing expeditions with his grandfather (who would sneak him out of school). Yet, Cardinale's own preliminary work seemed clear: it didn't make sense that more diversity was necessarily better.

"So, I started my career in this field by setting out to prove David Tilman wrong," says Cardinale, blithely, "and to show that scientifically there was no evidence that biodiversity was the key factor controlling the planet's productivity or sustainability. So. I was initially a big critic of the field, and I thought that it was overblown."

The caddis flies had other plans. Caddis flies are a group of insects best known as the slender, mothlike creatures flitting above streams and pools all over the world. The larvae live in the water, and several species have evolved a neat trick of weaving mini silk nets in bottom gravel to catch drifting food. In an elegantly simple experiment, Cardinale and his colleagues colonized a series of carefully controlled, outdoor streams with either one species of caddis fly or a mix of many. They then compared the amount of the drifting particles nabbed in each stream. What Cardinale saw startled him. Not only did the caddis flies trap more nutrients when more species were present (but with the same number of individuals), but adding species actually made the other species better trappers as well: different caddis fly species built nets in different areas of the stream bottom, catching particles normally out of reach. They also, as it turns out, altered the water flow in miniscule ways to make more food available to everybody. The trapping efficiency of many species together was greater than the sum for each species alone.[17]

The discovery was a game changer for Cardinale. He and others—most of them skeptics like himself—began looking at dozens of similar experiments involving different plants and creatures in different habitats around the globe. They gathered the data and, crunching the numbers together (a process known as "meta-analysis"), they looked at whether the more-is-better rule of species diversity applied in nature (outside of experiments) and whether the effects were widespread. "That series of meta-analyses led to literally dozens of publications that probably spanned a decade, and the bottom line from all of it was that David Tilman was right," says Cardinale.

"Basically, we saw the effects of biodiversity in almost every place we looked: the more diverse an ecosystem is, whether it's in oceans, whether it's in grasslands or in forests, almost always, the more productive a habitat is, the more efficient it is, and the more stable it is over time."

The evidence presented by Cardinale and others—much of it appearing in the pages of the leading scientific journals *Nature* and *Science*—made the case clear: biodiversity *is* at the center of many of the processes that keep life going. Species extinctions, on the other hand, almost invariably make ecosystems less productive and more vulnerable, sometimes in unpredictable and monumental ways. Less productivity—reducing nature's ability to trap and accumulate energy into useful living tissue—means other living beings, including people, often lose out. In the world's oceans, for example, places that have lost a species to overfishing have generally smaller, less dependable yields of other fish overall—and less food for societies that depend on them.[18]

"What biodiversity does" explains Cardinale, "is it basically makes things resistant to change. . . . An ecosystem that's more efficient—meaning it can take up a greater fraction of those nutrients or sunlight—and that's better at resisting an invasive species or harmful disease and that's also more productive, in almost all instances that I can think of, that's good for people. I mean, that's a healthy lake with a lot of fish. That's a healthy forest giving us a lot of lumber."

The variety of life, in other words, is no small thing. On the contrary, it may be the *biggest* thing. While governments and people everywhere wring their hands over the dire, earth-altering consequences of climate change, the crisis of wildlife extinction could be just as devastating—or worse. When Cardinale and his colleagues gathered studies exploring the effect of losing local species on ecosystems, they were amazed to find that the impacts of shrinking biodiversity on key ecological processes can be as large as or larger than those from global warming and other notorious and agenda-topping environmental problems. Even "intermediate" species losses as low as one extinction per five species (the same proportion of vertebrate animals already known to be at risk of disappearing around the world today) hit the productivity of these natural systems as hard as the damage done by climate shifts and thinning ozone. Greater losses to biodiversity do more damage still. "If the main thing that we care about is how productive the planet is—how productive natural ecosystems are—then all of the data that I've been part of, heard, and that I've seen and read seems to suggest that biodiversity and conserving it is probably what we need to focus on most," says Cardinale.[19]

"I don't want to give the impression that biodiversity is more important than all of these other environmental problems or that we shouldn't be focused on climate change," he says. "Climate change clearly is a big thing from a societal perspective. On the other hand, there are certain issues—water quality, the ability to take carbon out of the atmosphere, the ability to produce goods and services like lumber or fisheries—where the number one priority for keeping those goods and services is conservation of biodiversity. . . . There's some things that you get from nature that, if you take them away, you're not going to be able to eat, drink, or breathe."

Biophilia—so the theory goes—evolved to help our earliest ancestors survive by equipping them with attentiveness to hunt and forage. Today, hundreds of millennia later, this affinity for other life may rescue us again. If our inherent interest in other species becomes an inclination to save them, the benefits could be more than simply overcoming "nature deficit" or satisfying an indistinct fondness for wild creatures: an end to dwindling biodiversity could ensure natural systems keep doing the work they do. It could keep them from sputtering and losing power. Their ability to absorb insults—from climate change, species invaders, or pollution—would remain strong. Plants would keep gathering sunlight. Grazers would graze. Pollinators would pollinate. And predators would hunt. Nature would feed and nurture life as it does now. It would filter air and clean the water. And people—with our infant-like dependency on all of these natural processes—would avoid, perhaps, a calamity of our own making.

The problem is, as much as we can't live without nature and wild diversity, we seem to care about pets more. A pet may be just as four-legged and furry as any wild mammal, but having a place in our homes appears to give it another, more-rarefied identity in our imaginations. "For many of us," writes John Bradshaw, "our animals have become an extension of ourselves, an emotionally based form of self-enhancement." Pet ownership is nonsensical in this way. Most pet people, according to research, assume an emotional, even intellectual, connection to their pets that existing "animal mind" science doesn't support. Many dog owners talk about their pet's "unconditional love," for instance, while having no real idea if other, distant, and more-elemental loyalties are at work; our pets' apparent devotion to us may not resemble love as we know it at all.

That something imaginary is central to our relationship with pets shouldn't be a problem, but it is. Inspired, perhaps, by a projection of our own desire to reconnect with nature, we let pets do it for us; we let them run free outside or we bring animals from the wild indoors. Because, as John Bradshaw writes, pets "bring a touch of wildness into our otherwise regimented and technology-dominated worlds," we feel a reciprocal, imagined obligation to resuscitate some genuine wildness in theirs. Our suspension of disbelief is unmoved by the reality of thousands of years of domestication (in the case of cats and dogs), their frequent role as invasive predators, and the obvious unnatural advantage for prowling pets that comes with available pet food and shelter to keep starvation and violent death at bay. The result of this fantasy has become a serious decline in wildlife and an escalating threat to the wild diversity that Cardinale and other scientists say is so crucial. Losses to our biological diversity drain the power of natural ecosystems to keep the living world on course. Our pets may be a convenient antidote for our biophilia's ancient itch, but the price of their convenience is high and getting higher. It's paid at nature's expense.[20]

In the second-floor therapy room of the children's hospital in Ottawa, Xavier still isn't ready to touch the visiting golden retriever himself. Instead, he watches delightedly as another health-care worker scratches Chara's noble head beside him. Meanwhile, the dog's owner—the indefatigable Ann Lambert—explains how she began her dog-therapy work bringing retrievers to visit the young, the ill, and the elderly around Ottawa for more than 34 years. In the beginning, back before popular consciousness (or even much research) noticed that pets may help sick people to feel better, Lambert took her prized dogs to seniors' homes just to show them off. She has a kennel at her countryside home just outside the city and has been breeding retrievers for years. She and a group of other kennel owners simply came to the same conclusion: their love for their pets was more than enough to go around. "We were just so into our dogs ourselves, we just wanted to share them," she says.

One day, caregivers at one of the homes asked if she would take her dogs upstairs and into the rooms of the bedridden. The results, Lambert recalls, were immediate and striking. One listless, unresponsive woman—one of the first she visited—lit up with sudden glee after Lambert's dog (disobediently) jumped on the bed. A young doctor, comatose following an adverse drug reaction, blinked for the first time when Lambert's pet touched his hand. Another time, Lambert visited a dying nine-year-old from Baffin Island. The boy was congenitally deaf and blind and unable to move or communicate. Yet, he revealed a sudden, otherwise-elusive calm when Lambert pressed his fingers against the warmth of her dog.

"The nurse said, 'Look at the monitor,'" Lambert recalls. "His heart rate had gone way down. The room was so quiet. There were tears from everyone watching."

Lambert's stories are affecting, and her enthusiasm for her retrievers is endearingly bighearted. She's a committed disciple of the pet effect; her dogs, she believes, really do bring relief to others. And since there seems to be no bottom to the well of her dogs' healing magic, she's happy to spread it around. There's more: Lambert's animal affections aren't limited to her sleek, wispy-coated canines; she's happy to share her joy of wildlife too.

I look through one of the photo albums Lambert brings—along with her dogs—to amuse young patients. Her wildlife pictures are striking. She's a skillful photographer. Her home outside the city is surrounded by woodlands and fields, and she likes to take a camera when she walks. She snaps chance encounters with the area's wild animals or images of Ontario's bucolic, bright expanse. Several photos show a snowy owl hunting over a field. The powerful white bird, with flecks of black and imperious yellow eyes, is impressive. It lives in the Arctic much of the time. Its tribe is far from common here during most of the year, but the owl often shows up in winter as the cold and the search for prey push them south. "They're beautiful birds," says Lambert, admiringly. "Wonderful to see."

It turns out that the veteran therapy-dog handler—champion of regal, wheat-golden dogs and a committed missionary for the healing power of pets—is a lover of wild things too. Nature and being near to it are important to her. Nothing about pet keeping, or so it seems, makes it any less so. To people like Lambert, it's only natural. Pet ownership and a love of wildlife are both less like a hobby and more like a state of mind; it's an emotional and psychological belief system. Its characteristics, as author John Bradshaw points out, can be remarkably reminiscent of those of a religion: the conviction can seem deep, supernaturally inspired and unshakably resolute. Lambert believes in the power of creatures to heal but also in the restorative wonder of nature. No rule exists that the two—adoring pets and admiring wildlife—need to be mutually exclusive.[21] "I love animals," Lambert says, simply. "I do."

CHAPTER 3
Cat War Battles

Mary Jane Proulx wouldn't be here if it weren't for the cats. Proulx—resolutely breezy with shoulder-length, vintage blond hair—is, for the first time in her life, a candidate in a municipal election. The race is for a council seat in the Canadian city of Cornwall. It's October, and with the election less than two weeks away, Proulx is in the thick of things. Residents of three houses along Miron Avenue are gathered in a driveway, and Proulx is in the middle. She's cheerfully fielding questions about the cats. It's always about the cats.

"Well yes," says a woman, shrugging sheepishly, "of course I feed them. What are you going to do? The poor things are starving."

Proulx looks conciliatory. "It's not their fault," she nods.

Miron Avenue is a short two blocks long. It's typical of a tidy residential street in this hard-times town. Squat, siding-clad houses sit well apart on wide, often-treeless lots. Sheds and garages, among the street's notable features, come in a variety of sizes. The grass is trim. The shrubs are few. The cats—feral, unowned cats, beholden to no one and seemingly in brazen control of the neighborhood—are many. "At least thirteen now," says Sylvain Bougie, a longtime resident. "No, maybe fifteen."

Cornwall is a beleaguered former mill town of not quite 47,000 in Ontario's easternmost corner. For more than a decade, it has muddled along as a place of few prospects. In 2006, the closure of the Domtar pulp-and-paper plant dealt a staggering blow to this once-busy manufacturing city on the north shore of the St. Lawrence River. A few smaller industries filled in—distribution facilities, call centers, and so on—but the descendants of generations of factory workers are still struggling. The median income teeters at or below the poverty line, and, on the southeast side, the weariness is palpable. Battered row houses appear begging for repair. Worried pensioners peer from windows. And the cats—the legions of cats—wait for nightfall.

Cornwall may be Ontario's stray cat capital. Dozens of swelling colonies of wild, unowned cats—like the one on Miron Avenue—occupy neighborhoods throughout the small city. The Ontario Society for the Prevention of Cruelty to Animals takes strays from across the province, but Cornwall alone accounts for almost a third of its intake. None of the agency's 10 other regional offices face anything quite like it: Markham, a city more than six times Cornwall's size, accounted for a number that's hardly more than a quarter of the cats handled by the agency in Cornwall last year. Far more are sick or injured than elsewhere too (40 percent of the agency's intake compared with the 20 percent provincial average). Essentially, unowned cats are everywhere here. No one knows exactly why or even how many. As soon as the wary creatures are spotted, they usually slip away like quicksilver. Counting would be a trick, and nobody has really tried. What's easier to enumerate are the neglected and now cat-occupied sheds, most reeking of acrid urine, or the scores of feces-filled flower beds.

The residents of Bergin Avenue were among the first to call the city's attention to the problem. They demanded something be done. Fingers pointed at a neighbor on the street who persisted in putting out food for the cats. Outrage mounted as the subsidized cat colony predictably grew, along with its mess. The same scene was—and is—playing out all over town, says Proulx. A remarkable number of people, it turns out, are feeding the cats right across the city. The cat colonies—no surprise—are thriving. What's also no surprise is the growing indignation of neighbors alarmed by the sheer cat numbers. There are shouting matches on Bedford Street and feuding on Miron Avenue. "It's not my problem; it's Cornwall's problem," says Proulx, growing animated. "I'm dealing with neighbors who are fighting with each other. It's nuts. It's crazy."

Proulx, who works part-time as a group-home social worker, is far from neutral in these cat wars. She's the proud enabler of Cornwall's cat caregivers (the term preferred by the army of people who feed the now-wild domestic cats). Through an arrangement with a nearby independent cat welfare organization called Roy and Cher's Rescue Farm, Proulx says, the local Walmart donates mountains of cat food in unsaleable damaged bags. Proulx and another volunteer, Maarten McDougald, distribute the food to people who feed the feral cats in Cornwall neighborhoods several times a week. Occasionally, when money is available, the pair will trap the animals, ferry them to a vet to have them surgically desexed, and return them, infertile, to their colonies. Proulx believes the approach—known as trap, neuter, and return, or TNR—is Cornwall's only *humane* hope for bringing the cat population under control. "Somebody has to do something," she says, "so we're doing something."

Actually, the city wants to do something too—something else. In response to the Bergin Avenue brouhaha, Cornwall's supervisor of bylaw enforcement, Chris Rogers, wrote a six-page report urging council to outlaw (essentially) unowned cats. Rogers's proposed bylaw would insist that anyone found feeding a stray assumes its ownership and thereafter must keep it indoors. Owned cats, too, would be barred from wandering outside unsupervised. Rogers developed his plan after studying cat-control efforts in other cities across North America. While the plan includes municipal funds for TNR efforts, the bylaw would almost certainly sound a death knell for the hundreds of unowned cats already wandering Cornwall's alleys and streets; without food subsidies from kindly cat lovers, many—if not most—of the feral felines would find the cold Ontario winters fatal. "I can see it's controversial," Rogers tells me. "But I believe we have a problem here that's exceptional."[1]

Proulx's bid for council is her protest. She doesn't expect to win—"I only have one election sign," she laughs—but she's hopeful that by stirring the election pot she can convince Cornwall to back off from what she sees as a Draconian and ultimately cruel plan. Local and regional newspapers are watching her closely. A TV national news program did a spot, and a documentary filmmaker has promised to join Proulx on election day as the ballots come in. Now, everyone—the mayor, other councilors, and the many candidates in the election—find themselves forced to have a position on the polarizing subject of Cornwall's cats. Fence-sitting is no longer an option. Both sides of this divided town won't stand for it.

"It's our fault," Proulx says of the cat problem. "It's our responsibility. Why should the cats suffer?"

Robert Prowse has an answer. Prowse is among a couple of hundred townspeople who have come to an all-candidates' event arranged by the local chamber of commerce. It's the evening after my day on the streets with Proulx. The room on the city hall's bottom floor is long and narrow. The ceiling is high and bright. Candidate tables are arranged around the perimeter, and Proulx is behind one of them. She smiles—a little uncomfortably—as Prowse approaches.

Prowse is the owner of one of the most upscale hotels in town. He moved here five years ago from Toronto to renovate a centuries-old downtown building and to transform it into a high-end inn. He was Cornwall's "Entrepreneur of the Year" within a couple of years and has become an active and familiar voice for the town's economic development. He's an imposing-looking, serious man with the aspect of someone comfortable with showing impatience.

"She was just asking me what my opinion is," Prowse tells me, standing by Proulx's table and working his mouth as if something sour is in it. Proulx, undaunted and indomitably cheery, looks on. "And my opinion is, euthanize them," Prowse pronounces, resolutely. "I don't believe in release programs, because you're basically saying 'go eat a hummingbird for lunch, or go fight with another tom at night and get all torn up.' I mean, it's not good for the cats either.

"No other pet would you allow to run wild in the streets. Their way of thinking is to say, 'oh, but they're wild animals.' No, they're not. They're not native here. . . . They're an invasive species that has wiped out half the songbird population of North America, according to the Smithsonian."

"Are you a bird-watcher?" I ask.

"Not particularly," he says, "but I like birds in my trees better than I like cats shitting in my flower beds. . . . It's something council has to stop hiding from and deal with. It needs to be regulated. If you don't have regulations in place, it's chaos. Which is what's got us to where we are now."

Prowse moves on to another candidate's table. "Everyone is entitled to their opinion," sniffs Proulx, airily. Her smile remains. Her nonchalance is both formidable and obstinate. Proulx has no truck with the other side, she explains; they simply don't see the fundamental injustice of making feral cats pay when their only sin is the call of their feline instincts. Sure, it's a shame the cats eat birds. Proulx's own cats never go outside, she says. But the unowned cats of Cornwall's streets and alleys shouldn't have to die because Cornwall's citizens have created a crisis. "I would do it for any animal," Proulx says. "I'm an animal lover. You have to feel for these cats, if you love animals; it's not their fault."

A thousand kilometers south, in Washington, DC, Pete Marra describes himself as an animal lover, too. The conservation scientist and director of the Migratory Bird Center at the Smithsonian Institution says he grew up as one. Marra is a seemingly mild, serious, and often expressionless man with weary eyes and boyish blond hair. His childhood was spent in the woods near his Connecticut home, and experiences with nature and wildlife helped set him straight when he drifted into waywardness (underage drinking and pot) as a young teen. His curiosity about wild things fortified his better angels. ("I always knew that I wanted to do something with science and natural history and birds, and it was always pulling me back to center.") His mother, a single parent, encouraged his naturalist's inclinations. With her blessing, Marra brought home pets—salamanders, rabbits, raccoons. Strays were always welcome. An affection for other beings became a kind of birthright in the family. Pets attracted him naturally. In the years since, he's had many. In his work, he's a tireless champion of birds and other wildlife, but he's had several companion animals at home, too. He's been a cat owner. Objectively, he is an animal lover by almost any measure.

That hasn't stopped other animal lovers from threatening to kill him. "I got all sorts of death threats," he says, incredulously. "I mean lots of mainly e-mails or notices on Amazon, you know, saying what people are going to do to me."

The attempts to terrorize him have been Marra's ongoing reward for some fairly straightforward science. In a 2013 article in the journal *Nature Communications*, Marra and his colleagues gathered numbers from dozens of earlier studies, combined the data, and calculated that cats are a leading cause of wildlife death across the United States. America's domestic felines, they write, are likely "the single greatest source" of bird and mammal deaths linked to human activity throughout the country. Later, in 2016, the biologist teamed up with journalist Chris Santella to round out the paper's findings in a book called (provocatively) *Cat Wars: The Devastating Consequences of a Cuddly Killer.*[2]

The story revolves around a simple exercise in number crunching: cats—according to the researchers' estimates—kill between 1.3 and 4 billion birds and up to 22.3 billion mammals in the United States every year. That's *billion.* More wildlife deaths are attributable to cats, say the authors, than the effects of road kill, poisons, pesticides, wind turbines, skyscraper and window collisions, and any other human-related causes. (In 2019, Marra was among researchers who revealed—in the leading journal *Science*—that the total number of North American birds had plummeted by almost one-third overall [down 2.9 billion birds] since 1970.) The cat prey numbers are conservative, says Marra; they give cats the benefit of the doubt. The figures for American cat populations (owned and unowned), the proportion of household cats allowed out-side, the proportion that hunt and for how long, and the number of kills per cat come from more than 100 studies. The lower wildlife-death figures—1.3 billion birds and 6.3 billion mammals—reflect the bottom range for all the estimates used. While a lot of the killing is done by roaming household pets, most of the death is at the paws of feral cats—the millions of unowned and quasi-wild animals living and hunting in towns and across the countryside throughout the nation.[3]

It's not exactly news. People have warned about the impact of domes-tic pets on the natural world for ages. In the late 1980s, for example, research by University of Wisconsin–Madison professor Stanley Tem-ple and his student calculated that about 7.8 million birds annually were lost to free-ranging cats in Wisconsin alone. Two decades later, after reviewing studies from 120 islands around the world, Spanish ecologist Félix Medina and colleagues concluded cats were to blame for driving extinctions, decimating populations, or shrinking the ranges of at least 175 species of reptiles, mammals, and birds. Among them was the Hawaiian crow, which disappeared from the wild as recently as 2002. In 2013, Canadian bird biologist Peter Blancher estimated Canada's 8.5 million pet cats and roughly 1.4 to 4.2 million feral cats wipe out between 100 and 350 million birds per year. In Australia, feral cats—along with introduced red foxes from Europe—have been implicated in the extinction of more than 1 in 10 of Australia's 273 native land mammals in the last two centuries. Another fifth of these species are considered threatened with extinction. The merciless success of our favorite feline hunters has earned them a spot on a list of the 100 worst invasive alien species in the world.[4]

Dog aren't much better: our slavering "man's best friend" has received far less attention as a wildlife menace, but its destruction of nature is nevertheless alarming. Dogs hold "the number three spot after cats and rodents as the world's most damaging invasive mammalian predators," writes Australian biologist Tim Doherty. The devastation, he writes, is "grossly underestimated." While scientists consider predatory cats the chief culprit in 63 documented extinctions around the world so far, our dogs have been linked to 11. Many of these—the thick-billed ground dove of the Solomon Islands and the Cape Verde giant skink, for example—haven't been seen since the first half of the last century.[5]

In their research, Doherty and his colleagues searched the list of threatened animals compiled by the International Union for Conservation of Nature for creatures whose major or sole threat is known to be dogs. These dog-menaced species covered the gamut, from Tasmanian devils and iguanas to doves, monkeys, and turtles. The researchers say that along with causing species extinctions, dogs continue to slaughter and kill animals from another 188 species already at risk of vanishing. In New Zealand, a single German shepherd is believed to have dispatched as many as 500 flightless kiwis. The main problem, say the scientists, is dogs left free to wander and to hunt down wildlife—mainly mammals and birds. Sometimes they do damage simply by spooking native creatures or disrupting their efforts to breed, nest, or raise young. Sometimes they spread disease. Dogs inflict the most damage to biodiversity in Central and South America, Southeast Asia, and Australia, according to scientists. Like their wolf ancestors, they prefer to hunt in packs. They often target large prey, such as deer and other similar-sized mammals. Sometimes they scrounge for an easier meal.[6]

On a beach near the village of Colola, Mexico, for example, scientists tracked village dogs by means of radio collars and found almost half scavenged in the sand for sea turtle nests, gobbling down the eggs. The beach is a known nesting ground for endangered eastern Pacific green turtles. Six of the world's seven sea-turtle species nest on just over 30 known beaches along Mexico's Pacific Coast and the Gulf of Mexico. All are close to towns where most people have dogs. Scavenging by these pets is widespread. In their study, the researchers found the nest-raiding dogs often traveled in groups and dug for eggs at night. Most of the owners willingly let their dogs run free, and more than one-third were unbothered that the dogs were finding their own wild meals.[7]

"The typically omnivorous diet of dogs means they have strong potential to affect a diversity of species," Doherty and his coauthors write in the *Conversation* magazine. "For instance, dogs killed at least 19 endangered Kagu—a ground-dwelling bird—in New Caledonia in 14 weeks. Threatened species with small population sizes are particularly vulnerable to such intense bouts of predation."[8]

Taken together, it's a stark picture: our favorite pets—cats and dogs—are linked to more than half of all recent extinctions of bird, mammal, and reptile species around the world. They are, as Doherty and his colleagues conclude, part of a malignant team of invading mammalian predators (along with rats, pigs, and others) that continue to push almost 600 other species ever closer to oblivion's edge. The scale of the problem is extraordinary: as many as 987 million dogs and upward of 752 million cats pad about this planet—in and out of homes but also through fields and woods. By now, domestic dogs have become the most abundant carnivore alive. Cats are not far behind. Overall, numbers of wild animals, meanwhile, continue to fall.[9]

Nothing, therefore, should have been a total surprise in the 2013 killer-kitty findings by Marra and his colleagues. Unique about the paper, undoubtedly, is its thoroughness and scale. The follow-up book provides a fuller description of the cat conservation crisis along with additional dangers—to people as well as to animals—of cat-borne diseases such as toxoplasmosis. The book also characterizes TNR (trap, neuter, and release) as a likely waste of time for managing feral cat populations; no convincing evidence exists to suggest it's effective, and sterilized cats rereleased on the landscape still damage wildlife. Instead, the Marra and Santella book endorses euthanasia as the better choice: "From a conservation ecology perspective," the authors write in a passage widely cited by outraged cat people, "the most desirable solution seems clear—remove all free-ranging cats from the landscape by any means necessary."[10]

The 2013 article caught the attention of the *New York Times*. Other media piled on. Indignant cat lovers were quick to notice, too, and they heard in it—or so it seems—a call to arms. "I'm still surprised by the strength and the passion of the reaction," says Marra. "It's always surprising that people are so focused on cats and only cats regardless of everything else that's out there." A feral cat advocacy group called Alley Cat Allies ("a champion for the humane treatment of all cats") marched on the Smithsonian with a box of letters, says Marra, demanding he be fired. Protesters began showing up wherever the conservation biologist was invited to speak. Passionate cat people would stand, call out, and disrupt his talks from the audience. Others would show up in costumes. When the book was released, protesters demanded that its publisher, Princeton University Press, pull it from shelves.[11]

Then, there were the threats. They came thick and fast. Marra alerted police around his work and around his neighborhood. The Smithsonian instituted a kind of "lockdown" in Marra's building, he says. Nameplates were removed from the lobby so nobody knew where the offices were. "There were a few times when there were weird cars outside my house, and I called the police about it," Marra recalls, chillingly. "They turned out to be nothing. So, in the end, I think a lot of these threats were just bluffs by, you know, people in their basements, online, sending off e-mails and cards."

"The science is really clear, and I'm a conservation biologist," Marra tells me after I wonder aloud whether he wasn't daunted by the vitriol. "If I didn't continue to push on this issue—and I am continuing to push this issue—then I would be complicit to the problem," he says, stridently. "I can't *not* be vocal about this; to me, the biggest problem here is ignorance."

For biophilia—our possibly innate attraction to other life—cats may be the quintessential pet. No other popular animal companion resides in such a wild, mysterious, and liminal space in our imaginations— even as our own species becomes increasingly distant from nature. Their beautiful, fluid grace is wonderful and strange. ("The nearest kin of the moon," writes W. B. Yeats.) Their antics and quirky neuroticism are a hit, too—at least on YouTube. (More than two million cat videos were available on the video-share site in 2019, and they've been viewed around the world more than 25 billion times.) Cats are compelling. At the same time, few other animals leave us so ambiguous—and few pets seem so ambiguous toward us. It goes both ways. Cats have only ever seemed half-committed to their domestic role in our human world.

That's the liminal part: cats are tame, but not really; they're in between. They're crepuscular: they're not entirely night creatures but neither are they comfortable in the civilized light of day. Something of every cat still vibrates with its wildness.[12]

Their history speaks to it. When cats and humans came together 10,000 years ago, we didn't fall in love; we tolerated each other. Mutual sufferance was the basis of our relationship for millennia. The first of these early farm cats is thought to be an ancient ancestor of Near Eastern wildcats. Biologists describe our early interactions as "commensalism," which means literally "sharing from the same table": the cats weren't particularly thrilled to have humans for company, but they loved that we stored grain to attract mice. The dining was delicious. It wasn't until Middle Kingdom Egypt that cats allowed themselves to get closer, becoming—as 4,000-year-old art from the period suggests—something like pets.[13]

The important part of this tale is that cats appear to have chosen us, not the other way around. In other instances of animal domestication, we drafted creatures into our service. We selected the ancestors of goats and cattle because they lived in herds with natural social hierarchies that made confinement palatable and allowed us to take charge. The wolves that became our dogs were accustomed to heeding the leader of the pack. Cats, on the other hand, are solitary hunters that savagely defend their turf from others (i.e., cats of the same sex). They eat only meat. Most significantly, cats don't tolerate being bossed around. Their wild ancestors never had to take orders, and they won't either. Unlike many other domesticated creatures recruited from the wild and bred for particular tasks, cats can't be taught to do much that's useful. They've been in our midst for a long, long time, but they're still not much help. More importantly, they don't care. It's all the same to them. For cats, cats have always been number one.[14]

Paradoxically, it may be this aloofness that invigorates their appeal as animal companions. Some argue cats are the most popular four-legged pet on the planet. And most cat owners seem to find something essential and satisfying in their pet's disdain for "tameness." Cats prowl our lives and remain just one generation away from their wild state. Their predator's intensity and sharpened senses seem hardly dulled, even after years sharing in our constrained and typically pedestrian human existence. They stalk and pounce and twitch their tails. Their cool, lissome precision remains keen and astonishing. Their deadliness, elegant. Even in the dull thrall of city life, cat owners can imagine themselves allies in their pet's savage, pulse-quickening adventures. Allowed to skulk and hunt outdoors—especially—our cats offer an even more inspired entry into a vicarious experience of wildness. Nothing could seem more natural.[15]

"What's sad, I think," says Marra, "is that letting your cat outdoors has become a replacement for a wildlife experience. . . . People have cats and let their cats roam because—well, first, they think they're enriching their cat's life—but I think at some level they're replacing their own silent need for some kind of natural history experience."

The response is visceral—perhaps even part of how we're made—but its effect, ironically, may be to endanger the nature we might otherwise crave: not only are cats killing wildlife, claims Marra, but impassioned cat advocates are part of an organized misinformation campaign that's influencing conservation policy. It's undermining efforts to stop the devastation.

In their perhaps-biophilia-inspired devotion to their pets, pro-cat people have discovered an endless well of faith in their cause. The faith is a tool they pit against science. Their emotionally charged public relations campaigns "strikingly duplicate past approaches of cigarette and climate-change fact fighters," argues Marra. The biologist and his longtime collaborator Scott Loss published the warning in a recent letter to the journal *Conservation Biology* with the headline "Merchants of Doubt in the Free-Ranging Cat Conflict." Like Big Tobacco and Big Oil before them, cat advocacy organizations and individuals take aim at peer-reviewed research first.[16]

Loss and Marra use the example of Alley Cat Allies—the Maryland-based group that demanded Marra's ouster when news of the 2013 cat-impacts study first broke. Alley Cat Allies describes itself as America's "leading cat advocacy organization," with 650,000 supporters across the United States and more than $10 million in annual contributions and other funds. (Requests for an interview with Alley Cat Allies president and founder Becky Robinson initially prompted a quick and seemingly positive reply from media representative Peter Osborne. However, when I provided the sample questions he requested along with a description of the book, Osborne replied with "I'll let you know," and the e-mail thread abruptly ended. Repeated follow-up requests went unanswered.) According to its Web site, Alley Cat Allies aims to lobby for TNR programs on behalf of the nation's unowned cats. It vigorously works to end euthanasia as an animal-control tool altogether. "This is about coexisting," Robinson said during an interview a few years back. "This is about compassion. This is about humanity, how we exist, how we interact. This is about respect for life."[17]

The organization's fervor—for both owned and unowned cats—is daunting. There's something both profoundly earnest and magical in its thinking: "Cats have lived primarily outdoors alongside humans, sharing the environment with birds and wildlife, for over 10,000 years," the group suggests. "The truth is that community [i.e., unowned and feral] cats have always lived outdoors and have a place in the natural landscape. . . . Their home is the outdoors—just like squirrels, chipmunks, and birds. They are well suited to their outdoor home. The truth is that it's natural for cats to live outside. . . . Cats have coexisted outdoors with wildlife for thousands of years. Reliable science shows that cats are part of our natural ecosystem and do not significantly impact wildlife populations. As animal lovers, we want what is best for all animals."[18]

The pro-cat public relations appear to be having effect. According to the Web site, more than 240 local governments across the United States support TNR programs as an approach to managing feral cats—even though, at the end of the day, these efforts always return the animals to the outdoors. Of 91 US cities and counties that condone the programs (including New York City and San Francisco), 63 describe them as "the only effective way to address feral cat populations." In some cases, the cat advocates have successfully convinced policy makers to distrust the research altogether. When the Council of the District of Columbia in Washington held a roundtable to consider its cat management practices in 2015, testimony by feline defenders and TNR supporters prompted the chair of the meeting to erroneously describe Marra's 2013 paper as a "discredited study."[19]

"Many of these outdoor cat advocacy groups talk about cats as part of wildlife, as part of nature, and that's what they're promoting now," says Marra. "They're really distorting the truth in the hopes that most people won't even know the difference. And the really sad thing is that many people *don't* know the difference. They don't really think of the species as a nonnative invasive. They don't know what that means. They just care about the fact that it's an animal."

There's an irony in the protectiveness of these ardent cat champions: Cats—to go by numbers alone—are among the creatures least in need of protection of any on the planet. Dogs too. While wildlife figures have been dropping like a stone over the last half century, the surging numbers of these companion animals have been described as a "crisis" too, and for reasons that have nothing to do with conservation: pet overpopulation—as some call it—is described as the number one killer of dogs and cats in the United States.[20]

Between six and eight million American pets arrive unwanted, stray, or otherwise homeless in US animal shelters every year, and between one-quarter and one-half are euthanized. In Canada, about one in every five cats admitted to a shelter in 2016 was killed. While the situation has been improving somewhat in recent decades, more dogs and cats continue to die of homelessness each year than of preventable diseases. Tens of millions more of them roam the landscape as unowned and feral wanderers—so many that the estimated population of unwanted pets now rivals that of the valued pets in our homes. Nowadays, companion animals are as likely as not to live altogether companionless.[21]

Economics plays a role. People who earn less than $50,000 are far more likely to give up their pets because of housing issues and pet-keeping costs than those who earn more, according to a survey by the American Society for the Prevention of Cruelty to Animals. Almost half of renters across the United States said housing was the main consideration when parting with their pet. The animals prohibited by landlords don't always find their way to shelters or to other homes; many are unceremoniously left to the streets. That means poorer neighborhoods are home to far more unowned cats than wealthier parts of typical North American cities. (When entire towns suffer economically—places such as Cornwall, Ontario—animal abandonment becomes an even greater risk, sometimes on a large scale.) And just as people without money are those more likely to abandon the pets, residents in lower-income neighborhoods are also the ones most likely to step in and feed the unwanted animals, helping feral populations to become established. In one survey of more than 200 cat colony "caretakers" in Rishon LeZion, Israel, for example, researchers found most are single, middle aged, and female. And most live in poor communities.[22]

Bird-watchers, meanwhile, are different. They often have money. People passionate about birds are frequently middle aged and middle class with time and resources. They travel for their hobby. They spend millions on it. From this perspective, the tendency for cat people and bird people to misunderstand one another is nothing new. It likely goes back to a time even before history's earliest cats, back to when the have and have-not people first noticed a widening chasm between them.[23]

Dissonance is the goading cousin of conflict. Biophilia may explain our inclination to associate with animals, but its role in producing, supporting, and defending (often energetically) the unowned cats and dogs that menace wildlife is a paradox inviting trouble. The contradiction rubs. It gets irritated and inflamed. While most homeless cats and dogs have little to do with humans, the people in their corner are nevertheless fierce in their protection of them. When conservationists respond that holding pets responsible is the only hope for the creatures they imperil, cat lovers accuse these wildlife defenders of cat hatred. The confounding effect is to set one expression of biophilia against another. Our love of animals, it seems, is at war with itself. Skirmishes are becoming more common.

At the Silicon Valley doorstep of tech giant Google, for instance, a group of employees created "GCat Rescue" to provide feeding stations, straw cat beds, and TNR to the estimated 125,000 stray cats on the property. That's about 2,500 times more than the 50 or so burrowing owls that nest in the fields and grasses around the area. The owls are rare in many places and listed as a species of "special concern" in California. (They're endangered in Canada.) Nesting in the old burrows of grassy fields, the owls are also easy pickings for cats. Reports suggest some of the Google-subsidized felines are hunting them, especially in an adjacent 750-acre recreation area known as Shoreline Park. According to the

Santa Clara Valley Audubon Society, the burrowing owl population in the area has plummeted in the past decade, and they're pushing the tech giant to close down the cat-feeding stations. The GCat Rescue, now with national support from Alley Cat Allies, is urging Google to stand with the cats.[24]

Ground-nesting piping plovers are also sitting ducks (so to speak) for predatory cats. The small, stocky shorebird—like a busy, off-white tennis ball on legs—is considered "threatened" in New York. In other areas, such as around the Great Lakes, its populations are already endangered. That's why the Virginia-based American Bird Conservancy decided it had to act after multiple reports that a feral cat colony was thriving in Jones Beach State Park on New York's Long Island where the birds are known to nest. The conservancy sued the state parks department in March 2016 for violating the Endangered Species Act, saying officials were not doing enough to rid the park of the cats and to stop cat caretakers from supporting them. The case became a high-profile cat-people-versus-bird-people cause célèbre until the case was recently settled: the cats were "humanely" removed and placed in sanctuaries.[25]

Other cat–bird conflicts have become deeply personal. Newspaper reports tell of frustrated "ecovigilantes" nabbed for threatening or knocking off cats to save the animals they menace. Prominent birdwatcher Jim Stevenson of Galveston, Texas, may be the best-known example. A decade ago, Stevenson—the longtime executive director of the Galveston Ornithological Society—shot a feral cat he'd seen stalking piping plovers not far from the cat's colony under a highway overpass. He was cuffed, jailed, and tried on charges of cruelty to animals. Cat advocates called him a monster. Bird lovers raised money for his defense. The weeklong trial raised questions about whether the law really protected unowned cats and whether the Endangered Species Act similarly defended the birds. The queer split of animal allegiances resulted—perhaps unsurprisingly—in a hung jury. Days after Stevenson learned he was free and wouldn't be retried on the charges, someone—a person Stevenson believes was an infuriated cat lover—shot at him through the glass of his sunporch door.[26]

The case of Nico Dauphiné is also notorious. The scientist—and, at the time, a research fellow at the Smithsonian—was well known for her studies and views on cats killing birds. She had not been long in Washington, DC, before Humane Society officers showed up to accuse her of sprinkling rat poison in pet food left for feral cats outside her apartment building. (There was no evidence any cats were harmed.) Dauphiné denied the charge. Surveillance video, however, showed her taking something from her purse as she passed the spot. It was enough to convince a judge of her guilt. She was sentenced to a small fine and four months of community service. Representatives of Alley Cat Allies were at the trial, offering sound bites to news media and providing information about Dauphiné's earlier anti-TNR writing. The online blog, *Cat Defender*, complained the punishment didn't go far enough: "In dealing with low-life scumbags like her," it said of Dauphiné, "society can either lock her up permanently or idiotically turn her loose so that she can continue to kill cats with impunity; there is not any middle ground."[27]

Why would there be? Four of five American cat owners believe cats don't pose a serious problem for wildlife or conservation. In a wide-ranging survey of cat attitudes in six countries, an international team of researchers compiled more than 1,700 responses from the United States, the United Kingdom, Australia, New Zealand, Japan, and China. The study was conducted three years after Marra's widely reported killer-cat study. Only UK cat keepers are less likely than American cat owners to believe that cats preying on wild creatures means trouble (only one-in-eight cat owners think it's a problem at all). People who don't own cats are far more likely than their cat-accompanied compatriots to think that keeping cats should be regulated somehow. They're also more likely to think cats should stay in at night or should be restricted to their owner's property.[28]

The overall acceptance of free-roaming cats in Britain, however, is exceptional. Even the venerable Royal Society for the Protection of Birds doesn't condemn the practice. ("Despite the large numbers of birds killed by cats in gardens, there is no clear scientific evidence that such mortality is causing bird populations to decline," the nature-advocacy group argues.) Outdoor cats seem as sacred as tea. Australia and New Zealand, on the other hand, appear to have had a clearer view of their unique wildlife losses. Even cat owners in those two countries—both with distinctive, unique biodiversity and a record of recent extinctions—are more likely than both nonowners and owners in the United States and the United Kingdom to consider cat-caused wildlife deaths to be an issue. Interestingly, the large majority of both cat people and non-cat-owners in all four of the countries (more than 85 percent) heartily agree having wildlife around is a good thing.[29]

The differences in cat attitudes among countries is noteworthy. While American media continue to report the villainy of "cat killers," Australians, for example, have openly declared a "war on feral cats," recognizing them as the leading cause of native mammal extinctions across their continent. "The federal government will unleash every weapon in its arsenal to wipe out 2 million feral cats—about a third of the population—and will provide $5 million [US$3.4 million] to community groups to serve as foot soldiers in the battle," reported the *Sydney Morning Herald* in 2017. "It's a race to save about 124 species of native wildlife at risk of extinction from feral cats, which are notoriously hard to kill." Cats in Kosciusko and areas of remote Australia will be among those on the hit list; they're known to prey on mountain pygmy possums, bilbies, bandicoots, numbats, and night parrots. The government's massive national program—set to continue to 2020—includes plans to eliminate completely island-dwelling feral cats and to phase out domestic cats on Christmas and Kangaroo Islands as well as three other islands. About 211,000 cats were culled across Australia in 2016, according to reports.[30]

In New Zealand, cat owners and nonowners alike are also among those most likely to agree that cats are a danger to wildlife, but that doesn't mean cat lovers are always happy when their felines are in the crosshairs of severe conservation measures. In Omaui, New Zealand, for instance, cats in the town may soon be banned altogether. The local government plans to stop cat owners from acquiring any new cats as soon as their current pets die. In the name of local wildlife, the town is aiming to be completely cat free within years. Reports suggest some residents feel "hoodwinked" and "shocked" by the proposal, and they've vowed to oppose it.[31]

A middle ground may exist somewhere. The City of Cornwall's cat-candidate Mary Jane Proulx, for one, believes it does. Something that's recognizably common to cats—as animals, as sentient beings—and to the no-less-worthy wildlife must be out there that can stop the constant warring. "I've come across neighbors fighting and yelling, screaming at each other. I say, look, I don't care. Right now, just get along, okay? You know I'm here for the bloody cats. I don't care if you yell and scream and swear. Just think of the cats."

On election night, weeks after my initial visit to cat-ridden Cornwall, the countdown to the final tally is suspenseful to the last. For Proulx, there's a moment of added panic. Mingling with a crowd of other council-seat campaigners and supporters, she watches the results roll in on a big, arena-sized screen at the city's civic complex. She's pleased to see her early poll numbers climb quickly ("a vote for me was a vote for the cats," she says), but almost immediately feels a rush of anxiety as they keep on going. "I said, holy shit," she says, recalling the instant when her victory looked likely. "I mean, I'm counting how many polls are left, and I saw that there were about half. I got scared. I thought, there's no way in hell that I want to get in there. I know nothing about politics. This is just a spoof—like Trump."

To her relief, Proulx—the council campaigner whose only platform imagined a town at peace with the welfare of homeless cats—comes up short. Her final count, 1,532 votes, puts her in the bottom half of the pack. By the end of the evening, Proulx is thrilled with her surprising— and happily unsuccessful—results. She is mercifully spared the mantle of governance, and yet she manages to beat eight other more serious contenders. Her results, she says, suggest people are listening; the cats matter to Cornwall. More importantly, she succeeded in her trouble-making mission: "It was fun. I pissed off people, and that was my main goal. And I got people talking."

Proulx's campaign was a stunt, but her message—why can't we all get along—is sincere. Of course, she says, feral cats kill some birds and other wildlife. It can't be helped. Dead birds, however, change nothing concerning the blameworthiness of the cats. They aren't responsible. They didn't create the problem; we did. Proulx's earnestness reveals a lot about pets-versus-wildlife intractability. She really does—as she says— love animals. Cats, quite simply, are the animals she knows. Wildlife, not so much.

Cats have been padding around this continent since the arrival of Europeans. Domestic dogs have been here even longer. For pet owners like Proulx, thinking of our household chums as deadly invasive preda-tors takes some getting used to. We glimpse, instead, a contented pooch by the fireplace or a purring cat in the window, and we picture them wandering the great, adventurous outdoors. It's a happy image. Our pets have been in the picture for so long, they seem to belong everywhere. In our world, perhaps they do. In the wild world, however, it's tragically different.

CHAPTER 4
Aliens in Eden

Tom Rahill is sprawled on his stomach in the cool Everglades swamp water wrestling in a tangle of cypress roots and snake. "Da head! Watch da head!" The shouts and splashing shatter an otherwise serene wilderness morning. The towering trees huddle. The sun shines through in angled shards. "There's a hole! I think she's going for the hole!" Rahill—hat gone and glasses askew—looks uncomfortable. His companions—the other madmen in this seemingly ill-conceived venture—dance through the trunks and scrub, yelling directions. "She's coming back at you, Tom! Watch da head!"

The snake—all 3.6 meters (12 feet) of her thigh-thick, twisting, Burmese python length—has indeed doubled back, and she doesn't look happy. Rahill has her by the tail. After trying desperately to pull herself free, she's turned on her aggressor to offer him a taste of his own medicine. The snake's insistent power is terrifying. She strikes. "Tom! Watch it, Tom!" Rahill rolls slightly. "Watch it!" He pulls back on the tail to throw off her purchase. He gives his arm a quick shake; one of the snake's needle-sharp teeth (pythons have rows of them) found some unprotected skin. The wound is slight, but it stings. The massive snake turns again. Rahill scrambles. He can see she's slowing, exhausted now and not quite warm enough to muster her most spirited fight. Rahill moves. He pulls while snatching for her neck. He grabs and holds on. "Dat's it, Tom! Dat's it!" The python flexes and writhes, but Rahill has her firm. He squares himself and lifts her high, draped like a great, over-sized cable. "Dat's it! You got her!"

The others close in. Troy Landry—star of the popular History Channel reality series *Swamp People*—is among them. His spirited shouts and Louisiana accent animate the drama: "Look at dat!" he says with admiration. "Oh yeah, dat's a big snake!" Landry has wrestled reptiles in front of television cameras for years; he's a master of made-for-television awe. Landry steps forward, offering a pillow-case-like cloth sack. Rahill slings the python's 27-plus kilograms (more than 60 pounds) between his upraised hands, ready to lower her into the bag. His fellow python hunters, Joe Franco Medina and Ernesto Eljzaiek, slosh through the wet for a closer look. The cameraman and sound engineer step up behind. Executive producer Brian Catalina watches appreciatively. Through the trees a tranquil canal is visible along the narrow dike. Beyond is the Ever-glades' great flat expanse—miles over miles of saw grass and alligators. Cypress woods dot the distance, and egrets, slender and white, wait.

"She didn't like you," says Landry, laughing. "She was mad. She didn't like you at all."

The immense marshes, mangroves, and woodlands of Florida's Ever-glades make up one of the most famous and spectacular wild areas in North America. Covering more than 6,500 square kilometers (2,500 square miles) across a large part of southern Florida, the Everglades is a wide expanse of mostly shallow, slow-moving water tipping from Lake Okeechobee across the low, flat southern peninsula like liquid across a broad, even plate. Its plains of ragged saw grass and pockets of pine woods and cypress constitute one of the world's largest wetlands and an unparalleled wilderness jewel.

Hot, wet summers and warm, dry winters create a subtropical world alive with an extraordinary and rich biology. Endangered Florida panthers, leatherback turtles, and West Indian manatees are among its best-known inhabitants. Reptiles (including both alligators and crocodiles in the only place on earth where they live side by side) include about 50 different species. Bird varieties number more than 360. Scores of mammals—deer, marsh rabbits, opossums, raccoons—live here too, along with a remarkable diversity of plants, insects, and coastal and wetland fish. Open, grassy swamp and soaring, primeval-looking cypress lend an almost *Jurassic Park* feel to the place. The large numbers of big reptiles help.

"I had read about it as a kid," says Rahill of his decades-long Everglades enchantment. "Then, once I saw it, man. . . ."

Rahill leaves off. It's been a half hour since the snake wrangler's intentionally theatrical, made-for-TV python fight, and we're back in his dusty truck. It's a late-nineties Ford F150 with a well-used canoe slung above. The other members of the team and the television crew are gathering gear. The swamp around us is peaceful again. The long, remote levee road that brought us here is dry and quiet. Rahill is looking through a pile of tools, flashlights, gloves, and other clutter, searching for antiseptic for his snakebite.

Rahill is a stalky, energetic man with a sharp wit and a grizzled beard. His glasses are smudged. Under a battered brimmed hat, a black bandana is tied just above his short, gray ponytail. Rahill first came to the Everglades in 1975. He was a wayward, troubled teen at the time, he recalls, and the swamp spoke to him. The wilderness here has been central to his life since. He knows it as few others do. "The beauty," he says, finally, "and also the inherent dangers of the Everglades matched the angst I felt within. The turmoil, the roiling inside my soul, was met by this beautiful and yet brutal environment." Now, Rahill is fighting desperately to save it—by tangling with massive snakes.

Rahill is a contractor hired by the US and state governments as a frontline soldier against a curious invasion: an onslaught of hundreds of thousands of former pet Burmese pythons and their descendants. Scientists say the enormous serpents—native to South and Southeast Asia and one of the largest snakes in the world—first came to the state as the exotic companions of snake-loving pet owners before they escaped or were released into the South Florida swamp. They soon found the subtropical Everglades suited them fine. They happily breed, and they happily hunt. Now, hundreds of thousands of them call the Everglades home. The native wildlife, meanwhile, is disappearing fast. In a region that's suffered hundreds of species invasions—including dozens of tropical birds and lizards—over the past century, the pythons stand out. Their predatory success is remarkable. Their ecological havoc, according to researchers, is profound. "Everything's being wiped out, basically," says Rahill. "The snakes have just had a field day."

Rahill was hired to catch them, to try to slow the invasion and protect the wildlife, and then he had an idea: he created an entire team of python hunters comprised entirely of US Army veterans, most of whom are former combat soldiers from Iraq or Afghanistan. He calls the group the "Swamp Apes" and says its chief aim is therapy. Some of the members struggle with physical injuries or more psychological battlefield scars, such as post-traumatic stress disorder, says Rahill. They hunt the enormous snakes—usually watching for pythons while driving the long dikes at night—not only for the sake of the Everglades but for the relief that comes with a sense of aim and adventure. It helps them to help. "I wanted to do something," explains Rahill. "One of the common themes of loss for veterans when they get out [of the service] is a lack of camaraderie and the lack of purpose. Swamp Apes provide a purpose."

In the meantime, they catch a lot of snakes—101 so far between January and November 2018, with another promising month ahead, says Rahill. They've also attracted a lot of attention. The group has appeared on CNN, NBC, PBS, and scores of other national and international media. An episode of *Swamp People* is just the latest spotlight. The reality television show, which has entertained its History Channel audience for most of a decade, interrupted its usual diet of Louisiana gator hunting to follow Rahill's python patrol. Reports that Everglades' Burmese pythons were breeding with escaped Indian rock pythons to create a "super snake" hybrid added sensational appeal to the visit.

"It's amazing that this all got started with a bunch of meatballs who released these animals into the swamp," Rahill reflects. "In Everglades National Park, I actually caught some guys releasing a snake. I was actually looking for snakes, and there were three guys, and they pulled a snake out of their trunk. . . . You know, they really love these animals." Rahill smirks and shakes his head. "'Go free, Fluffy.'"

One of Rahill's snake bosses is a biologist named Michael Kirkland. I travel to meet him a couple of days later, a few hours north at his West Palm Beach office. Kirkland is young, sharp, and intense in a way that Rahill—with his breezy ease—could never be. The snake invasion and his army of snake hunters are his focus. The scale of this pet-release catastrophe and its consequences are gathering momentum, and if it can't be stopped, it must be slowed. Kirkland, the chief of defense in this battle, is determined. "I work seven days a week, and I haven't stopped," he says. "I've had to get special agreement from my wife now. . . . So, yeah, it's absolutely consumed me, but she knows that I'm really passionate about this. We don't have children so our [snake hunter] contractors are kind of like my kids now."

Kirkland is an invasive animal expert with the South Florida Water Management District (SFWMD). The agency manages most of South

Florida's wilderness—not including Everglades National Park and the Big Cypress National Wildlife Area—and is the area's largest landowner. Huge tracts of wetlands fall under its control, including the extensive Everglades and Francis S. Taylor Wildlife Management Area. The agency's aim is to manage and protect water across the southern half of the state, covering 16 counties from Orlando to the Florida Keys. Restoring the Everglades to bolster the ecosystem and its natural water-purifying powers has occupied the agency for the past few decades. The project, according to the agency's Web site, is the largest environmental restoration effort in US history.

Kirkland's role in this massive endeavor is to try to get rid of the pythons. He's as close as it gets to Florida's St. Patrick. Rahill and his Swamp Apes hold just one of the python-hunting contracts with SFWMD. There are 23 others. Kirkland oversees them all. (Most snake hunters, like Rahill, also share their time with the US National Park Service, catching pythons in the area parks.) Stopping or at least managing the pythons is critical. The snakes appear to be eating their way to a radical disruption of South Florida's entire watery ecosystem. "I call this a wildlife emergency," says the biologist. "We've seen a 99 percent reduction of fur-bearing animals in the Everglades National Park." One well-watched video shows a 3.4-meter (11 foot) python in the park coughing up a 65-kilogram (35 pound) deer. The big snakes have not only replaced alligators as the Everglades' apex predator, they're eating them as well. They've become an ecological juggernaut here, and their numbers have soared. Kirkland estimates between 500,000 and 1 million of the massive pythons now live and feed across the region. It's a staggering figure considering it all began with pets.

"Miami is ground zero for the exotic pet trade business in the United States," Kirkland tells me. "I mean, the exotic pet trade business is a billion-dollar industry, and I think a lot of Floridians, in particular, really enjoy owning some of these pets. You buy one in a pet store, and they look reasonable to own. But, you know, some of these species like the Burmese python, the reticulated python, and so on, quickly grow in size and become not practical to own. . . . And so unscrupulous pet owners will just set them free. And because of our climate here, a lot of exotic species are able to thrive."

Pythons aren't the only ones. An estimated 50,000 nonnative species have been introduced into the United States, and South Florida is home to hundreds of them. It is, after all, the Sunshine State—a comfortable, welcoming place. "I think it's somewhere around 50 percent of our plant population down here is exotic," says Kirkland. And it's not just the greenery. Budgerigars (originally from Australia), mynahs (from Asia), and bulbuls (Thailand) fill the trees. Rhesus macaque monkeys (Asia) perch there, too. Scarlet ibis (South America) scour the marsh bottoms for apple snails (Brazil), while Cuban tree frogs (the Caribbean) chorus nearby. Lionfish (the Indian and Pacific Oceans) swim coastal waters, and big, dinosaur-like black and white teju (Argentina) prowl the forests. The place has become an ecological hodgepodge. And, says Kirkland, pet owners are the main cause behind the mess. "Eighty percent, if I were to guess," of the region's alien animals were introduced as released or escaped pets, he says. The pythons just happen to be among the best known—and among the most devastating.[1]

"It's hard to compare these things," Kirkland explains, "but just as far as the predator–prey wildlife interactions, the Burmese python is probably our number one issue."

The first invading constrictor was spotted in Everglades National Park in 1977. Sightings soon became frequent. More of the pet snakes kept coming: federal figures for live animal imports suggest more than 99,000 Burmese pythons were brought into the United States between 1999 and 2006 alone. By the late 1990s, scientists witnessed "a population explosion" of the Everglades pythons, says Kirkland, and the animal's impacts were becoming increasingly hard to miss: numbers of

Everglades' wildlife—especially marsh rabbits and other mammals, reptiles, and birds—began falling fast; the snakes were swallowing them whole. "Anything on our endangered species list is potential prey for this species," says Kirkland. At least 68 animal and plant species that naturally live in the Everglades are now listed as threatened or endangered. The most famous include the Florida panther, the American crocodile, the West Indian manatee, and the snail kite.[2]

Many other species—especially small mammals and birds—have seen their populations plummet as well. Not all of this is the work of snakes, of course; land-use changes and other human impacts have had a hand as well. But abandoned and escaped former pets are nevertheless doing their part to shake things up here. While the Everglades National Park is internationally recognized as one of the world's great wilderness wetlands, it now has the dubious distinction of being the only developed-country UNESCO Natural World Heritage Site that's considered by the international body to be "in danger" of losing its heritage status. In 2012, the US Fish and Wildlife Service placed the Burmese python on its list of "injurious species," preventing anyone from bringing them into the United States or transporting them across state lines. "That legislation," says Kirkland, wryly, "probably came a little late."

Meanwhile, Kirkland's agency and the US National Parks Service, the Florida Fish and Wildlife Commission, and the US Fish and Wildlife Service share the seemingly quixotic task of trying to stop the snakes. (Nongovernment groups, including the Nature Conservancy, Auburn University, and the University of Florida pitch in where they can.) New science suggests "rapid evolution" is helping the pythons adapt to the cool and enabling a northward push—to where the Everglades lap against more populated areas and the creekside yards of unsuspecting homeowners. So far, professional snake catchers—Rahill, the Swamp Apes, and the rest of the "surly Everglades python hunters," as Kirkland calls them—add up to the best weapon these agencies have been able to muster. "Not only is it the most effective management effort to date," the biologist declares, "it's cost effective."[3]

Actually, the price is about $250 per snake. The python hunters earn minimum wage for each hour in the swamp—Kirkland tracks them using a GPS app on their phones—and receive another $50 for each snake caught. Pythons longer than 1.2 meters (four feet) pay out an extra $25 for every additional 30 centimeters (one foot). A 2.4-meter (eight foot) python, for example, earns $150. Snakes with eggs add $200 more. Almost three-quarters of the pythons rounded up so far have been longer than 1.2 meters. About half have measured more than two and a bit (more than seven feet). Altogether, Kirkland says, the python rustlers have dispatched about 2,000 animals in the program's first 19 months (it began in March 2017). It may seem a drop in the bucket, but considering the number of large and pregnant females among those caught, the impact is likely far more significant, he says.

"Essentially, we've removed tens of thousands of pythons from the Everglades, if you look at it that way," Kirkland explains. "If you were to put all these animals together, they would weigh over 22,000 pounds [9,980 kilograms] and be over 12,000 feet [3,360 meters] long, which is over two miles [3.2 kilometers]. . . . We don't know what the population is, so we can't say that we're putting X amount of dent in the population. I can't mathematically tell you that. But I will say that we haven't seen any other management programs that have had results like ours." He pauses and adds, gravely, "And I consider doing nothing not a good option."

Increasingly more scientists agree: invasive alien species are one of the single greatest threats to life's diversity the modern world has seen. In its 2019 summary report, the Intergovernmental Science-Policy Platform on Biodiversity and Ecosystem Services—an independent international science group monitoring biodiversity and often likened to the United

Nations climate panel—determined that worldwide records of new species invasions have increased by 40 percent since 1980. In 21 countries that keep careful records, the numbers of invaders have climbed about 70 percent in the last 50 years. People, for the most part, are the ones who put them there. Where these human-facilitated invasions occur, meanwhile, wildlife numbers have dropped by a fifth—or by even more in biodiversity hot spots.[4]

Species are disappearing, too. The wild works of nature—after 3.5 billion years of imagination-defying evolution—are being erased from the planet thanks to creatures and plants living where they shouldn't be. These invaders—transplanted to where other life and ecological systems are simply unprepared for them—have been linked to the recent extinction of *one-third* of all vanished animal species around the planet and one-quarter of all obliterated plant species. These numbers are new and come from recent work led by scientists at Britain's University College London. After examining 935 extinctions over the past 500 years for which the cause is known, researchers determined that invasive alien species have played a greater role in extinguishing animals and plants than any other factor so far, say the researchers. The impacts of over-hunting, overfishing, pollution, and disease appear far smaller (although these threats often work in concert). Climate change has had less impact too (for the time being; it's expected to grow worse). The destruction done by other native species (run amok) doesn't compare. Invasive aliens, according to the scientists, have been the *real* chart-topping annihilators.[5]

"By definition, *we* are the problem with aliens," says Tim Blackburn, the University College London professor who led the work, "because aliens are species that, you know, either deliberately or accidentally are, by human activities, moving to areas where they don't naturally occur. . . . We are continuing to introduce alien species to new areas all the time—pretty much every day, on average, a new established alien population is discovered somewhere around the world."

Blackburn is a bird nerd. He can't explain why. He grew up in a suburb outside London with little nearby wildlife (beyond the usual company of house sparrows and squirrels). He had no pets. Somehow, a fascination for birds showed up anyway, like a kind of early life bolt from the blue. "Apparently, I've been interested in looking at birds since before I could talk." His fascination steered him to the study of ecology and, eventually, to New Zealand during postdoctoral work. That's where the magnitude of invasions by nonnative species really hit home.

For millions of years, New Zealand's islands evolved a remarkable and unique biology without predatory mammals (beyond a few bats, seals, and dolphins). More than two dozen species of flightless birds emerged in this mammal-free idyll, and they lived unmolested. When the first Polynesian settlers showed up, everything changed. These pioneers brought dogs and rats. Hundreds of years later, British and European colonists added cats, possums, stoats, and anything else they could think of. Now, introduced mammals in New Zealand make up more than 30 species. The number of native species threatened with extinction, meanwhile, tallies to 219. Among these are 71 threatened birds.[6]

After Blackburn's plane touched down in New Zealand, he wasn't so much alarmed by the birds that were missing but by the common ones from elsewhere: "Initially, I was just struck by the incredible abundance of European bird species there," he recalls, speaking to me from his London office, "species that aren't supposed to be in New Zealand but are there in incredible numbers. . . . I went to a place on the south side, and there were just really large numbers of things like yellowhammers, buntings, greenfinches and goldfinches, blackbirds and song thrushes, and house sparrows and skylarks. Not only were they there, they were there in the kinds of densities that you just never see anymore in the

UK." Birdlife in New Zealand, in other words, has been turned on its head. Fifty-nine bird species have gone extinct—including many of the flightless ones—since first human contact, while almost 1 in 10 bird species now living in the country comes from somewhere else. For the rest of New Zealand's birds, close to half are also either threatened with, or at risk of, extinction. The most common menace facing the nation's threatened birds, meanwhile, is the risk from introduced alien invaders.[7]

Versions of this topsy-turvy ecological story are playing out all over the world. While biologists acknowledge most successful invasions by alien species seem to do no harm, the few that do are often especially destructive. In some places—Australia and Indonesia, for example—native mammals rather than birds are hardest hit by introduced invaders. In other regions, reptiles and amphibians are feeling the pinch. Different parts of life's diversity are affected differently as the geography changes: invaders contribute less to extinctions across continents—where their spread might not reach every corner and refuge—while alien invasions on islands are particularly deadly.[8]

Three-quarters of all birds, mammals, amphibians, and reptiles known to have gone extinct over the past 500 years have blinked out of existence on islands. And while these typically isolated, water-ringed lands make up hardly more than 5 percent of the planet's surface, more than one-third of all species currently considered "critically endangered" by the International Union for Conservation of Nature live on them. Most (more than 80 percent) are being nudged out of existence by the same handful of invaders: feral cats and dogs, rats, mongoose, pigs, and goats. All of them were introduced after humans came ashore.

While most extinctions have more than one cause, 126 of all recently vanished species are thought to have disappeared because of the impacts of alien invasive species alone. "Once they're in the environment, it's really, really difficult to put those worms back in the can," says Blackburn.[9]

"Part of this is just the fact that we are homogenizing environments as well. So, you know, we're moving to a situation where everywhere you go in the world you encounter the same few common species," he explains. "We live on a planet where millions of years of evolutionary history overlain on our ever-changing environment have given us biogeographic regions with different habitats containing different sorts of species. And you go to different places, and you have these wonderful distinctive floras and faunas. And, you know, do we really want to lose that?"

The problem is quickly getting worse. When Blackburn's team gathered together almost 3,500 records for nonnative bird introductions around the world over the last 500 years, it found as many invasions occurred in the years between 1983 and 2000 as occurred during the first four centuries of the period. In the old days, it seems, colonists took a long time to screw up the environment. They brought nonnative birds to hunt as game (e.g., ducks and geese) or to keep around as farm-friendly pest control (e.g., insect-eating songbirds). Some brought aliens for sentimental reasons and to fill forests with familiar birdsongs for homesick settlers. (One of the most abundant birds in North America, the European starling, was introduced in New York's Central Park by drugmaker and theater lover Eugene Schieffelin; his wish to fill Manhattan skies with birds that appear in Shakespeare's plays unleashed one of the most successful avian invasions ever.) But ships in the old days were sluggish, and travel was slow. Invasions were ponderous by today's standards. Now, people and creatures move constantly. Invading birds no longer arrive primarily from Europe. Most come from subtropical Asia and Africa bound for rapidly developing countries in the Middle East and elsewhere. The speed of this movement of wildlife is dizzying. And the purpose, mainly, is to satisfy a widespread yearning—for pets.[10]

"The rate at which things are being introduced has just increased enormously," says Blackburn, "and a lot of that—*most* of that—is going to be from the pet trade."

In his *Naturalis Historia*, Pliny the Elder argued that keeping caged birds as pets is a Roman invention; it was created, he wrote, by Marcus Laenius Strabo, a Brindisi-based bird lover in the first century BC. "From him," Pliny said, "began our practice of imprisoning within bars living creatures to which Nature had assigned the open sky." But the claim may have been a few thousand years off. More likely, keeping bird companions began as far back as civilization's dawn, during the early days of Mesopotamia or ancient Egypt. Even the Sumerians who ruled modern-day Iraq thousands of years ago had a word—*subura*—for birdcage. It's far from new. Our desire to lock up feathered things, to own the exaltation of creatures with wings, or to bring their wild music into our homes seems to be age-old if not altogether ancient.[11]

And almost from the time we began caging birds for pets, we began releasing them again. Often, they were freed into unfamiliar landscapes. Alexander the Great, for example, returned to Greece from India with native parakeets in iron cages, and wild populations of what are now known as Alexandrine parakeets soon made themselves at home across much of southern Europe. Early Babylonian, Polynesian, and Norse sailors brought caged birds on ocean voyages and released them as a way of determining when land was near. (The freed birds would return if they saw nothing but the sea.) Chinese Buddhists, a thousand years ago or so, started practicing *fangsheng*, or "release life," a custom of liberating caged birds or other animals to generate positive karma by an act of kindness.[12]

Today is different only in degree—a large degree: releases and escapes are now the most common pathways for alien vertebrate animals to invade unfamiliar environments around the globe. As exotic pet keeping gathers momentum—accelerated by increasing trade and traffic across a tirelessly traveled world—the chances of people setting free their exotic pet birds, snakes, lizards, or fish are growing as well. It happens all the time. Exotic pets are, by definition, no strangers to the wild. Many owners who grow tired of their pets believe they belong back there—even if the local "wild" is thousands of kilometers from the animal's native home. Released pets, say researchers, are most often those commonly available in pet stores, cheap to buy, long-lived, and capable of growing unmanageably large (compared with their cute baby selves at the time they're purchased). Pet owners who let oversized snakes slip silently into a swamp, say, or who unleash other exotic reptiles, amphibians, birds, and mammals into unknown landscapes can inadvertently change the world. One-third of the earth's most destructive aquatic invasive species, for example, come courtesy of aquarium and ornamental fish hobbyists who let their pets free or dump their water into wild waterways. More than half of all reported reptile and amphibian introductions have succeeded, creating entirely new populations in often far-flung lands. If the climate is right, the predators few, and the food plenty, exotic pets sometimes find paradise in unexpected wildernesses.[13]

"People get pets that turn out to be more difficult to keep or to handle than they realize or they get too big," explains Blackburn. "And people don't like to have their pets put to sleep, essentially, so they think that the most humane thing to do is to let them go to finish out their lives in the wild. But that, of course, is not the place you necessarily want them. . . . The situation we have here is that—through no fault of their own—these nonnative aliens are running around in areas—and it's not their fault that they're there—chewing their way through the native flora and fauna." The biologist pauses, as if readying pet-loving listeners for the inevitable. "There are many cases where eradication is going to be your best approach."

Recently, research led by the California-based group Island Conservation and published in the journal *PLOS ONE* suggests that wiping out island-dwelling feral cats and dogs, rats, pigs, mongoose, and goats could have outsized benefits for biodiversity around the world. The study suggests almost 1 in 10 of earth's most threatened bird, mammal, amphibian, and reptile species could be rescued from imminent extinction simply by ridding these human-introduced mammals from just 169 select islands (from among the planet's roughly 465,000). New Zealand is home to 11 of these islands. In 2016, the government there launched an ambitious, US$6 billion program to eliminate all invasive rats, cats, stoats, and other predators from every corner of the country's 268,000 square kilometers (103,475 square miles) by 2050. Australia shares a similar idea; its seven-year invasive species strategy aims to rid all of its 8,300 islands completely of invasive rats, cats, and rabbits. Around the world, more than 1,200 programs to eradicate invasive alien mammals have been tried in recent decades and most (85 percent) have succeeded in improving the fortunes of beleaguered native wildlife.[14]

"We're in a situation, essentially, where we have a duty to those native species that are just going to get chewed up by those aliens and potentially go extinct," says Blackburn. "We have to do something."

Unfortunately, annihilating some creatures to save others has never felt comfortable for animal lovers or fit well with conservation. People intent on rescuing species are often the same ones who think animals are fellow beings that deserve our solicitude. For this group, biophilia is less an abstract notion and more of a wellspring of human values. Our relationship with other living beings becomes clearest not when we think about their populations, but when we chance upon an individual and lock, for a moment, with its solitary gaze. We identify with them—as we do with people—in the singular. The suffering of one can weigh as heavily as the larger calamity of nudging entire species to the brink. When former pets are the issue—when our released or escaped creatures maraud native wildlife in unfamiliar environments—the paradox is magnified.

"For me, killing's off the table," Marc Bekoff declares, resolutely, from his Boulder, Colorado, home. "It's just not something that I'm going to support."

For Bekoff, an activist and emeritus professor of ecology and evolutionary biology at the University of Colorado, there's nothing particularly paradoxical about it. Bekoff is a prolific writer and champion of what he and others call "compassionate conservation." The movement—which many consider to be growing in popularity—directly challenges thinking that we can sacrifice individual animals in the name of life's variety. An essay in the journal *Conservation Biology* (Bekoff is a coauthor) sets out the argument: "With growing recognition of the widespread sentience and sapience of many nonhuman animals, standard conservation practices that categorically prioritize collectives without due consideration for the well-being of individuals are ethically untenable." In other words, morality makes the difference: it's what biophilia looks like up close and personal.[15]

"The basic tenets of compassionate conservation are, first, do no harm," explains Bekoff, "and that the life of every individual matters." The longtime animal biologist—he began in medical research but left his first doctorate because the lab work involved experimenting on live animals—is a passionate advocate. In recent years, he seems to be making his case everywhere at once. He's the author, for example, of an early and frequently cited *HuffPost* review of Peter Marra's book *Cat Wars*, portraying the Smithsonian scientist as something of a wannabe cat killer. He's published pieces decrying the cull of wolves to save elk at Yellowstone National Park or to help beleaguered caribou in Canada. He's fiercely critical of the alien predator eradication programs of Australia and New Zealand. He's also a dizzyingly fast talker. The hurtling pace has something irresistible about it. Our conversation clips along, lively and smart, until—almost imperceptibly—it's suddenly weirdly disorienting.

"Really, if an individual is alive, then, you know, we can't harm it, and that's really what it comes down to," he says. "I mean, you can cash it out, saying that they have the right to live and stuff like that, but I just look at it focusing on the life of each individual as being valuable in and of itself because they're alive. . . . It's not about saying, well, we've got a conservation problem out there, and as long as we minimize the pain and the suffering and the deaths then we're doing okay. It's really about saying killing is off the table. I just don't think that I've been granted permission to kill animals to save other animals."

And if native animals are dying because people release nonnative species that, in turn, kill them? Maybe, answers Bekoff, the native-versus-nonnative distinction is overblown: our obsession with eradicating alien species to save local ones may be ignoring the realities of inevitable ecological change (even if humans are mixing it up with the speed of a turbo-powered blender). Maybe, argue the compassionate conservationists (with disarming sincerity), there's something odiously political involved, the conservation equivalent of knuckle-dragging nativism: "A staunch commitment to maintaining historic [species] assemblages," they write in the *Conservation Biology* essay, "appears unrealistic and may be rooted more deeply in xenophobic ideology than scientific understanding." Perhaps it's more humane, if not more politically palatable, to think of aliens as simply wildlife that hasn't been around long enough to be considered native yet, says Bekoff.

"There's disagreement on a couple of levels," he explains. "One is, are the introduced animals really doing all the damage for which they're blamed, and the other is, is getting rid of them going to really solve any problem. . . . As a biologist, one of the arguments I make is that our ecosystems are evolving entities. They're not static. They're dynamic. And so, removing one species—say, an invasive animal with individuals that supposedly do this damage—doesn't necessarily stabilize an ecosystem."

These kinds of arguments worry Tim Blackburn. The thinking, he says, has the potential to worsen what is already one of the most alarming environmental threats to face our living planet in modern times. And it's a perspective that seems to be gaining popularity. More people embrace it because a fondness for animals—an expression of biophilia, ironically—is behind it: "People do love their animals," says the biologist, "and I can understand why they would get uptight about a situation where scientists or conservationists or managers are going in and potentially killing large numbers of more or less sentient vertebrates."

Even black rats attract sympathy. When authorities tried to eradicate the invasive rodents from Channel Islands National Park off Southern California a couple of decades ago, the outcry got ugly. Native species, including the endangered ashy storm petrel, Cassin's auklet, Scripps's murrelet, and the Anacapa deer mouse, were being devastated by the rats and, in some cases, teetered near vanishing altogether. A lawsuit by opponents stalled the rat extermination almost immediately, and when it finally got underway again, park rangers had to wear bulletproof vests. Local newspapers wrote of the outrage: "Who are humans to call other species invasive?" When the way was finally cleared to use toxic bait to eliminate the rats on the islands, men in an inflatable boat landed on one of them, Anacapa Island, and scattered pellets of vitamin K around the place as an antidote to the poison.[16]

Invasive species biology has been a target of scorn from popular science writers and some academics for years. The fact that many alien vertebrates are former pets (or their descendants) likely worsens the emotional stakes. Scientific uncertainty—expected when trying to anticipate alien impacts into the future—leaves plenty of scope for skepticism. Ignoring principles of precaution, some writers prefer to highlight the benefits of a few aliens over the disproportionate havoc wrought by others. Science journalist Fred Pearce, for instance, attracted attention with his 2015 book *The New Wild: Why Invasive Species Will Be Nature's Salvation*. Similar articles and essays followed. Two researchers at Montreal's McGill University tracked how many; they found the popularity of arguments discrediting invasive species science has grown exponentially in recent times. Blackburn and his New Zealand colleague James Russell likened the trend to antiscience efforts by climate-change skeptics and antivaxxers. They invented a term for it—"invasive species denialism."[17]

"I mean partly, you know, you could argue that for most species, there isn't evidence that they're having an impact, so actually we shouldn't get too upset about it," says Blackburn. "I think that's essentially the position of most invasion biologists I know anyway. But when you actually see all these new species, we don't necessarily know what the effects of those species are going to be. So, it's possible that the next big thing in alien invasions is just being introduced at this moment or being established at this moment, and we don't know what that's going to be or what effect it's going to have. So, you know, it's a dangerous game to play here.

"There are thousands of species that have populations in trouble around the world already," says Blackburn. "So, this is already a major issue that we are going to have to face up to if we want to maintain our biodiversity in a reasonably intact and reasonably distinctive way. . . . It's almost inevitable that any human activity is going to have some sort of value system involved in it. I would just argue that our sort of moral responsibilities in this case are weighted towards preventing the loss forever of these unique species that evolved over millions of years and are going extinct a hundred to a thousand times the natural background rate." The biologist's voice betrays his sense of urgency. "I think you have to look at it from the perspective of both sets of species, as it were: do we have a moral responsibility to the individuals of this alien species or do we have a moral responsibility to the individuals of this native species that our actions are driving to extinction? I think the balance probably tips toward the latter."

To kill a python, Everglades snake wrangler Tom Rahill carefully presses a metal rod against its head and, with a special weight, gives it a sharp, forceful whack. The tool scrambles the animal's brain and kills it instantly, he tells me. The euthanasia is required by the agencies that hire him. He's not thrilled to talk about it—the Swamp Apes is intended as a therapeutic group, and Rahill fears any publicity around killing the creatures could detract from its rehabilitation aims. It might also divert attention from the larger issue of the future of one of the world's great wildernesses. "There's a lot of folks that, you know, would rather see the pythons live their lives naturally," Rahill explains, "but they don't understand the devastation they're causing.

"My answer to them is, why don't you like rabbits? Well, because if you like rabbits, you'd want us to remove these pythons. They're devastating the native rabbit population as well as other animal native species that belong here—thanks to irresponsible pet owners coming out after two or three years and then having this snake grow to gargantuan proportions and then releasing it."

Rahill is telling me this as the two of us drive the levee looking for more snakes. By now, the *Swamp People* film crew has gone. They've moved on closer to the coast to shoot another segment. This time, it's about invasive green iguanas. The huge iguanas, which can grow to more than 1.5 meters (five feet), are driving wealthy, beachfront homeowners crazy. They're digging in banks and gardens, defecating across lawns, and fouling power lines. Water management authorities don't like them much either; the enormous lizards have a nasty habit of burrowing into dikes and dams, compromising Florida's canal and water system. The prehistoric-looking beasts are native to the Caribbean and South America but arrived in the state almost half a century ago—as pets. Like the pythons, they were released or escaped and soon found Florida's subtropical landscape quite comfortable enough to make themselves at home. Climate warming has made it more so; the seasonal cold snaps that once kept iguana numbers in check don't happen often anymore. The population—now estimated in the hundreds of thousands—is thriving. For Troy Landry and his team, the iguana hunting also promises good TV.

Rahill hopes his python bit makes the show, too. The Swamp Apes could use the exposure. Rahill is hoping to grow his organization and to help more veterans. Ideally, he'd like to coax the state or federal government to provide some funding. (Right now, Rahill says, much of the Swamp Apes overhead is paid for out of his pocket.) He also wants the wider world to know what his beloved Everglades is up against with these invading pets. Rahill has spent more than four decades tromping through this beguiling wilderness, and he knows it intimately. He's watched, ringside, as invading plants and animals have transformed it. He's no trained scientist, but he's an expert in the biodiversity losses that have impoverished this rich, wild wetland forever. His enchantment has turned to worry.

"It's the wildlife, man," he says, as dust curls behind the rattling truck. "The wildlife has diminished significantly. Mainly mammals. Started really seeing it in the mideighties and into the nineties. It started just really being evident. On this road, back then, you'd see raccoons, possums, cottontail rabbits, marsh rabbits, in particular—they use the same runs that the pythons hunt in." Rahill rubs his scruffy chin. "It's a changed place, man," he says. "It's just changed."

CHAPTER 5
Fire Lizards and Plague Dogs

Lost Bay Nature Reserve in eastern Ontario is tiny by the standards of great world wildernesses—not quite 2.5 square kilometers (one square mile) all told. In environmental importance, however, it punches above its weight. The woods, the pine trees, and the rich, black-water marshes are a small part of what conservationists consider a crucial ecological "bridge." They call it the Frontenac Arch, and it's more of a ridge than a bridge. The narrow stretch of granite and marble, covered for the most part by scattered woodlots and rocky fields, links the stony expanse of the Canadian Shield to the Adirondack Mountains of New York. It's noticeably more rugged than the surrounding landscape. Five different forest types intersect along the arch, bringing together a startling array of plants and animals from every direction Almost no other place in Canada has a greater variety. Recognition of the fact earned it a designation as a UNESCO World Biosphere Reserve. The reserve itself boasts 24 species rare enough to be considered at risk of extinction. The wonderful diversity is much of the reason John Urquhart loves the place.

Urquhart is a young ecologist who, when we meet, is leading an ongoing effort to uncover and map the whereabouts of all the salamanders, frogs, snakes, turtles, and lizards found in Ontario, Canada's second-largest province. The project, called the Ontario Reptile and Amphibian Atlas, was created to gather observations by hundreds of volunteer naturalists who scour large areas that comprise squares of a grid superimposed on a map of the province. When an area needs special attention or when an important grid square isn't being covered by volunteers, Urquhart and his colleague, Joe Crowley, take to the field themselves. Other regional or even larger amphibian monitoring projects—including the Global Amphibian Assessment run by the International Union for Conservation of Nature—compile similar information around the world.

When I pull into the reserve, Urquhart emerges from the lone cabin with long, bouncing strides. Lanky with boyish, dirty-blond hair and a broad, infectious smile, the young field biologist is in his element; the work on behalf of a nature-and-conservation organization known as Ontario Nature (with support from the provincial government) suits him perfectly. Field biology is his passion, he tells me. (Down the road, well after our meeting, he'll go on to establish his own fieldwork-based ecological consulting company, Blazing Star Environmental.) As I step out of the car, the biologist greets me eagerly, keen to show me around. Reptiles and amphibians comprise some of the province's most secretive and enigmatic creatures, and Urquhart is expert at revealing their secret world. Salamanders, in particular, are among the province's most elusive wildlife groups. "We just need to know more," Urquhart tells me. "It's a big data gap."

We talk for a time before starting what quickly becomes an energetic, loping hike through the open, midsummer forest. It's work to keep up. Urquhart's long legs move fast. He heads up the first slope, moving back and forth in a sort of zigzag pattern. Here and there, he stops, rolling back logs the way a kid in a just-discovered corridor opens door after hallway door. Moving from one fallen tree trunk to the next, he lifts each log and peers intently beneath, studying for a moment as if looking into a strange, dark passage. "There," he says as I hurry up behind him. A tiny black shape suddenly skitters from the shadows. It looks at first like a fast-escaping beetle. Urquhart deftly scoops it up and reveals an impossibly small, fully formed salamander. Its glistening eyes were no bigger than punctuation. "Baby redback," he explains. "This might have hatched a week ago . . . maybe just days."

For a moment, even Urquhart looks startled at its proportions; an animal this tiny is a rare find even for a regular visitor to the cryptic places a rolled log reveals. "Redback salamanders are the only amphibians in Ontario that don't have an aquatic larval stage," he tells me. "Other young salamanders and frogs live as tadpoles in ponds and streams. Baby redbacks like this are the only ones to hatch on land looking like miniature adults."

Urquhart knows his salamanders. Not many do. As a group, amphibians are among our least familiar and most poorly understood noninsect animals. Outside of the spring chorus, when marshes thrum with the peep and croak of singing frogs and toads, the world's amphibians are extremely successful at remaining inconspicuous. Even for many naturalists, they're often a question mark—a kind of natural-history blind spot. The irony is that our forests are home to greater numbers of amphibians than to any other land vertebrates, including birds and rodents. Salamanders, in particular thrive: North America is the global center of salamander biodiversity. More than half of all the world's 738 recognized species live here (205 in the United States, 151 in Mexico, and 21 in Canada). More significantly, few other animals are as vital to local ecosystems—as food for other creatures and for moving nutrients into the forest from enriched pools and ponds as they metamorphose from water to land dwellers. Meanwhile, their typically dual citizenship in both aquatic and terrestrial domains makes them especially qualified as harbingers of environmental change.[1]

This canary-in-a-coal-mine role is sobering—especially considering that, right now, salamanders, newts, frogs, and toads constitute the most at-risk class of animals on the planet. Almost one-third of all critically endangered creatures on earth belong to the group. Scientists say 32 percent of the world's more than 6,770 known and assessed amphibian species are now threatened with extinction (compared with 13 percent of all birds and 21 percent of mammals). Already 34 species are formally listed as gone from the wild forever, while 138 others are now possibly or presumed extinct as well. In the tropics, the rate of vanishing amphibians is threatening to rival some of the great mass extinctions of history. It is, by many accounts, among the greatest conservation calamities of all time. "We're already losing these animals fast," Urquhart says. "What the future brings could be worse."[2]

The sad news is that, according to many researchers, what the future brings almost certainly will be worse. Urquhart's comment is a portent of a new and deadly killer on the horizon. Recently, amphibian biologists have been sounding the alarm about a previously unknown fungal disease that's devastating salamander populations in Europe and threatening to cross the Atlantic. The arrival of the skin-eating fungus *Batrachochytrium salamandrivorans*—meaning "devourer of salamanders"—could spell a wildlife disaster in North America. And what makes the situation so bleak, according to experts, is the disease's seemingly unstoppable means of getting around. The contagion hitches rides with internationally traded pets; its accomplices, as it turns out, are unwitting and pet-loving humans.[3]

Salamanders—secretive, far from cuddly, and not inclined to do much—are surprisingly popular household pets. For centuries, amphibian fanciers have been drawn to them for their cartoonish appearance and often brilliant coloring. Their bright yellow, orange, and red markings earned them the nickname "fire lizards" and the folkloric belief they can walk through flames without consequence. Some people associate them with other mythic qualities as well, such as immortality, because of their ability to regenerate lost limbs. Newts, or at least their eyes, have been linked to witchcraft and the occult (thanks, in part, to the cauldron incantation from Shakespeare's *Macbeth* and the zany sketches of Monty Python). Collectors especially prize exotic species. According to the US Fish and Wildlife Service, an estimated 2.5 million live salamanders, representing 59 species, were imported into the United States between 2004 and 2014. In 2014 alone, as much as $1.3 million worth of salamanders (at market prices) entered the country to join the homes of eager pet aficionados. Experts consider the creature's popularity as an animal companion to be the biggest concern. Encounters between released or escaped pet salamanders and their unsuspecting wild cousins may be inevitable, say scientists; the spread of *Batrachochytrium salamandrivorans*—or Bsal, for short—to natural populations may be equally as certain.[4]

There's another reason scientists are worried. The fungal disease has a chilling precedent: mass deaths of millions of frogs around the world over the past few decades have been linked to another similar pet-trade-fueled pandemic. A sister variety of fungus—this one named *Batrachochytrium dendrobatidis*, or Bd—has been wiping out populations and species of frogs and toads with fearsome alacrity. In lush equatorial jungles and tropical mountain forests, outbreaks of Bd have been particularly catastrophic. About 500 species of frogs have seen their numbers plummet, and 90 are now thought to have gone extinct altogether. More than half of the roughly 1,300 species of frogs and toads that have been tested for the disease show signs of the fungal infection. Colorful harlequin frogs in South and Central America have been particularly hard hit, including the revered-but-now-disappeared Panamanian golden frog.[5]

Batrachochytrium dendrobatidis is found almost throughout the globe—in 52 of 82 countries that have been sampled. Recently, a team

traced its genetic trail to the likely birthplace of the disease in Asia, probably somewhere on the Korean Peninsula. The researchers conclude that
the massive spread of the disease was almost certainly caused by a growing global trade in exotic pet amphibians that began in the early 1900s.
"The international trade in amphibians has undoubtedly contributed
directly to vectoring this pathogen worldwide," the authors write; Bd is
now regarded as the worst case in recorded history of a single pathogen
affecting vertebrates.[6]

In North America, outside the tropics, Bd's impact is less dramatic;
many amphibians on the continent have been infected but apparently
without causing mass deaths. *Batrachochytrium salamandrivorans*, on the
other hand, is unlikely to be so forgiving. Lab tests involving Bsal have
already shown that the new disease is deadly for at least a dozen North
American salamanders and newts. While scientists don't know exactly
how Bsal kills, the fungus is known to invade the salamander's skin,
which plays a crucial role in the animal's immune system and its breathing. Susceptible infected salamanders grow listless, unwilling to eat, and
die within a week or two. In experimental tests, for example, intentionally infected Eastern red-spotted newts, a common animal often kept as
a pet, and rough-skinned newts, a widespread species that ranges from
Mexico to British Columbia, suffered symptoms soon after and invariably died. These common creatures, or so the thinking goes, are well
positioned to spread and amplify the disease among other salamander
species if Bsal makes it to the continent's shores. Our cold winters—a
factor that can often freeze out other diseases from flourishing here—is
unlikely to help. Researchers say that if the fungus infects North America's wild salamanders, stopping it may be next to impossible.

In 2019, more than 40 academics writing in the top journal *Science*
warned that the impact of Bd and Bsal together—the health consequence of both is known as "chytridiomycosis"—is so far responsible
for "the greatest recorded loss of biodiversity attributable to a disease."

Nine of every 10 species hammered by the disease since the 1980s still show no signs of population recovery, say the authors, while about 4 in 10 continue to see their numbers dwindle. Other better-known animal-killing diseases, such as West Nile virus in birds and white-nose syndrome in bats, don't come close to the devastation chytridiomycosis has wrought so far. The scientists caution that far more amphibians will die if these fungi—Bd or Bsal—are allowed to spread to new regions.[7]

The National Amphibian Monitoring Program of the Netherlands has been keeping tabs on frogs, toads, and salamanders in that country for more than two decades. Like the Ontario Reptile and Amphibian Atlas in Canada, the Dutch monitoring program compiles reports from amateur naturalists throughout the country. The small, low-lying nation is among the most densely populated in Europe and not the first place people think of for its variety of wildlife. Nevertheless, green space is abundant, and the Wadden Sea National Parks along the North Sea coast comprise the biggest tidal wetland in Europe. Sixteen species of Dutch amphibians make their home in the Netherlands. Although nine are listed on the national Red List of threatened or endangered animals, none were considered at risk of disappearing—until recently.

In 2008, conservationist Annemarieke Spitzen-van der Sluijs was working as the Dutch equivalent of John Urquhart—as a project manager with the Netherlands monitoring program—when the first dead salamanders began to show up. Lifeless bodies of adult endangered fire salamanders were discovered again and again lying on forest footpaths in the south of the country where the species is known. The dead creatures appeared simply stopped in their tracks; no signs of injury were visible. In 2010, concern escalated: the number of live fire salamanders spotted by monitoring volunteers began to fall dramatically, and by 2012, only two animals were seen (despite increased efforts to find them). When 39 salamanders were captured to start a captive-breeding program, half of them died too. Postmortems found no evidence of the usual amphibian diseases, including Bd. The population had crashed by 99.9 percent within seven years.[8]

It was a mystery. For Spitzen-van der Sluijs—who, along with her conservation work, had simultaneously embarked on a doctorate studying amphibian diseases—the puzzle fell neatly into her lap. Her doctoral advisers, An Martel and Frank Pasmans, happened to be leading wildlife pathologists at Ghent University in Belgium and experts in Bd and other frog-and-salamander-killing illnesses. The researchers began to look for clues in the livers, spleens, kidneys, and skin of the dead salamanders. After ruling out the usual suspects among deadly diseases, they discovered a strange fungus growing in one of the petri dishes. Genetic analysis revealed it to be something none of them had ever encountered. As it turned out, Bsal was a species of fungal killer never described by science before. The research team was gobsmacked.[9]

Using genetic markers, the scientists carefully tracked the new killer back to its native home. Like Bd, they found it thousands of kilometers away in Asia, likely Vietnam. In that part of the world, the fungus appears to live harmlessly among Thai, Vietnamese, and Japanese salamanders that have grown resistant to its lethal effects. So how did the disease reach the Netherlands? The researchers analyzed skin samples from more than 1,700 amphibians in European pet shops, at London's Heathrow airport, and at the warehouse of a Hong Kong amphibian exporter. Three captive Vietnamese crocodile salamanders—making the rounds in the international pet trade—tested positive for the disease. Two had already been imported to Europe in 2010. The research team had their smoking gun, and they reported it in the journal *Science*: The source for the deadly infection killing endangered salamanders in the Netherlands was very likely a pet.

The new conservation catastrophe had been unleashed by a Dutch pet lover's fancy for exotic Asian amphibians. Now, the diversity of salamanders across Europe—almost an entire taxonomic order of animals—could be in peril.[10]

By 2016, the fungus was reported in the wild in Belgium and Germany and in a pet store in the United Kingdom. Researchers tried to determine what would happen next. They used computer models to anticipate how bad it might get. An "unlimited spread" of the disease is possible, they reported. It was beginning to look more like the arrival of the fungus on the shores of North America may only be a matter of time.[11]

When Europe's first trans-Atlantic links with North America were forged more than 500 years ago, tragedy was among the first to make the voyage. Columbus's landing on October 12, 1492, marked the beginning of waves of European infectious diseases that, for centuries afterward, killed more native North Americans than were born each year. Plagues of smallpox, measles, influenza, and other murderous viruses carried by European settlers swept like wildfire through indigenous communities lacking immunity to Old World pathogens, killing millions. In the same way epidemics accompanied the human colonizers, diseases associated with their domestic animals did too. In 1889, for example, colonial Italian soldiers in Africa brought along livestock and, unwittingly, a measles-like virus known as rinderpest. The alien disease quickly decimated millions of African cattle, sheep, and goats, as well as 90 percent of Kenya's buffalo and countless giraffe, wildebeest, and other wild animals. Unable to herd or hunt, one-third of Ethiopians and two-thirds of the Maasai people of Tanzania starved to death within a few years.[12]

"When you translocate a person or an animal, you translocate a zoo of bacteria, viruses, and other things with them," explains Canadian wildlife health expert Craig Stephen. "It's no different for you or me than it is for a dog than it is for a frog. When we bring an animal from one ecosystem into another, we bring parasites, bacteria, or viruses that the animals in the receiving environment have never seen before and may be more susceptible to."

Stephen is head of the Canadian Wildlife Health Cooperative, the vanguard of Canada's efforts to stop new wildlife diseases before they find a foothold here. The earnest but friendly scientist with a broad moustache and a ready grin took the helm of the organization in 2014. His headquarters are connected to the Western College of Veterinary Medicine at the University of Saskatchewan near the country's geographic middle in Saskatoon. The Canadian Wildlife Health Cooperative's main task is to coordinate and compile the work of frontline wildlife research labs—the places with the gurneys, examining rooms, and microscopes—located in Canada's five veterinary colleges scattered across the country as well as at the British Columbia Animal Health Centre.

The Canadian Wildlife Health Cooperative operates independently from government, but its funds come from about 30 different federal and provincial ministries that recognize the importance of wildlife health to everyday human lives. Wildlife diseases can spill over into agriculture, for example, and can affect food security. Some diseases disrupt trade. Others—think HIV or avian flu—infect and kill people directly. This last concern is, of course, a big one. Scientists believe most emerging infectious diseases that threaten people today are "zoonotic," meaning they originate (sometimes as mutants) from the host-switching diseases of animals. A vast and largely unknown reservoir of these bugs exists among wildlife. The Canadian Wildlife Health Cooperative functions as a kind of early warning system, says Stephen. It fulfills the Canadian and provincial monitoring obligations under the World Organization for Animal Health (originally called the Office International des Epizooties) of the World Trade Organization.[13]

Wildlife diseases are also important to conservation. The impact of wild animal health on biodiversity has been a longtime interest for

Stephen. He got his start working at a nature reserve before becoming a vet and, later, completing a doctorate in epidemiology. His thesis explored infections in wild salmon. Not long ago, wildlife diseases were viewed as simply nature's way of culling the weak or rebalancing oversized animal populations, Stephen explains. "And that was the dogma for many years. But now in this era of emerging infectious diseases, we are seeing diseases driving some species to extinction or on to the endangered species list." The big difference today is "cumulative effects," he tells me. A century ago, before the widespread impacts of climate change, habitat loss, urbanization, and globalization, wild animals were often resilient and could bounce back when illnesses struck. "But now, when we start thinking about all these different challenges wildlife face, the addition of a disease can push them over the edge."

That's what makes our biophilia-inspired love of pets such a pernicious problem for those worried about wildlife health. Stephen, who has spent years studying how animal sickness gets around, considers pets accompanying globe-trotting humans to be especially nimble as vectors of wild creature infections. Many pets are unaffected by the diseases they carry. They can live and travel with otherwise deadly disease wherever their pet-owning humans care to take them. Pet-borne illnesses have been blamed for battering biodiversity all over the world. Mass animal deaths—from Africa to Hawaii and elsewhere—have been linked to viruses and parasites released into the wild by companion animals.[14]

Many consider the situation to be particularly bad, but Stephen warns that the scale of the problem remains difficult to put a finger on: "For starters, it's difficult to measure disease-related deaths in the wild," he says. It's harder still to apportion blame when animals are already beleaguered by many other human impacts. "The challenge is not to get into a 'he said, she said' situation" concerning how much wildlife disease is linked to pets," he explains. "The challenge is to advocate for responsible pet ownership. . . . We need to think about this when we're thinking about what we want to bring into a country and about what assurances we have that whatever the pets bring with them—their internal zoo—is not going to be released into the environment."

One environment known for some of the world's most impressive wild animals is the Serengeti region of East Africa. Home to two UNESCO World Heritage Sites and two Biosphere Reserves, its sweeping plains are famous for thunderous migrations of wildebeest and zebra as well as for magnificent elephants, giraffes, baboons, and other celebrated creatures. Safari-traveling tourists flock by the thousands to witness the spectacle themselves. What they won't see anymore, however, are African wild dogs. The rare, pack-hunting creatures went extinct in the Serengeti in 1991. They disappeared, say scientists, at the same time their population was being ravaged by illness.[15] Not long after, in early 1994, lions became sick as well. Researchers watched as six of the big cats convulsed with grand mal seizures. Other lions wandered nearby, disoriented or lethargic. The lion body count began to quickly mount, and before the year was through, more than 1,000 of the majestic animals had died a wrenching death. One-third of the Serengeti's lions perished in a proverbial blink of an eye.[16]

Scientists needed little time to identify the culprit: the killer was a virus known as canine distemper (CDV), and the probable source of the disease, say researchers, was pet domestic dogs from villages nearby. The strain of the lion-killing virus matched the strain found in the pets. Canine distemper is a terrible killer, causing lesions, diarrhea, and deadly swelling in the brain and spinal cord. The lions, said researchers, had never been exposed to it, and they had no immune defenses. The African wild dogs were similarly vulnerable (both to infection by CDV and to another great, pet-linked killer—rabies). A half a decade earlier, CDV—likely passed along by dogs in towns near Ethiopia's Bale

Mountains—almost annihilated the last of the world's rarest canine, the Ethiopian wolf. Outbreaks of CDV that also implicate pet dogs (as well as coyotes and foxes) have been similarly linked to die-offs of gray wolves in Yellowstone National Park in 1999, 2005, and 2008 after the once locally extinct animals were reintroduced just a few years earlier.[17]

For many conservationists, CDV—along with rabies—is one reason to view pet dogs less as man's best friend than as wildlife's enemy. Our four-legged companions can become wellsprings of inadvertent animal death among a lot of wild populations. While both CDV and rabies are now found almost everywhere, even among wild creatures, dogs—often living in close quarters in towns and villages—provide an ideal reservoir for the diseases, and pups offer a continual supply of new, susceptible hosts. When conditions are right and the domestic–wild contact is made, a reservoir will overflow, and an outbreak can take hold. What makes CDV especially alarming is its capacity to switch hosts. The disease doesn't simply travel between dogs and wild canines, such as wolves; it has infected animals as varied as harbor seals, dolphins, tigers, and monkeys. A few decades ago, CDV came close to rendering extinct the last black-footed ferrets in Wyoming.[18]

For other rare and threatened animals, infected cats are a greater worry. The world's most endangered wild cat—the Iberian lynx—was dealt a devastating blow when feline leukemia virus was discovered among its meager numbers in southern Spain between 2003 and 2007. Out of a total global population that barely tops 150, 6 of the stricken lynxes died. Scientists blame virus-carrying domestic cats for the outbreak. Feline leukemia virus is the world's second greatest killer of cats (after deadly trauma, such as being hit by cars). More than 8 of every 10 infected cats that fail to shake the virus die within three years. Several wild cats have been shown to be susceptible as well. Along with the Iberian lynx, jaguars, puma, bobcats, and even endangered Florida panthers have been sickened and killed by the virus. The panthers have seen their numbers dwindle to barely 200 adults in recent decades. In the early 2000s and again during the period from 2010 to 2016, outbreaks of the virus spread among the struggling panthers after being first passed along by domestic cats. In the rare animal's only known home in South Florida—a region where biodiversity has already suffered its share of insults—three of the rare wild cats infected by the disease died.[19]

In the world of wildlife extinctions, however, Florida can't hold a candle to Hawaii. The Pacific island paradise is, according to the American Bird Conservancy, "the bird extinction capital of the world." Since the arrival of humans on the archipelago more than a millennium ago, the group says 95 of 142 bird species found nowhere else on earth have disappeared forever. Many belonged to a family of extraordinarily varied finch-like honeycreepers. The colorful and distinct songbirds diverged from a single island ancestor over just a few million years (a more dramatic illustration of adaptive evolution than even Darwin's finches of the Galápagos), and now most of these species are gone. What's more, the tragedy continues. Thirty-three of Hawaii's remaining native (endemic) birds are listed under the US Endangered Species Act, and 11 of them have not been seen for decades and are likely already extinct. On Kauai, six of seven honeycreeper species remaining on the island face possible extinction in the coming decades, say researchers. Hawaii's biodiversity train wreck is, by all accounts, still underway.[20]

Pets and disease are in the thick of it. In particular, pet birds brought from other places and released—accidentally or intentionally—play a large supporting role in Hawaii's ongoing extinction crisis. The other usual suspects are involved, too: invasive predators (such as rats and cats), logging, hunting, development, and so on. But among the main villains, say researchers, are bird-killing avian malaria and, especially, introduced mosquitos that transmit the disease. Mosquitos didn't exist in Hawaii before the nineteenth century, when larvae in shipboard water arrived with the *Wellington* in 1826—or so one story goes. Things have gone badly for Hawaii's birds since. The arrival of pets has made it worse.[21]

Early immigrants to the islands often arrived with caged pet birds as companions. Asian songsters, like the melodious laughing thrush or the Japanese white-eye, were favorites, along with colorful show birds, like India's red avadavat. These birds got loose on the islands in the early 1900s. Several finch species arrived as pets, too, before they escaped into Hawaii's landscape during the 1960s. Released pet parrots, more recently, followed them to lush forest freedom. At least 58 bird species from elsewhere now make their home on the islands, and more invasive land birds live and thrive in the state than land birds known to occur there naturally. The problem is that most of these feathered aliens come from places where mosquitos also live and have lived for millennia. Some of these birds have a natural tolerance for mosquito-borne malaria and can survive quite well as malarial carriers. The consequence, according to some researchers, is that escaped pets and their descendants likely now act as reservoirs for the disease, where it can survive and fester. The more vulnerable native birds—encountering infected mosquitos only in recent times—face a greater risk from the deadly illness as a result.[22]

In a review of these and many other examples, University of Georgia ecologist Peter Daszak and his colleagues conclude that it's time for conservationists to take wildlife disease seriously. Emerging infections affecting wild animals around the globe have become a substantial threat to the diversity of life on earth. Writing in the journal *Science*, the researchers suggest a name for the problem—"pathogen pollution"— and they lay the blame squarely at the feet of humans. People, they say, are transporting contagion-carrying creatures to new, naive ecosystems. Meanwhile, the success of disease is encouraged by wildlife stress brought about by the human-caused destruction of forests and climate change. While the wildlife disease crisis seems to be getting worse, it's probably not new. Infections linked to human colonization have been implicated in 40,000 years of wildlife extinctions across vast continents and islands, say the authors. According to one theory, these contagions may have helped annihilate mammoths, mastodons, camels, horses, ground sloths, saber-toothed cats, and the other big mammals across the Americas following the arrival of our species some 14,000 years ago.[23]

Pets, of course, didn't do all of that. Many wildlife epidemics in which people had a role involved food and farm animals, as in the case of rinderpest brought with cattle to Africa or virulent strains of avian flu linked to Asian poultry. Others have been traced to infected stowaways, such as the shipboard rats that brought sleeping sickness (trypanosomiasis) to the now-extinct rodents of Christmas Island. Nevertheless, our pet dogs, cats, birds, and even fish have been implicated in many wildlife-killing outbreaks.

Toxoplasma gondii, for instance, is a parasite that reproduces when it colonizes cats, but it infects, sickens, and kills a lot of other animals, from seals and dolphins to people. The domestic cat carriers of the disease, meanwhile, are everywhere. On the coast of California, endangered sea otters have been washing ashore dead for years. Scientists eventually found toxoplasma disease is the culprit. The tiny organism infects the otter brains, killing them outright or scrambling their expert swimming skills until they struggle, flounder, and drown. Rain runoff is believed to carry the sickness from nearby cat scat to the sea. There, it swirls in kelp forests where the otters like to feed. Recently, researchers used genetic markers to trace the link to domestic cats on shore. The study ended speculation that wild bobcats and mountain lions might be the source; the otter-killing strain has a direct connection to the feral domestic cats living in the nearby hills. Meanwhile, herpes virus continues its deadly march as another pet-borne killer. The continuing global spread of the disease among carp, for instance, has been tied to the trade in pet goldfish and koi around the world. Another similar, deadly microparasite called ranavirus, has also been found infecting frogs and salamanders for sale in pet stores in several countries.[24]

As the worldwide problem of emerging wildlife diseases gathers attention (not least because of their recognized threat to human health), more connections between wild animal death and diseases spread by the pet trade are revealing themselves.[25]

The US Fish and Wildlife Service spotted the link between pets and the salamander-killing Bsal immediately: in January 2016, the agency banned 201 species of salamanders from international or interstate trade as part of its North American defense against the disease. The decision was touted as the best bet for trying to prevent what scientists believe could be a biodiversity crisis if the disease reaches North America. Pet salamanders were declared illegal to import into the country or to move across state lines. Penalties include up to $5,000 in fines and six months in prison. "With the highest biodiversity of salamanders in the world here in the United States, we're very concerned about the risk this fungus poses," David Hoskins told the *New York Times*. Hoskins is assistant director of the agency's Fish and Aquatic Conservation Program. The blocked species, including 67 native to the United States, are considered those most likely to act as carriers of the disease. Never in its history has the agency listed as "injurious wildlife" so many native animals at once. "We needed to move quickly," Hoskins said.[26]

More than a year later, a Canadian ban followed but with a wider prohibition. The decision to bar *all* salamanders from entering Canada is a preliminary step in efforts to keep the new fungus from these shores, says Samuel Iverson, a biologist with Environment and Climate Change Canada's wildlife health unit. The ban is aimed at the estimated 17,000 salamanders—including newts—that arrive in the country each year to supply the pet trade or for researchers who use them as study subjects.

The rules, announced at the end of May 2017, prohibit the import of every salamander species, unless authorized by a permit, for a period of one year. "We're going to start out with a very precautionary one-year restriction," says Iverson, "while we learn a bit more about the disease and zero in on a bit more of a targeted, long-term management regime."

Many amphibian enthusiasts and some scientists affected by the move have called the ban a bad idea. John Clare, a Cuyahoga Community College chemistry teacher who has been photographing, writing about, and keeping salamanders for years, is one of them. Clare describes the bans as a death sentence for the salamander hobby across North America. Clare is the founder of Caudata.org, the "longest-running community for amphibian enthusiasts on the Internet" and a site through which people buy and sell captive animals. The agency's ban, he says, will likely put safe, responsible salamander breeders and sellers out of business. An internal report by the US Fish and Wildlife Service confirms that pet retailers will likely see direct sales losses of about $3.8 million—$10 million when salamander tanks, habitat, and other products are factored in. Clare believes most of these loses are being felt by hobbyists and small-time vendors that only trade domestic species. "Rather than destroy a wonderful hobby passion and doom animals through isolation [preventing breeding from taking place], a simple treatment and testing requirement could be accomplished," he tells me.[27]

Others warn that pet-lover frustration following the ban may actually increase North America's risk of the disease, tempting a salamander black market that makes Bsal's backdoor arrival even more likely. "Inevitably it will," says Rob Conrad, owner of Global Exotic Pets in the Canadian town of Kitchener, Ontario. "That's with anything, not just amphibians and reptiles. As soon as you tell people they can't have it, it's the first thing they want." Conrad sells and ships exotic creatures across the country. Some of them are salamanders, and many come from abroad. In his store, as we speak, a display tank holds several available-for-sale fire salamanders from Europe—the same animals currently being devastated by Bsal's deadly spread across that continent. The truth is, he says, applying the brakes doesn't often work. Prohibited species become more attractive to collectors because of their perceived rarity in the trade or because of higher prices. At the same time, a greater ban-inspired business in local, wild-caught species might exacerbate the transmission of fungus across the country once it gets here.

"Look, if they really want to protect the planet, they'll have to go to extreme measures, and banning the importation of a certain type of amphibian is not going to do anything," Conrad tells me. "People keep living. People keep traveling. We live on a global scale. So, trying to protect one little thing is not going to do anything."

Université de Montréal professor Stéphane Roy learned of the ban in Canada only after he was suddenly barred from ordering axolotls from the main research breeding facility in Kentucky. Each year, Roy imports about 400 of the salamanders—unique among vertebrates for their capacity to regrow severed legs, nerves, and other tissues—for use in limb and spinal cord regeneration research. Environment and Climate Change Canada officials told Roy acquiring a permit (after proving the salamanders will be properly housed and quarantined) could take up to 70 days—long enough for Roy effectively to lose his summer research season. "I understand the reason they're putting the ban in place," he tells me. "We want to protect the environment. Of course, I hope I won't be collateral damage because of that."

In 2016, a team of US researchers led by Katherine Richgels of the US Geological Survey used computer models to explore the Bsal threat to the United States more closely. The models tried to predict its arrival and its subsequent spread around the country. Numbers of pet stores in every county across each state were key predictors. The most likely places for the fungus to enter North America, the researchers said, were near large ports where pet retailers are many. These places include central and southern Florida, New York City, and Southern California. Los Angeles, with its 283 known pet stores, is particularly vulnerable. In other words, given the size of the pet trade and given Bsal's main *agents de voyage* are passionate pet owners, many scientists think the odds of a North American outbreak are close to a sure bet.[28]

"Oh yes. Certainly," predicts Bsal's codiscoverer, Annemarieke Spitzen-van der Sluijs, when I ask about the spread of the fungus to North America. "If it's not there already. It's such a massive country and mortality in aquatic newts can be hard to detect, especially in remote areas. And not all owners might be aware of the symptoms, yet, so they might discard animals and not report a possible Bsal record." The young biologist considers for a moment: "But perhaps," she offers, "I'm too pessimistic right now."

CHAPTER 6
The Emptying Jungles

The yellow-throated warbler, crudely wrapped in tape, was tucked ignominiously behind a trash can. It was recovered at a terminal of the Miami International Airport the week before I arrived. A smuggler— likely spooked by customs and border protection officers on a routine check—apparently stashed it there. It was still in its wrap, immobilized for the trip. No telling where the bird was bound or where it was from. (Yellow-throated warblers are small, lively birds that live throughout the southeastern United States and around the Gulf of Mexico.) Its journey, brutally begun in a forest trap somewhere, was cut short. A life of singing for its food as a caged pet was spared. Finds of this kind are not uncommon. Abandoned songbirds—bound tight or squeezed into hair curlers or pill bottles—are an almost regular occurrence at the airport these days. The yellow-throated warbler was unusual for another reason: prior to the discovery, the US Fish and Wildlife Service (USFWS) kept a list of 40 bird species known to be targeted by smugglers and trafficked across the country and abroad; the yellow-throated warbler marked the first time for intercepting its species.

"So that was number 41," says David Pharo. "It came in on one of the many flights that happened that day, and the people got nervous and ditched the bird." Pharo is a special agent with the South Florida office of the USFWS. He and a team of about 20 other wildlife inspectors and agents enforce wildlife protection laws—including endangered species legislation, the Migratory Bird Treaty Act, and others—across southeast Florida, Puerto Rico, and the US Virgin Islands. His work is often clandestine, sometimes involving long, in-depth investigations and elaborate sting operations. Vice-squad drug cops may get the glamour, but wildlife enforcement work—according to Pharo—is no less pulse quickening. ("We use the same tools, techniques of any law enforcement agency.") Pharo is serious about it. He might just be serious about everything—perhaps even a little gloomy. His obvious gift for grave inscrutability is probably gold in the world of undercover police work. He doesn't seem interested in smiling much.

Pharo is speaking to me in a windowless meeting room at the South Florida USFWS headquarters in Miami, just a stone's throw from the airport. Eva Lara is here, too. She's the supervisory wildlife inspector of the office, and, to my relief, she's cheerfully enthusiastic. The contrast to her furrow-browed colleague is striking—good cop, bad cop. The room is overbright. The building—squat and brick with a couple of bay doors and little else to let the outside in—has all the charm of a well-kept warehouse. Planes pass low overhead. Nearby, Miami International Airport extends like a bustling sprawl of runways, jet traffic, and terminals. It is, according to the airport authority, America's third-busiest airport for international passengers and number one for international freight. In 2018, almost 415,000 domestic and international flights came and went from MIA (as the airport is often called), and 45 million passengers passed through. More flights leave here for Latin America and the Caribbean than from anywhere else across the United States.

All of this, of course, helps explain Miami's reputation as a top international hub for the multibillion-dollar, worldwide trade in wildlife. Every month, about 1,200 to 1,500 legal and declared wildlife-related shipments pass through the South Florida region, says Lara. Of these, the vast majority (more than 85 percent) are live animals, and most—by far—are intended as pets. Many are tropical aquarium fish, she explains. Snakes, lizards, other exotic reptiles, and amphibians are popular too. Big spiders are big. Mammals are a little less so. Caged birds—a favorite in this city's thriving Cuban community—have seen aboveboard shipments drop off here in recent years. The reasons aren't entirely clear, Lara says, but improved captive breeding might have something to do with it. What's certain is that not as many birds are traveling through Miami as once did. She catches herself: "Not legally."

Across the table, Pharo assumes a meaningful look. "There's been a persistent, ever-growing problem of bird trapping down here in southeast Florida," he says, offering an officious-sounding clarification. "It's readily expanding and growing throughout the United States."

Pharo and Lara believe the number of wild birds *illegally* trapped, traded, and trafficked between Florida and elsewhere has been climbing for years. More of the smuggled birds began showing up at the airport in the mid-2000s, and it's getting worse. The animals are being moved about—sewn into pants, tucked into waistband pouches, hidden in luggage—to feed a growing and eager appetite for colorful, musical, or simply rare caged companions. Some supply contestants for illicit song competitions. Others go to gamblers who pit them against each other in featherweight fights, like cocks. Increasingly, they're smuggled as individuals or in small groups to avoid detection: "People are smuggling between 20 to 45 birds within either body-carry-on or luggage into the country," says Lara.

Many of the trafficked birds from Cuba or Puerto Rico end up in Miami, while species trapped in Florida often make the opposite journey. Blue grosbeaks and painted buntings are probably the most trafficked, say the officers. The rest of Latin America—home to the greatest diversity of wildlife on earth as well as its most rapidly dwindling animal populations—provides scores of other sought-after bird pets. "I don't have enough of a pulse to really quantify anything," Pharo says. "We don't have really a good grip of how much of this is going on. It's such a clandestine thing, and they're bringing them in now in smaller, much smaller shipment sizes than they used to. . . . They know it's a risk, a real serious risk now, so they only bring one or two on their person at a time."

The risk to the smugglers, as Pharo describes it, comes from the US government's recent and ongoing crackdown—a rare instance in which President Donald Trump has endorsed and continued one of Barack Obama's environmental initiatives. After a 2013 congressional report linked poaching and the illegal wildlife trade to drug traffickers, arms smugglers, and even terrorism, Obama issued an executive order declaring wildlife crime a national security issue. An interagency task force was created. Money to battle the problem went from a few hundred thousand to tens of millions of dollars. One of President Trump's first executive orders was to keep the fight going.

"Operation Ornery Birds" is part of it. That's the name the USFWS came up with for an ongoing and largely undercover effort to infiltrate and pull apart the tangled web of illegal bird trappers and traffickers operating in South Florida and beyond. (The initial title was "Operation Angry Birds" until agency brass worried about copyright infringement.) The initiative—which began in 2012 and has so far nabbed six bird traffickers in six separate cases involving more than 400 birds—is considered one of the largest of its kind in US history. Pharo is the agent in charge. "These aren't just bird enthusiasts and fanciers," he says.[1]

Earlier investigations twigged agents to the sheer scale of the problem. Back in 2006, illegal bird dealers and three Miami pet stores were caught for illegally selling protected species, and in 2012, a 76-year-old man who touched down in Miami from Cuba was stopped at customs with 16 Cuban bullfinches sewn into his pants. The species can fetch up to $5,000 a bird on Florida's black market, says Pharo. Operation

Ornery Birds picked up where earlier efforts left off. An agent posing as a buyer answered an Internet ad for a prohibited songbird known as a Puerto Rican spindalis. The agent made secret recordings as the seller, who called himself "El Doctor," boasted of other illegal sales, including 60 northern cardinals to a California buyer the previous week. In another early bust, a man arriving from Havana was arrested with five Cuban grassquits, a Cuban bullfinch, a yellow-faced grassquit, an indigo bunting, and a blue grosbeak immobilized in hair curlers and concealed in his underwear. A search of his Florida property revealed other birds, several cages, and a mist net for trapping. "The mortality is very high," Pharo says. "We see birds with missing feathers, infested with mites, with really bad muscle atrophy. . . . A lot of birds, the species that are associated with Operation Ornery Birds, are species that are, over time, in decline." Pharo looks at me, gravely. "So, there's impacts."

One-third of every kind of bird on earth is caught up in the growing and often-murky market for wildlife. More birds are traded and trafficked around the globe—most as pets—than any other nonfish vertebrate animals. Some of it is legal. Some is not, involving caged birds in desperate circumstances sold by shadowy smugglers to underworld gangs. There are, as Pharo says, impacts. The birds themselves suffer and often die. The consequences for biodiversity around the world are more difficult to measure. What we know is that one out of eight of the planet's bird species is now threatened with extinction. In places where scientists have identified causes, the pet bird trade has emerged as a dangerous—and often previously overlooked—prime suspect.[2]

"It's a really big deal," says biologist Bert Harris, "It turns out that the pet trade is a big deal, especially in Southeast Asia but also in Africa and parts of Latin America, like Brazil and Mexico. . . . Trapping is causing extinctions."

For years, Harris and his colleagues have been tracking the wild birds trapped to supply pets—mostly to local bird lovers—from Indonesia's rich and heat-drenched jungles. What they've found, so far, is stark. Trade is the main threat facing 13 bird species and 14 separate sub-species now believed to be at risk of global annihilation. In all likeli-hood, say the researchers, five of the subspecies—the scarlet-breasted lorikeet, three races of white-rumped shama, and the *miotera* race of hill mynah—are already extinct in the wild. The demand for caged birds is seemingly insatiable in the region, and the results are dire. Scientists call it "the Asian songbird crisis" and describe it as the top reason many of the region's most spectacular bird species could soon vanish altogether. Indonesia's bird-focused biophilia, ironically, has put the survival of the nation's birdlife in jeopardy. "And it's really hard to breed these birds in captivity," Harris explains from his home in Virginia, "so there's a constant demand on the wild. A lot of them are dying in the markets. A lot of them are dying on the way in transport. So, I don't know if there's more demand, but it's definitely unsustainable."[3]

The toll on Indonesia's birds is also heartbreaking, he says. Harris is a research adviser to the international wilderness preservation group the Rainforest Trust. He was the organization's director of biodiversity conservation until his recent appointment as the executive director of the Clifton Institute—a Virginia-based environmental organization focused on ecological restoration, education, and research. Harris is a thin, bookish-looking biologist with a rich, slightly taut voice and an audible sense of urgency. Since he was a kid, he says, he's been in a kind of unshakeable thrall to the wondrous feathered life of the tropics. He recalls the spell cast by a boyhood trip to Belize and subsequent summer fieldwork in Costa Rica. His love of bird-watching was a gift from his dad, and the sheer splendor and diversity of Central American birdlife was arresting.

After college, he volunteered in Ecuador, where he quickly discovered just how little we know about the lives of these extraordinary creatures. More startling still was the dawning realization that many of the species were disappearing. "I really recognized the conservation crisis that was happening," he recalls. It was a few years later, during his postdoctoral studies of the pet trade in Indonesia, when Harris began to appreciate fully the magnitude of problem. "It turned out that there were a bunch of empty forests where everything looked just fine and, then, when you go in there, there were no birds. They had all been trapped out."

The effect was eerie. It was also worrying: conservationists often estimate the population health of a species by means of satellite photos of suitable habitat, assuming the birds must be there. In photos of the Indonesian islands of Sumatra and Java, many forests appeared to be perfectly suited for abundant birdlife, but when researchers visited, they found the jungles were silent. Nothing stirred in the empty treetops. Harris and his colleagues then walked the village markets. They soon found some of their missing birds; they were hanging in bamboo cages, for sale in market stalls.

In a recent paper published in the journal *Conservation Biology*, Harris and his coresearchers combined information they gathered from 14 years of bird counts in a Sumatran jungle with interviews with trappers and local market prices for a variety of species. The findings show that as the pet-trade value of a species goes up, numbers in the wild go down. The inverse relationship is plain; price changes drive some bird populations into a tailspin. While being hunted for food and forest loss have long been considered the main threats to bird biodiversity in Indonesia, the work by Harris and his fellow researchers suggests the biodiversity impacts of pet trapping may be as bad—or worse. "Price, actually, is the best predictor of decline. So, that's pretty good evidence that trapping is the main driver."[4]

For three critically endangered songbirds, for instance, the connection is devastatingly clear. Black-winged mynahs, gray-rumped mynahs, and gray-backed mynahs are closely related starlings with a sleek pale body, black wings, and a bare, bright-yellow patch behind their eyes. They were once considered a single species, and they're still commonly called "black-winged mynahs" for simplicity. These handsome birds are at home only on the west side of the Indonesian island of Java. At least, they used to be. As recently as two decades ago, the birds were common in the area, whistling and trilling high in the leafy branches. Then, their popularity as a caged pet triggered a mynah-trapping rush. Bird lovers prized them for their brilliant music and striking looks. They quickly became a favorite contestant in Indonesia's ever-popular songbird competitions.

A research team lead by Oxford Brookes University tracked the trend. They followed local sales of the birds between 2009 and 2018 across seven area bird markets as well as online. By 2014—as the black-winged mynahs were becoming increasingly rare in treetops—the price of just one of them peaked at about $140 in the markets. That's about three-quarters of the monthly minimum wage for people living there. Scientists estimated that between 1,300 and 2,300 mynahs—both trapped and captive bred—were sold every year. That's about $170,000 in annual sales—not counting money for hundreds of others peddled in separate bird bazaars across Java, Bali, and elsewhere.[5]

The impacts of the mynah craze soon became obvious: the birds, proudly celebrated as musical pets, are now all but gone from Java's jungles. While some 40,000 of them currently live in bamboo and wire cages in homes throughout Indonesia, less than 500 fly free in the wild. Beyond the nation's birdcage bars, say researchers, black-winged mynahs may already be ecologically extinct—that is, with numbers too few to sustain the population. The affection of Indonesia's bird lovers may have settled a new silence in the wild jungles of Java. "The birds that have the nice songs are the ones that are the most threatened," says Harris, solemnly.[6]

And it doesn't stop there: when the best singers are gone, trappers simply turn to the next species in line. Harris calls it "trapping down."

Throughout much of Southeast Asia, for example, straw-headed bulbuls were the pet trade's top recruit for years. The bulbuls look quite
plain, but they're extraordinary vocalists. That's likely why they've been
trapped out of existence in Thailand. In Malaysia and Indonesia, they're
barely hanging on, and in the Sumatran jungles of Harris's study, they've
almost vanished completely. "So now," says the biologist, "trappers have
switched to shamas, and the shamas are declining quickly. So, now,
they've switched to greater green leafbirds. It used to be a really common bird—and in some places, it's still a really common bird—but now
it's becoming valuable, and they're trapping it really fast because it has a
nice song. So, basically, they're running out of preferred birds.

"It's pretty much all illegal," Harris explains, "because people don't
get the permits they need to do this legally. And there's zero enforcement. They're all for sale out in the open in all the villages."

Owls are there, too. Far more now, since *Harry Potter* showed up. The
blockbuster books and movies about the famous boy wizard arrived
in Indonesia as a global cultural force in the early 2000s and brought
owls—as pets to the wizards and lovable if somewhat clumsy couriers
of the mail—to the attention of the nation. Legions of Asian bird trappers returned to the forest to find them. British anthropologists Vincent
Nijman and Anna Nekaris documented the trend. Owls—referred to
locally as *burung hantu*, or "ghost birds"—were a rare find in surveys of
birds available in local markets during the 1980s, 1990s, and early 2000s.
After *Harry Potter*, they began showing up in far more bird-selling stalls
far more regularly. More species became available, too, including barn
and bay owls as well as several large and stately owls such as wood owls,
fish owls, and eagle owls. The birds became known as *Burung Harry Potter.* In the crowded, clamoring, larger bird markets of Jakarta and Band-
ung, buyers began to find 30 to 60 owls typically on offer, and as many
as eight different species in the dim light of the tarp-draped stalls. The

fictional Eeylops Owl Emporium had become a reality. Thanks to what Nijman and Nekaris call "the Harry Potter effect," wild populations of Indonesia's ghost birds may be edging closer to jeopardy.[7]

"The really worrying thing is that trapping hasn't been recognized as a big problem, but it *is* a big problem," says Harris. It's also a hard problem to solve. For instance, halting what is often a generational tradition is unthinkable to local trappers. Harris and his team interviewed many and found most learned the skills from their fathers and relied on the income to feed their families. Most had no idea the practice was hurting wild populations, and science simply knows too little to educate them. Many of the magnificent jungles of the region have hardly been penetrated by researchers, and much of their luxuriant mystery remains. Species are still being discovered, even as they blink out of existence. For many creatures in Asia's forests, we don't know what we've got till it's gone.

"There is very little taxonomic research going on for the birds of Southeast Asia," Harris explains. "So, actually, we have a lot subspecies that should be split and elevated to full species status. But there just haven't been studies or that hasn't happened yet—and, in the meantime, they're being trapped out of existence."

It's not just birds. For almost a thousand species known to be at risk of extinction, a cause of their peril is—at least in part—the international trade in wildlife. Researchers suggest that literally billions of plants and animals—worth about $300 billion—change hands in legal commercial exchange every year. The trade in pet fish, mammals, birds, reptiles, and others is a sizeable part of it, generating about $5.27 billion. Few animal groups have escaped the pet industry's notice—or the yearning of pet owners to keep them as companions. There are pet lions and pet sloths for sale. Pet snails and pet giraffes. Some creatures have scales. Others fur. Some have fangs and poison that kills. Many are in trouble in the wild. Countless die in transit or in pet stores. (One investigation of a major international wildlife wholesaler a few years ago confiscated more than 26,400 animals of 171 species and subspecies and found about 80 percent of them were seriously ill, injured, or dead. Almost 3,500 dead or dying animals were being discarded by the company every week.) Our longing to be near wild things is forcing literally millions of creatures from hundreds of taxa to come indoors with us—or die trying. Outdoors, meanwhile, life's richness grows poorer.[8]

More bird species (585, according to one estimate) are caught up by the exotic pet business, globally, than species from any other animal group, but reptiles (485 species) are also frequently bought and sold. The variety of marketed mammal species is only somewhat less (113). Meanwhile, reptiles targeted by the pet industry are five times more likely to be threatened with extinction than reptiles that are not. Pet-trade-targeted mammals are almost three times more likely to land on the International Union for Conservation of Nature's list of imperiled species. Parrots, meanwhile, are not only the most popular pet bird group throughout the world, they're also the most endangered—one in four of every parrot species on the planet is at risk of vanishing from the wild.[9]

"I'll start by being a pessimist here," says Sheldon Jordan, the Canadian government's top wildlife cop and, until recently, chair of the INTERPOL (International Criminal Police Organization) Wildlife Crimes Working Group. "I'll start with a quote from the Duke of Cambridge, Prince William, at the Hanoi conference on the illegal wildlife trade which happened in November of 2016. He said, 'If I were a betting man, I would bet on extinction.'"

Jordan is a plainspoken and down-to-earth man with neat, parted hair and square glasses. His trim Van Dyke beard frames a warm smile.

Today is one of the rare days that he's actually at his Gatineau, Quebec, office, across the river from the Canadian capital, Ottawa. As head of Canada's Wildlife Enforcement Directorate, Jordan is among the government's more peripatetic bureaucrats. His work includes executive roles on key North American and Canadian wildlife enforcement networks as well as on the world stage. He's spent more than 25 years fighting global crime—beginning with drugs and, then, on behalf of wildlife—and his is a respected, sought-after voice. When I reach him, he's newly returned from London, England, and a British conference on the illegal wildlife trade and a separate meeting of the INTERPOL wildlife group. Before that, he was in Sochi, Russia, for the 70th Standing Committee meeting of the Convention on International Trade in Endangered Species of Wild Fauna and Flora (CITES). "I think I can count on my two hands in the last month and a half the number of times I've slept in my own bed," he says.

The closest thing the world has to global rules governing the trade in wildlife is CITES. Signatory countries put their own laws and regulations in place to abide by its terms. In the United States, for example, the Endangered Species Act gives the USFWS power over CITES-relevant regulations. Canada has a CITES law with an absurdly protracted name: the Wild Animal and Plant Protection and Regulation of International and Interprovincial Trade Act. ("WAPPRIITA," says Jordan. "It's easier.") Other nations have their own rules and science advisers for fighting illegal wildlife trade. A growing CITES appendix now identifies more than 34,000 species in need of protection and for which permits are needed to cross borders. Other international agreements also have a role. The Commission for Environmental Cooperation, for instance, emerged as a pan-continental conservation force after Canada, the United States, and Mexico became partners to the North American Free Trade Agreement (now the Canada–United States–Mexico Agreement). Long before that, the 1916 Canada–US Migratory Bird Treaty—the world's first international conservation agreement—was penned and still has active bird-protection legislation in both countries. "We've got lots of laws out there," says Jordan. "What you actually have to do is to be in a position to not only enforce them but make sure that the public is behind them."[10]

It's a problem. In countries where keeping or selling wildlife is a traditional or cultural practice, enforcing any wildlife rules can be difficult. For instance, some conservationists worry CITES export permits from some nations are granted when they shouldn't be. Each year, about 317,000 live birds and 2 million live reptiles, as well as millions of reptile skins, pieces of coral, and hunting trophies, are cleared for international trade, but the sheer number of the allegedly captive-bred animals in this group has been called "implausible" by researchers; some breeding facilities are cover for illegal trapping from the wild. CITES has also been criticized for not being nimble enough: the convention can take years—more than 10 on average—to regulate the trade of species known to be suffering from the impacts of trapping. Of 958 species traded on the international wildlife market and, at the same time, considered threatened with extinction, more than one-quarter currently have no CITES protection at all. Many are endangered and even critically endangered. Reptiles, in particular, are poorly served by the convention: of 355 threatened species directly targeted by the pet trade, 194 remained unlisted and unregulated by CITES in 2016.[11]

If the legal trade in wildlife is a problem for diversity, the black market only makes thing worse. Few criminal enterprises in the world are considered as lucrative. Some estimate the illegal wildlife trade is easily a third as large as its lawful counterpart. Every year, about 350 million plants and animals are sold on the black market globally, and millions of prospective exotic pets are among them. The value of this illicit trade falls anywhere between $10 billion and $30 billion for animals alone, says Jordan. And the problem is gathering momentum. "Environmental crime is rising at a rate of 5 to 7 percent per year," explains Jordan, "that was in 2016, which is almost double the rate of world economic growth."[12]

Wildlife law enforcement agencies everywhere are trying to step up their game. Not long before our conversation, for example, Jordan led a monthlong INTERPOL crackdown on global wildlife trafficking involving 92 countries. Operation Thunderstorm—"the largest wildlife crime blitz that's ever been organized"—netted mountains of elephant ivory, tons of wild animal meat (such as whale, elephant, bear, and zebra), and tens of thousands of animals—many taken from the wild to furnish the pet trade. The 27,000 reptiles included 869 alligators and crocodiles, 9,590 turtles, and 10,000 snakes. Among the almost 4,000 birds, there were parrots, pelicans, ostriches, and owls. The appetite for exotic pets has not only grown, its tastes have broadened, the variety of creatures desired as human companions grander and stranger. A Florida couple kept a pet elephant for 34 years (along with a menagerie of other creatures) before it was finally seized by authorities. A few years ago in Thousand Oaks, California, a pet 1.8–meter (6 foot) albino cobra escaped, attacking a family dog and terrorizing the community until it was captured several days later. In 2019, a 75-year-old man in Gainesville, Florida, was gored to death by one (or more) of his pet cassowaries—huge, flightless birds found on the other side of the world and equipped with daggerlike talons.

The impacts of this weird, wild pet trend are toughest for the most vulnerable animals. Parrots and primates have been particularly hard hit. In a 20-year tally of poaching problems during 23 different wild parrot studies across 14 different countries, almost one-third of the more than 4,000 parrot nests being observed were raided by people taking eggs and young, likely to sell as pets. Meanwhile, more than a 110 known parrot species are now threatened with extinction. Our evolutionary cousins are suffering too. Between 2005 and 2011, about 1,800 endangered chimpanzees, gorillas, and other apes—many intended as pets—were intercepted while being trafficked in 23 countries. About 3,000 great apes are lost from the wild every year as a result of illegal trade, according to the UN Environment Programme. Meanwhile, as many as 700 pet chimps (many of unknown origin) now occupy living rooms, basements, and other quarters in private homes across America.[13]

To an exotic-pet owner, the rarer a species the more desirable it can be—and the more valuable. As scarce creatures become harder to get, prices climb. The traffickers never lose, and the pressure on wildlife never lets up—even as populations plummet. Red line torpedo barbs, for example, sell in pet stores for several times as much as similar aquarium fish. They are also endangered, heading inexorably toward extinction in the wild. In the remaining few suitable streams burbling through India's Western Ghats, the fish—locally known as *Chorai Kanni*, or "bleeding eyes"—has seen its population halved in the past few years. Of India's total $1.54 million in exports of live aquarium fish a decade ago, red line torpedo barbs accounted for two-thirds. For most aquarium fish, however, the damage done by the pet trade isn't known. Often, no one's keeping track.[14]

While scientists consider the aquarium-fish business to be a major threat to the biodiversity of these animals, too little is known to even guess how most wild populations respond to their popularity as pets. Trade in coral reef fish, for example, involves more than 1,800 species from more than 40 exporting countries, and yet, their wild numbers are rarely tracked. Similarly, little is understood about the kinds of fish and how many are sold and shipped around the world. Figures for the United States alone suggest between 9 and 12 million individual aquarium fish arrived in the country every year from 2000 to 2011. When scientists recently assembled what's known about the biology of 72 Asian fish loved by US aquarium keepers, they found that many share life cycles and other biological characteristics that put them at high risk of overfishing and population collapse.[15]

The United States not only imports more aquarium fish than any other country, it's one of the largest markets for exotic pets, period. Europe is up there too. More recently, a fascination for owning exotic animals has begun to gather steam in the wealthy countries of the Middle East. And in Asia and South America, meanwhile, exotic pet keeping has a long, cultural history that's being rekindled as more affluent and aspiring pet owners can afford the hobby. Demand, by all accounts, is climbing everywhere. For some species, captive breeding fills the bill. For many others, however, mating in a cage or aquarium isn't an option. Or at least not much of one. For these, wild capture is just easier. Trappers and fishermen—often rural, poor, and with few other opportunities—are frequently eager to do it. Wild creatures, meanwhile, have no way of keeping pace.[16]

"The human population is more than 7 billion and expected to increase by another billion in the next 20 or so years," says Jordan. "So, the pressure on resources is obviously going to continue having an impact. . . . Obviously, law enforcement isn't going to solve the situation. Number one is reducing demand."

Unfortunately, tackling demand won't be easy: the allure of exotic pets is, by many accounts, powerful and strange. People who have never lived with a wild animal—according to those who have—simply don't get it. Exotic animals are viscerally enchanting. It's an experience that's not easily explained. The feeling has the ineffable quality of something ancient and elemental. The animals themselves can be magnificent, the way lions are, or glorious, like songbirds, and still the grandeur of their forest-forged beauty remains—even as they're surrounded by living-room furniture. In their daily presence, biophilia is tangible. The awe in it becomes real and affecting. The creatures are the wild within our reach. We can feel their warmth and hear them breathe. "I'm telling you," says Tim Harrison over the phone from Ohio, "there's nothing like it in the world to have a tiger react to you like you are friends. . . . To be around a huge predatory animal, like the world's largest predatory cat, the tiger, and have it rub up against you or chuff at you every time it sees you. You get connected to it."

Harrison is a boyish-looking retired police officer with a thick moustache, a ball cap, and a busy life just outside Dayton, Ohio. He's kept pet tigers. He's wrestled around with them. He's had lions, too. Bears, cougars, venomous vipers, pythons, and countless other wild creatures have all been at home at Harrison's place—although, he says, he didn't plan it that way. Harrison spent 29 years as a public safety officer—the job of police, firefighter, and paramedic rolled into one—working for the Ohio city of Oakland. As a teen, he worked as a veterinarian's assistant and at a couple of local zoos, so in his adult job he was the go-to officer for calls involving escaped and dangerous exotic pets. There were a surprising number of them. Harrison—who at first couldn't understand people who kept big cats and dangerous snakes as pets—began to care for the animals he rescued when he couldn't find accredited shelters and zoos to take them. That's when something clicked. "There is a spiritual connection," he says. "You become the wolf. You become the lion."

Harrison became known as the wild animal guy. He began speaking at area events and schools. He believed educating people about responsible exotic pet ownership was important. News stories about his work as Ohio's dangerous-animal cop were followed by guest appearances on talk shows. He became something of a regular on the nationally syndicated, breakfast-television show *The Daily Buzz*. He brought his beasts along. The viewers loved it.

"I thought I was doing the right thing," he says. "I thought that's how you educated people. Then, I learned that it's getting worse—which reality TV started. That was the whole thing. It was like flipping a light switch on. When reality TV started and Steve Irwin on *Animal Planet* and all those shows came out with some of the most dangerous creatures in the world, I went from 5 to 6 calls a year to 112."

The shows Harrison hoped were educating people actually inspired viewers to acquire strange animals for themselves. By handling his wild creatures on air, Harrison says, he had become an accomplice. Bringing his tamed wildlife on television was fueling the crisis, actually stoking an already-growing appetite for exotic pets. "I was part of the problem," he says. Telling people, "kids, don't try this at home," did no good, he explains. And the pet trade was always at the ready to meet the new demand. "When people see it on TV," says Harrison, "it's for sale the very next month."

By the time he traveled to Africa for the first time, Harrison's doubts about exotic animal ownership were mounting. But what he witnessed on the savannah stunned him. "You've got to remember, I'm the guy who took a giraffe out of somebody's garage outside Troy, Ohio," he says. "Somebody had bought a giraffe and put it in a garage. Its neck was down for almost a year. It was so atrophied that when we got it out, it took almost eight months to raise its head back up again. I knew there was something wrong with that, but I didn't know where to go with it, how to handle it. So, I went over to Africa, and I'm riding in the vehicle with everybody else, and I look up and see these giraffes. They're running across the land. They're just running. I'm going, 'Look how beautiful that is, look how magnificent.' And I've got tears in my eyes thinking about the giraffes they're selling at the auction. And it hit me: this isn't right." Harrison stopped bringing his animals to television appearances, and the shows soon lost interest. He wasn't sorry.

In 2001, Harrison and other police officers, firefighters, and paramedics created the nonprofit group called Outreach for Animals. Their aim is to educate people about the perils of keeping wild creatures— especially dangerous ones—as pets and to encourage exotic animal laws to regulate the practice. In jurisdictions with loose laws, people were dying when their huge pet predators switched their cub-like affection for their adult killer's instinct, he says. Before the so-called Zanesville Massacre, for example, Harrison's home state of Ohio was one of the worst offenders. Many towns required tags for dogs, but there were no rules to target keeping tigers and other exotics. In 2011, however, the situation turned tragic: a distraught Zanesville, Ohio, exotic animal collector named Terry Thompson released more than 50 lions, tigers, leopards, pumas, monkeys, wolves, and bears into the countryside. He killed himself outside his home in a mess of chicken parts and blood to encourage his animals to devour his body. No other people were hurt, but sheriff's deputies were forced to shoot 46 of the big, dangerous animals for fears that someone eventually would be. In 2012, the state enacted some of the strictest exotic pet regulations in the country.

Even so, Harrison admits, it remains an uphill battle. Many US states and a few Canadian provinces—Ontario, for instance—have limited regulations and are still the Wild West for wild pets. More people, meanwhile, seem drawn to the idea of having wild animals in their midst. In this technological, urbanized world, the appeal of these creatures may be stronger than ever. Our biophilia has turned from an urge to a craving, and the more wildness the better. "People pay the most for ones that are closely related to the wild," Harrison explains. "And they get them from people that will actually, through the black market, bring them in as cubs from the wild. . . . People pay double for those. The closer to the wild, the more they want them."

Back in Miami, USFWS Agent Pharo believes culture plays a role too. Florida's seemingly untamable hunger for wild birds, he says, is far more common in particular communities in town. For Caribbean and South American residents, for example, filling a home with the treetop music of a jungle bird is tradition. Acquiring birds from local trappers is something many people in Latin countries have always done. Biophilia—in this sense—is a time-tested custom. "Miami and South Florida are a kind of the melting pot of Latin America, and, of course, a lot of these

Latin cultures bring this type of activity here to the United States," Pharo explains. "They are very, very enthusiastic about certain bird species, and it just has grown from there."

Pharo echoes Sheldon Jordan's view that laws and more agents can do only so much; awareness is key. In April 2018, Pharo and other Miami wildlife enforcement officials invited television cameras and other media to the middle of Everglades National Park. They wanted reporters to watch as they carted cages holding about 130 birds from a white SUV and released them into the surrounding trees. The birds were among those rescued during Pharo's Operation Ornery Birds investigations. Images show photographers lined along the ground as the door of one large cage is lifted and dozens of colorful birds explode into the air: "I am thrilled that our more than 1.5 million visitors who visit Everglades National Park can once again see these birds fly free in their native habitat," Justin Unger, the park's deputy superintendent, announced to reporters. The officials were hoping the elaborate news event might bring home the conservation side of the story.[17]

It was a grand hope. Wildlife crime has exploded in the past 10 to 15 years, and trafficking in wild species is now the fourth largest criminal trade behind illegal drugs, counterfeiting, and human trafficking, according to the World Wildlife Fund. It's worth up to $20 billion annually. Across the United States, the equivalent of about 60,000 wildlife shipments, representing perhaps millions of individual creatures and plants, illegally change hands every year. The Internet and social media exacerbate the problem, opening fluid new avenues for faster and more-difficult-to-track exotic pet sales. America's particular brand of biophilia, as it turns out, has helped distinguish the country as one of the largest consumers of illegal wildlife in the world. Miami is its epicenter. "This is a recurring issue here," Pharo says, grimly. "It'll probably never go away in my lifetime."[18]

CHAPTER 7
Cat Got Your Fish

The road from Alberta's capital of Edmonton to the little town of Morinville some 35 kilometers (22 miles) north is flat and straight. Views of sweeping prairie fields and endless horizons lie scarcely broken by distant stands of scrawny poplar and spruce. Little else is out here. It's gray and colorless in early November, and—across the fields, at least—it's mostly featureless. The sky, on the other hand, is something else. Prairie skies almost always are. It's enormous and arresting. It stretches wide and around, drawing inward and up, like a limitless Gothic arch. And, today at least, it's crowded with dark, menacing action. Small, scudding clouds stampede ahead, like frightened cattle, while higher up and behind them, others—mountainous, black, and boiling—build over each other and tumble forward.

When Morinville comes into view—as a huddle of low, dark buildings—its smallness is striking; the stormy sky dwarfs it. Any significance to the place seems stripped away, scoured by clouds. It would all be overwhelming, if people here weren't used to it. Feeling puny seems to come with the territory. Nature in this place is vast and insistent. It's a fact Albertans seem to understand intuitively. While people in the province have a reputation for being environmentally tone-deaf—mainly when in defense of their oil sands, the rapacious engine of Alberta's turbulent economy—no one really lives that way here. It's not possible. Feeling insignificant beside nature's bigness is part of the deal: a leviathan sky churns; a limitless plain stretches; and not far off, the Rockies tower like giants. If residents of this place seem unfazed or even reckless about protecting their wilderness and wildlife, it's likely because they don't think we're capable of inflicting much damage; sheer grandeur makes nature seem invincible.

Closer to town, the importance of a key Morinville industry—pet food—becomes obvious. The oven smokestack and the dry-ingredient silos rise over the facility, over the town's houses, over commercial warehouses and the nearby rail yard. The community's buildings seem almost gathered around them, like visitors to a monument. Champion Petfoods—although a little south and east of downtown—is at the figurative center of this place. It's a vital part of Morinville's economic life. It's also one of those rare, rural Alberta success stories that has nothing to do with oil.

Champion is now considered one of Canada's largest independent pet food producers. It began three-and-a-half decades ago as a tiny, five-person outfit in a remote Alberta hamlet. Reinhard Mühlenfeld launched the idea. He was a local feed-mill operator who thought his rural clients might appreciate a heartier, meat-first meal for their sturdy Alberta farm dogs and cats. Mühlenfeld's recipes, emphasizing large amounts of beef, chicken, and fish products, impressed the pets. That was enough for their humans. Demand climbed. By the early 1990s, the company became an export business, and a Toronto investor came aboard. The game plan was straightforward: charge more as a premium brand—currently about double the price of other brands—but offer high-end food with more meat. The company dubbed it "Biologically Appropriate™" pet food made with "WholePrey™ standards." The kibble and canned products use 50 to 100 percent meat, including "free-run poultry from our prairie farms, wild-caught fish from Vancouver's Pacific waters, or red meat from Alberta's fertile ranches." This, Champion's marketing materials argue, is the diet our animal companions were built for: it's the food that the wolf and wildcat ancestors of our pets would—if they could—choose from a menu.

"We've always focused on creating foods that use ingredients that reflect the kinds of foods that cats and dogs have evolved to eat," explains Frank Burdzy, Champion Petfoods president and CEO. "We focus on including larger quantities of fresh and raw meat, and minimizing the amounts of carbohydrates that are typically found in pet food."

The idea was a masterstroke. Business surged, and the company grew. In a global dog-and-cat food market worth $84.5 billion and expected to grow at 6 percent every year, Champion's products attracted notice, becoming (in the words of the company's Web site) "the world's most awarded pet food." Orders arrived from around the globe. More than 80 countries now import the food, and two-thirds of Champion's sales are exports. The company built its large-scale "kitchen"—that's food industry lingo for the production plant—in Morinville and another in Kentucky. Its workforce grew to 500 employees. Rumors recently swirled that food giant Nestlé wanted to buy the organization for $2 billion, but Champion denies it. News or not, it speaks to the company's winning recipe for success. "There's a belief that if we nourish our pets as nature intended," Burdzy tells me, "our cats and dogs will not just survive, but that they will thrive and be the healthiest and happiest that they can be."[1]

When I finally arrive at Morinville's Champion Petfoods facility, I meet Scott Sobel in the parking lot. He's a smartly dressed US-based public relations consultant who arranged for my tour of the place. Jeff Johnston, senior vice president for Research, Innovation, and Product

Development, is inside with Leigh Newton, the company's business development manager. We gather in a boardroom in the pet food research building—the "Discovery Kitchen"—separate but adjacent to the far-larger food preparation and packaging plant. Everyone's very friendly. Johnston, in particular, is easy and gracious with prairie warmth. He's a heavyset, gentle man with big hands and an earnest humility. Before we sit, the group looks at me with seriousness and tells me, frankly, that I can't report anything they say.

I look around, puzzled. This tour was arranged weeks before, and no mention of conditions came up. Sobel speaks first: if I'm to visit the plant, everything I learn will be background only. My voice recorder will stay behind, and I won't quote anyone directly. (Burdzy's comments above arrive later by e-mail. They come via Sobel's public relations office; crafted and vetted, they're the only attributed words I can use.) Today, traveling through the operation, there'll be no interviews. The visit is for context. No secrets can slip, no confidence risked. Sobel, with a gray beard and deep, brown eyes, appears at least somewhat apologetic: surely, he says, I can appreciate Champion's position.

It's true that the company has to be careful. Following decades of successive business triumphs and awards, Champion now unexpectedly finds itself legally on the ropes. After years selling pet food with the tagline "trusted by pet-lovers everywhere," some of those same pet lovers are taking the company to court. It began with a 2017 report by the Colorado-based "Clean Label Project" suggesting products made by Champion and other top pet food companies contain arsenic, mercury, and a variety of menacing heavy metals. ("Are We Slowly Poisoning Our Pets? Science Warns YES!" exclaimed the group's press release.) Class-action lawsuits by pet owners—with eager lawyers—have demanded action and compensation for what they call Champion's "negligent, reckless, and/or intentional practice of misrepresenting" the safety of its foods.

Champion didn't see the lawsuits coming. It couldn't. As far as the company is concerned the heavy metals named in the court actions are naturally occurring and impossible to avoid. According to the company's research, any traces in Champion's pet food fall within existing regulatory and suggested guidelines, including US Food and Drug Administration benchmarks. None, according to scientists who have looked, pose a known risk to animals in such tiny amounts. Champion's own pet food development and testing is already complex and impressive. Its Discovery Kitchen research facility here is big. In one room, a group of nutritionists conspire behind computer screens (with, for today at least, dogs at their feet). In another, white-coat technicians and scientists test formulations. There's a mini production facility at the back for testing ideas. Johnston's manner and obvious love of his job add to my impression that Champion is sincere about pet health, about a pet's eating experience, and—most importantly—about giving pet owners what they want.

Ironically, that appears to be the problem: pet food buyers want more fresh meat and fish in pet meals. They want their four-legged family members to eat dinners similar to their own. But, more fresh meat and fish—Champion's chief marketing boast—is naturally (but apparently not dangerously) higher in concentrations of heavy metals. The cause of the pet owners' consternation may have more to do with their own pet-diet choices than anything else. Happily, they are choices that appear unlikely to actually put their pets at risk.[2]

The risk of these pet-diet choices to wildlife, however, is another story altogether.

"Trends in pet foods closely follow trends in human diets," nutrition expert Marion Nestle tells me later. "Current trends are toward increasing 'humanification' of pets, turning them into members of the family." Nestle is an emerita professor of food science, nutrition, and public health at New York University. She's also the author of several books on food for people and pets. Her *Feed Your Pet Right*, coauthored with a colleague, is billed as a popular road map to pet nutrition. "If humans are eating paleo or keto, they want their pets to do so, too," she explains, "and will dream up all kinds of rationales to justify those choices."

So-called paleo and keto diets are popular in the world of human food these days. They reflect a kind of evolutionary nostalgia for the food of our early forebears: people are better off, so the thinking goes, when what we eat resembles what early humans ate before farming brought copious grains, dairy products, and beans to the table. Pet foods that mirror the presumed diet of wild, ancestral dogs and cats follow a similar logic. Champion's "biologically appropriate" pet foods ensure dogs and cats eat—as they did in days of yore—more lean meat and wild-caught fish.

"You can see a continuing shift in our own lives toward eating foods that nourish our bodies more naturally," writes Burdzy in his e-mail. "People today are interested in knowing where ingredients come from, and are increasingly seeking out foods from local farmers and growers. We see similar patterns when it comes to feeding our cats and dogs. The natural nutritional requirements of pets and the transparency around how their foods are made along with the sources of the ingredients used to make them are increasingly key components to pet lovers' decisions about the foods they buy."

Jumping aboard these new dietary trends has been a key to Champion's success. The poultry, fish, and eggs used in its dog food, for example, are described as being "deemed fit for human consumption" before they are considered as Champion ingredients. More companies are following suit. While the big multinationals—such as Nestlé Purina, Mars, and J. M. Smucker—still dominate supermarket pet food shelves, hundreds of smaller players have propelled so-called natural pet foods to sales of about $8.2 billion (in 2016) and to a significant claim to one-quarter of the total US pet food market. The absence of good evidence that these high-protein diets actually *improve* pet health apparently hasn't made a difference. While these pet foods continue to grow in popularity, research so far has yet to demonstrate dogs and cats are better off as a result.[3]

"We simply do not know whether more expensive products are better than cheaper products or whether higher-protein diets are better for pet health and longevity than lower protein," suggests the nutritionist Nestle. "Pet food companies are not interested in doing that kind of research; they mainly do research on how well their products are accepted by pets and, therefore, pet owners."

In other words, the pet food trend toward more "whole-prey" meat and more wild-caught fish may not make much difference to our animals at home. For animals in the wild, however, it matters a lot.

Gregory Okin, a geography professor at the University of California, Los Angeles (UCLA), credits a sleepless night with his sudden realization that America's pets actually eat enough animal flesh and fish every year to feed a midsize country. Okin says he was lying in bed, carried along by a restless mind, when the immense scale of meat consumption by pets occurred to him. "I was actually thinking about backyard chickens first," he laughs. Urban backyard chickens are the same as having protein for pets, he reasoned, while pet dogs and cats are nothing but protein consumers. The contrast struck him: how much do our pets eat, anyway? He got out of bed and grabbed a pencil.

His discovery that night, after a few straightforward calculations, was pretty close to his final answer after more careful consideration and more data. It was published a couple of years later in the journal *PLOS ONE*, and summarizing it is simple: our pets eat a lot, especially a staggering amount of meat. "Dogs and cats—if they were their own country— are about the fifth largest global meat consumers," says Okin, speaking by phone from his UCLA office. Only Russia, Brazil, the United States, and China could be said to eat more. In the United States alone, household pets gobble down about one-third as much animal-derived calories as the nation's more than 325 million humans. All told, the total food calories consumed by American pets—including meat and everything else—equals roughly the same dietary energy gulped down by the entire population of France. "It was actually those calculations that I did that first late night that made me think, there's something here, this is a pretty interesting question," Okin recalls. "These numbers are big enough that they might actually surprise people."[4]

For the world's wildlife, it's not just surprising, it's a potential crisis. Meaty pet food is creating a disaster for wild animals—including creatures in danger of extinction. The problem is the sources of the meat. Raising beef for humans is increasingly recognized as a leading reason for the devastating and ongoing conversion of wildlife habitat to farmland. Growing beef for pet food is no different. Similarly, a massive fishing industry is trawling the oceans for forage fish that many marine creatures depend on for prey. Humans use a lot of this fish ourselves, but mountains of it is fed to our pets. Occasionally, say researchers, some pet food recipes use the flesh of threatened fish directly.

Okin is especially interested in meaty pet food impacts on available land: as worldwide meat production has tripled over the last four decades, about 70 percent of all farmland—and almost one-third of the earth's total land surface—is now devoted in one way or another to raising farm animals. As I write, world leaders are wringing their hands over the almost 80,000 fires that have affected the Amazon rainforest so far in 2019—most have been set by farmers clearing land, and more than three-quarters typically will be converted to livestock pasture and feed crops. Wild creatures, meanwhile, are feeling the squeeze. They're running out of room to live.[5]

Researchers blame the business of raising cattle and other livestock for a role in one-sixth of all modern biodiversity losses around the world. Of more than 8,600 species described by the International Union for

Conservation of Nature as "threatened" or "near-threatened" with extinction, almost two-thirds (5,407) achieved their unfortunate status thanks, at least in part, to impacts from farming. Livestock, in particular, is a chief menace. It's linked, for example, to the ongoing tragedy of the vanishing numbers of cheetahs in Africa. There, the steadily shrinking populations of the world's fastest land mammal are being devastated by local herdsmen who blame them for preying on cattle and kill them to ensure they don't. Huemul deer in South America, meanwhile, are being driven from their forest homes by grazing livestock and the clearing of pasture land. More than 2,300 other species in almost every cranny of the planet are directly affected by the growing need for more land to raise meat or to supply dairy products. At the same time, land cleared for crops—including the immense quantities grown to feed farm animals—jeopardize more than 4,600 species, including the Fresno kangaroo rat (squeezed out of its San Joaquin Valley, California, home by walnut and orange groves or other fruit and vegetable farms) and African wild dogs in sub-Saharan Africa.[6]

Livestock farming is also a large-scale menace to the larger natural ecosystems that keep the planet going. According to the UN Food and Agriculture Organization, the soaring production of cattle and other farm animals threatens about 306 of the world's 825 land-based "eco-regions"—places recognized for their distinctive kinds of life and geography. Livestock farming, says the organization, is expanding fast in the tropics rich with wildlife, and it now menaces more than two-thirds of all known global "hot spots" for biodiversity. No cause of nature's undoing (on land, at least) is more catastrophic than the changes we're busily making to the earth's surface—especially through farming.[7]

The pet food question—and Okin's startling answer to it—was really a result of intellectual wanderlust. The geographer's chief work is studying deserts. He looks at the soils and plants of arid landscapes. They're

austere places, says the geographer, but enchanting. ("It's just beautiful there. Plain and simple," he says.) His thrall with their stark but
breathtaking expanse began years ago during hiking and camping trips
in America's western wildernesses when he was young. He's been working to understand them since. Desert dust, in particular, attracts much
of his scholarly attention. The minerals and nutrients swept up and carried by the wind can have profound effects on plants and other life
across long distances, often in surprising ways. It sounds capricious and
freewheeling. In Okin's description, it seems a close fit for his breezy,
ranging intellect.

Okin did his pet food calculations as an exercise in mental diversion,
but the findings add to other evidence that pet ownership's environmental footprint is large. A decade ago, for example, Australian architects
Brenda and Robert Vale at Melbourne's Victoria University calculated
the amount of carbon released into the atmosphere by the act of keeping
an average pet dog. The number—taking into account the effort and
energy that goes into the dog's food—is about twice that emitted by
a 4.6-liter SUV driven 10,000 kilometers (6,200 miles) a year. Their
intentionally provocative book, *Time to Eat the Dog: The Real Guide
to Sustainable Living*, advocates—among other things—keeping non-
carnivorous pets (or better yet, edible ones such as rabbits or backyard
chickens) to improve the sustainability of a typical modern household.[8]

Okin's math—painstakingly derived using American Pet Products
Association estimates of US pet numbers, average dog and cat body
weight figures, and estimates based on popular and premium pet food
ingredient lists—looks at the costs of feeding pets from a variety of
angles. Consider, for example, the mountains of poop our pets produce. If feces from all the US dogs and cats was left out as curbside
trash, the bulging, foul-smelling bags would equal the weight of all the
garbage produced annually by the State of Massachusetts. The quantity
of greenhouse gases generated by the consumption of US pet products,

meanwhile, is similarly scary: Okin estimates these climate-altering gases are equal to about 58 million metric tons (64 million tons) of carbon dioxide per year—more than is produced by entire nations such as Ireland, Sweden, or Denmark. Supplies of freshwater are at growing risk, too, he says.[9]

Farming is responsible for consuming more water than any other human use—by far—and raising livestock is especially draining: estimates suggest about 15,415 liters (4,072 gallons) of water are used to produce just a single kilogram (2.2 pounds) of beef. For every four burgers worth, in other words, we need more water than the amount carried by a typical water tank truck. At the same time, farming and eating animals is also responsible for almost one-third of water pollution (mainly from manure, antibiotics and hormones, fertilizers, pesticides, and dust and dirt from eroded pastures.) In the United States, livestock farming is blamed for more than half of all erosion and sediment affecting waterways, more than one-third of pesticide use, half of antibiotic use, and one-third of all nitrogen and phosphorus found in the nation's streams, rivers, and lakes.[10]

Okin's estimation of how much of the problem is linked to filling dog and cat bowls was not intended as an outright challenge to pet ownership; he's allergic to dogs and cats, but he likes them well enough. When he wrote his paper, Okin was only curious—and hoping for a good night's rest. The paper, however, sparked an almost immediate backlash. Like Peter Marra's cats-and-birds study, Okin's publication was seen as a salvo launched at the pet owners' way of life. Wagons were circled, and Okin bore the brunt of a vigorous counteroffensive. "I got *a lot* of negative responses," he remembers, "and I think they're hilarious. The people who made negative comments on this—actually, both Sarah Palin and Rush Limbaugh mentioned this thing in passing, which I consider a badge of pride—most of the people who said anything negative about it didn't even read the press release, which I wrote very carefully to make sure that I wasn't saying people shouldn't have dogs and cats."

It didn't matter. Commentators stepped forward to assail the work. Pet advocates were indignant. The Humane Society of the United States said Okin's estimate of pet numbers was inflated. (The American Pet Products Association numbers are often questioned because the organization prefers higher pet figures for mercantile purposes.) Okin was— and is—unfazed. Even if fewer pets mean the final calculation of pet food consumption is 10 to 20 percent lower, he says, it still adds up to a staggering amount of meat. "Pets are a little bit of a sacred cow," Okin tells me, "and this is basically showing that the sacred cow has some costs. That's all I'm trying to say is, it has some costs. . . .

"It's my job as a scientist to actually try to give information about what I consider objective reality, and my role is to stay out of it. That's why I'm not trying to tell people to eat their pets." He laughs. "You know? That's not my job. My job is to tell people here's the deal: if you care, pay attention to this; if you don't care, don't pay attention."

Maybe. But it's harder, perhaps, to ignore the fish: while mountains of the meat eaten by our creature companions come from cattle, chicken, and pigs, thousands of metric tons of this fleshy protein is also pulled from the sea as wild-caught fish. Much of it emerges in sagging nets as silvery schools of sardines, anchovies, herring, and other small, shimmering fish—known to scientists as "forage fish." These gleaming multitudes support the largest fisheries on the planet (earning about $5.6 billion every year) and make up one-third of all fish humans catch (by weight) around the world. Pet food is just a part of this, but it's significant nonetheless: if separate boatloads of fish were brought ashore for different human uses—for example, as food for people or as animal feed—one of every seven of those ships would dock exclusively to feed our pets.[11]

"You look at the big fisheries in the world, and most of them are fishing for these small, schooling, silvery fish," explains University of Washington biologist Tim Essington. Essington is a plainspoken scientist with a wide grin. He's studied the ocean's little fish for years. Forage fish are close to the bottom of the food chain, but they're a critical link in ocean ecosystems everywhere. They eat tiny plankton and other diminutive life and, in turn, serve as food for vast numbers of seabirds, whales, seals, and bigger fish. They're famously productive, spawning in uncountable numbers. They're tasty, too. "From an animal's perspective, these things are like the Kobe beef of the aquatic world," Essington tells me. "They're as fat as all get out, these plump little morsels, and it looks as though they play a really important role in a lot of food webs. Essentially, they're really, really effective at eating little tiny things and packaging them into a morsel that is then easily found and captured by these other predators."

Or by humans. People have caught these little fish to feed ourselves since time immemorial. As more of us occupy this planet, more forage fish are swept up by our trawlers. These days, the fish aren't simply being used to feed us; they're used to feed our farmed animals and farmed fish and, increasingly, to nourish our pets. The problem is we're taking all this fish from the same shimmering schools that other wild creatures need to survive. "They're super important to us," explains the biologist. "At the same time, it's really clear that these are really, really important and preferred types of food for a lot of things we also care about, like a lot of marine mammals, a lot of seabirds, and a lot of those fish that we like to catch, tunas and cods and things like that."

Including large amounts of fish in pet food is a growing trend. Hundreds of thousands of tons of mackerel, herring, sardines, anchovies, menhaden, and others are shipped to pet food kitchens around the world every year. The fishy flesh is canned as cat food, or it becomes an ingredient in high-protein dry-food recipes. In Australia alone, household cat food consumes about 2.5 million metric tons of fresh or frozen fish per year. That's about 13.7 kilograms (30 pounds) per cat every 12 months—and an amount that's more than all the fish and seafood eaten annually by the average Australian person. In some cases, pet food may contain products from threatened large marine fish such as tunas and sharks. Recently, researchers in Ottawa reported that several pet food Web sites advertise Pacific salmon in their food, even though some of these salmon species are listed as at risk of extinction. With global pet ownership climbing and pet food trends veering toward premium, higher-protein diets, impacts on forage fish stocks and on the birds, fish, and other wildlife that depend on them appear to have become a growing conservation concern.[12]

Unfortunately, understanding the size of the problem is difficult. The confounding fact is that forage fish populations have always gone up and down, sometimes wildly. Long before people were around to catch them, these small fish have been affected by multiyear or decade-long shifts in ocean currents or other large-scale environmental changes. Sometimes these shifts help the fish, fueling surges in their numbers. Sometimes—just as often—they send populations crashing. It's hard to know how fishing affects this seesaw—and, in turn, how it impacts other wild animals that eat them. "One of the interesting defining traits of these things is that the populations have these boom-and-bust periods," Essington explains. "And they definitely fluctuate at different time scales. Two species in the same system—one will have, like, a 30-year time frame and then another will have, like, a 10- or 15-year cycle. . . . So, we're admitting, of course, there is an important environmental process going on here, but the key question is how does fishing act on top of that."

Not long ago, Essington decided to tackle this ecological Gordian knot: "I was just exhausted by conversations with people or in management circles where someone would say it doesn't really matter what we do since these things are all driven by the environment anyway." In an influential paper in the *Proceedings of the National Academy of Sciences*, he and his colleagues managed to loosen the tangle—at least a little. By figuring out how much of the swing in numbers occurs naturally, they were able to back-calculate the forage fish fishery's influence on the population roller coaster. "If we say, hey, what's happening to this thing is a combination of the environment and fisheries, then if we know what one of them is, we can figure out the other one."[13]

The "punch line," as Essington describes it, is that fishermen around the world fish hardest for the schools of tiny fish precisely when populations are on their way down. While sardine, anchovy, and other forage fish rise and fall naturally, Essington's work shows that fishing can "sharply amplify" how far their populations dip. That means populations plummet further and more often. And, once they drop below one-quarter of their typical strength, many fish stocks (about half) crash altogether. "Basically," the biologist explains, "the sort of natural population collapses become amplified through this sort of accidental acceleration by—in some cases—a considerable degree. It could be 30 to 40 percent lower than it would have been otherwise. Which, from a predator's perspective, probably really matters. Because you're really talking about lowering the abundance at a period where food is now scarce."

For millions of seabirds—including many gulls, terns, petrels, gannets, auks, and others—along with sea lions, bottlenose dolphins, and scores of other wild marine creatures, that's a problem: collapsed forage fish stocks could mean these other wild animals go hungry, fail to breed, and die. Among seabirds alone, one-third of all global species are considered threatened with extinction and half are known or thought to be dwindling in number, according to the International Union for Conservation of Nature. In the six decades between 1950 and 2010, populations of average seabird communities fell by 70 percent. More than 40 species are considered by the world conservation group to be either "endangered" or "critically endangered," including 18 kinds of petrels, 9 albatrosses, and 3 penguins. Many forage-fish-eating seals, whales, and other ocean-dwelling mammals are also in bad shape. In March 2019, a Mexican government committee reported that the world's most endangered marine mammal—a small porpoise called the vaquita—now numbers no more than about 10 in the wild.[14]

Plummeting forage fish populations didn't necessarily imperil these creatures, but research suggests the fishy shortfalls can leave them without enough prey, struggling to feed their young or even to survive themselves. One study suggests that, while the yearly catch by fisheries around the world increased by almost 10 percent within the 20-year periods of 1970–1989 and 1990–2010, the amount of food eaten by seabirds decreased by almost 20 percent at the same time. Some seabirds are considered "extremely dependent" on forage fish and need them for fully three-quarters or more of their diet. In some places, the importance of the tiny fish to other ocean life is especially profound. Off the coast of California, for instance, 19 species of marine mammals, 33 species of marine birds, and more than 40 species of marine fish depend on sardines and other abundant forage fish species. Among these are endangered birds, shrinking rockfish populations, and eight species of whales. In the early 1970s, the forage fish fishery was famously linked to declines in the California brown pelican that resulted in it being listed as an endangered species. While thin eggshells from pesticides likely hit the birds hardest, northern anchovy—their favored prey—were being netted by the truckload in areas next to the pelicans' breeding colonies.[15]

A few years ago, scientists reviewed the previous studies exploring whether faltering forage fish populations have a role in the changing fortunes of wildlife. They calculated how many of the little fish must be available in the sea before the animals that eat them go hungry. They came up with the magic fraction of one-third: if the available forage fish prey is allowed to fall below about 30 percent of their full complement, seabird nesting efforts begin to fail and adults begin to die. If the food scarcity doesn't improve, the miserable reproductive success of the birds continues and populations—and possibly species—take a downward turn. Leaving "one-third for the birds" when scooping up net loads from forage fish shoals, conclude the scientists, is vital to ensuring marine ecosystems remain healthy. "Basically, what we know from some of the seabird studies," says Essington, "is that when you dip below average abundance for these forage fish, that's when you see correlations between the bird reproductive success and the abundance of food."[16]

Fish matter. A shortage of fish matters a lot. These days, the lesson couldn't be more relevant. Fisheries are faltering around the planet. Concern over the pet food industry's growing appetite for fishy meals is a growing part of a far larger worry: About half of *all* global fish stocks are being fished to the max, according to scientists, while almost one-third either are being overfished now or have already been hammered by fishing in the past. Predictions suggest the last remaining wild fish stocks on the planet will collapse—or come very close to it—by midcentury. That's a lot of bad news for humans: 10 percent of us need fish to make a living, according to the UN Food and Agriculture Organization, and 4.3 billion of us eat fish to get 15 percent or more of our animal protein. And it's bad news for wild, fish-dependent animals too. The fishing industry is already remaking—or has remade—the ecological features and machinery of large parts of oceans everywhere. In a few cases, it's even rerouted the path of evolution for some of the marine creatures that live there.[17]

"People through time are harvesting a wider and wider swath of the food web," Essington says. "And, you know, it's not good to be doing this without any thought about it. . . . These patterns in fishery development are—to a certain extent—flagging some trade-offs, because it doesn't seem like you can continue to grow your landing swath from the top while simultaneously gutting the middle of the food web.

"Forage fish basically function in two roles that we really benefit from, as food for us and as food for the things we want to eat or for animals that we really care about for other reasons. The question is how do we achieve a balance."

Months after my Morinville visit, the legal clouds over Champion Petfoods appear to be lifting. In Wisconsin, a federal judge ruled class-action claims against the company in that state weren't worth more of the legal system's time. In a summary judgement, the court said evidence against Champion didn't make a convincing case. Nothing presented could support a conclusion that the pet food risked pet health or that it wasn't all it was advertised to be. Trace amounts of naturally occurring arsenic, cadmium, and other heavy metals don't seem to be the menace that some claim. A month earlier, similar judgements were reached in other class-action lawsuits against Champion in Illinois and Massachusetts. (As I write, the initial California case has yet to reach a conclusion.)

The legal teams behind the lawsuits are undoubtedly disappointed. The plaintiff pet owners may be too. The irony is strange. Being discouraged is an odd response when learning that the meaty, Biologically Appropriate™ food you've been feeding your dog isn't poison after all. But, two years of complex, expensive legal wrangling can be disorienting. And confusion was likely there from the start. In its pet food industry rating report at the center of the fuss, the Clean Label Project didn't measure heavy metals relative to what's known or widely suspected to be harmful; it measured them relative to amounts found in other pet foods. The consumer awareness organization believes companies that have less are better than companies that have more—even if trace levels across the board have no discernible impact.[18]

"What it comes down to," the group's executive director, Jackie Bowen, tells me by phone, "is our belief at the Clean Label Project that exposure to less industrial and environmental contaminants is always better than more exposure." The organization has been criticized for similar rating reports grading companies in the baby formula industry and others that make protein powder. The thinking—none is the edge of too much—isn't shared by everybody. From what's known, most of these elements aren't a worry in tiny trace quantities. They're also generally unavoidable in the foods we eat—especially in fish and animal tissue where they tend to accumulate.

What's more disorienting is that high-end, high-meat pet food may come with other consequences: your pet may not be at risk from traces of scary-sounding elements, but wildlife may be threatened by losses of prey and habitat increasingly consumed by pet food's voracious supply needs. As pet foods become more humanized and influenced by paleo-diet fashion—as more pet owners believe dogs and cats should eat like us or, at the very least, like their red-in-tooth-and-claw ancestors once did—the threat worsens. "There's gourmet food, and there's regular dog food," UCLA's Professor Okin explains. "In the seventies, every dog ate regular dog food, and now there's this push for gourmet food. One of the things that makes this sort of high-end dog food high end—and the same for cat food—is that it has more meat in it. Not just more meat, but better meat.

"I think people need to be really, really critical about marketing. You know, there's some pet food ad on TV that characterizes dogs as wolves that need to be chasing down buffalo. Well, dogs aren't wolves, and they don't need to chase down buffalo. . . . I'm not trying to tell people not to have pets," Okin adds, almost apologetically. "I'm just letting them know that if this is something you care about, then this can go into your decision about what kind of pet to have. You could just, you know, instead of that Great Dane, you could have a miniature poodle, and that would make a huge difference in terms of your impact."

Okin considers for moment: "Or, instead of a golden retriever, you could have a hamster."

CHAPTER 8
Nearest and Dearest

From a side door to the Toronto Christmas Pet Show, the clearest path to the thronged and milling center of the event is past Santa's Village. The tinsel-and-tree decorated space occupies a corner in the largest of three huge convention halls devoted to the fair. There's a small, open arena for doggie athletics next door, but it's empty; nothing's scheduled there for a couple of hours. A long line of people and pets waits in front, anticipating a turn with Saint Nick: a photo of their dog or cat with the jolly old elf, seated adorably in his big, red chair, is a guaranteed hit with family and friends. It's only C$10 (about US$7.60) for each easy-to-distribute digital copy.

Beyond Santa, a view of the wider room opens up. Its immensity, teeming with people, is startling. The sound is a murmuring roar punctuated by barks and squawks. About 240 booths are there, representing more than 170 different businesses. Almost every imaginable pet product and service can be had. The booths squeeze together in tight rows back and forth across field-size floors. About 28,800 square meters (310,000 square feet) of the massive Mississauga International Centre—low and stretched beside the wide runways of Toronto's Pearson International

Airport—is filled with them. Thousands of the 17,000 visitors expected at the three-day event (admission just C$18 per person) are pressed into slow-moving rivers of humanity. Many have brought their dogs, cats, and other pets. (Animals get in for free with a signed waiver of vaccination status and pet-owner responsibility.) Smiling vendors—testing the limits of their enthusiasm after hours in stale air and colorless light—appear glad to see them.

Megan Vickell's space is in the second row back from where I begin. The variety of pet merchandise I pass before I get to her makes my head spin. The guy at Politically Incorrect Pets! offers chew-and-shake dog toys resembling US President Donald Trump (C$25 for the large; C$12 for the small). The musician selling his wife's book, *Jake the Road Dawg* (about their real-life canine roadie), tells me they're a fine read for only C$25 per copy. One booth peddles officially sanctioned sports jerseys for dogs and cats. If any of the National Hockey League, National Football League, or other sports teams aren't on the racks, they can easily be ordered. (The C$35 price for a medium-size shirt is a show special; they're usually C$40.) The Barkley Bites dog treat vendor says packages of dried chicken feet cost about C$10, while the Best Friends Apparel staff claim the human clothes they peddle are developed by dog owners to reflect a true "dog-owner lifestyle." (A crew-necked sweater that reads "Can I pet your dog?" gives you the feel for just C$40 plus tax.) At the Sparkle and Barkle Doggie Boutique, an elegant, shimmering pet choker—with Rosaline Swarovski pearls among crystal Aurora Borealis balls and rondelles—has a variable price: C$93.95 to C$127.95 depending on your pampered animal's neck size.

Vickell's booth, however, brings me up short. Her sign and materials are understated and tasteful. A logo advertises a "Modern Day Dolittle." There are glossy cards and printed information: "Are you experiencing issues with your pet and can't get to the bottom of it? Would you like to better understand your animal's wants and desires? Perhaps you are just curious what they are thinking." The brochures promise that Vickell can help: "Like a Modern Day Dolittle, she talks to animals."

I stop and reread the line. A young woman steps forward. She's disarmingly friendly with shining eyes. She's also trim and sharp and attractive. Her slacks are crisply ironed. Her blouse is bright. Her long hair is carefully (expensively?) cut. She strikes me as the model of a young, eager, urban professional—one of the beautiful achievers found in Toronto's downtown professional firms. My impression, as it turns out, isn't far off: this is Vickell, and she's been a public relations expert for most of the past five years. She was the head of public relations and marketing for eBay Canada before striking out on her own as a consultant. She specializes, she says, in brand development and marketing. Most of her work is with companies that want to play in the big-money game of pet products. A year ago, however, she began to change course. Most would describe it more as a radical veer: "My career is in PR and marketing, pet-brand communications," she says, cheerfully. "This is a different kind of animal communications."

Being an "animal communicator" is Vickell's new job, and she's just getting started. Her title says it all; she "talks" to animals. She asks them questions. She finds out what they're thinking and feeling. It is, she explains, her gift and highest calling. For about C$100 (about US$76) per session—more if she visits in person—Vickell will have a two-way telepathic chat with your pet and tell you all about it. Messages, she says, are shared through symbols, signs, and pictures. Often a window into the pet's emotional state is there as well. The pet, on the other hand, doesn't need to be; Vickell can communicate without meeting or even seeing the animal in the flesh (or even in a photograph)—"for that is the beauty of telepathic communications," she explains. Technology helps, though. The young clairvoyant says she conducts a lot of her work over Skype, Viber, FaceTime, and even Instagram. Many of her clients are thousands of kilometers away or on the other side of the world. "Singapore and New York are huge markets for me," she says.

Demand for her service is considerable, Vickell tells me. The allure of understanding our pet's thoughts and desires is becoming increasingly irresistible to a lot of people. Pet owners love the company and affection of their companions, but sometimes it's not enough. Many are burning with curiosity, too. The mystery of the pet-and-pet-lover bond is profound and affecting. It's also murky, deep, and enticing. So much so that the frustration of such essential ignorance can be vexing. Biophilia yearns for a deeper connection. For the most passionate pet people, the irritation can worsen with time, like flourishing fleas in a coat of too-dense dog fur. The not knowing cries for a remedy. Vickell offers one.

"Typical questions would be, is my dog happy?" she says, describing her usual session playbook. "Is their diet okay? Are they okay with me taking it to this place or this place? Why is it acting out against this kind of dog and not that kind of dog?

"Sometimes we go deeper, depending on how openhearted and open-minded the owner is. Depending on that, we can go deeper into past life stuff. Like has my—or will my—dog reincarnate. A lot of people who have lost an animal will do a reading with me, and they want to know. They also want to know the signs and symbols around them. Like, is my dog trying to communicate with me? What are you seeing? How are they trying to deliver messages?"

I feel myself both mesmerized and struggling to keep up. Vickell, meanwhile, is charming and patient. She watches me closely. She's trying not to leave me behind. Her eyes are alive. Most disarming is her bold matter-of-factness: she could be a lively business professor explaining the principles of brand development and consumer psychology. Reincarnation, she instructs, is common for pets. ("I have one dog of my own right now. She's a rescue, and she's—this is where you really have to be openhearted and open-minded—she's actually been with me in past lives.") Pets returning to their owners in a different pet body isn't unusual, Vickell tells me. It's also not a sure thing. "Sometimes they're undecided," she says. "If the owner is grieving, and they have to move through stuff, [the pet] wants them to grieve properly. . . . They won't come back just to appease the owner. It's all lessons, right?"

The animal communicator pauses. She looks at me steadily for a moment. In the crowded, overlit convention hall—swimming with people and clamoring with noise—I imagine a lone cloud of doubt, tiny in the rafters: "Is your mind blown yet?" she asks. Her laugh is gleeful. "For some people, it's too much when I tell them all this. Sometimes it's too much for people to digest."

The Toronto Christmas Pet Show and its sister Canadian Pet Expo in the spring are the largest indoor consumer pet shows in the country. Few pet-product fairs aimed at pet owners outsize them anywhere in North America. In the estimation of organizer Grant Crossman, the events sit near the top among all of the pet-owner-focused pet shows held in cities and towns across the continent. (The several massive pet industry trade shows—such as SuperZoo in Las Vegas—are aimed at pet businesses.) It's no small boast: hundreds of consumer pet shows are held in every corner of the United States and Canada every year. Mega shows—such as this one, America's Family Pet Expo in California, and the huge out-door pet-product festival known as Pet-a-Palooza—attract vendors and visitors from all over. Vast numbers of dollars change hands. Crossman, who has been involved in the pet world one way or another since he was 14, counts himself lucky: his career in the industry happened to corre-spond with the most explosive growth the pet business has ever seen.

In the last 25 years, the amount of money we shell out to feed, groom, and pamper our pets has soared. In the United States alone, spending on household animals has almost quadrupled in that time. In 2019, Americans were expected to pay about $75.38 billion (up almost $3 billion from 2018) into the pet industry. Worldwide, the figure topped $116.6 billion in 2017, according to the London-based market research group Euromonitor International. And the market shows no sign of slowing—growing at about 3 percent per year. It's staggering: if pets were their own country, they'd be economically outperforming all but the top richest 60 nations in the world.[1]

Our biophilia has become a hulking global economic engine. For every $100 spent by US households in 2011, $1 of it went to pets. Given all the things that daily demand our money—the mortgage, the food, cell phones, Netflix—it's remarkable to contemplate. If pet owners cover just the basics for their pets—including training, shots, regular medical checkups, and pet insurance—the yearly cost of keeping a puppy, according to veterinarians, is about $2,816 while keeping an adult dog comes in at $2,463. Kittens cost $1,788 in the first year, while adult cats cost almost $1,583 every year thereafter. If your cat or dog lives to a ripe old age of, say, 13, it's worth reflecting that the cost of your animal over its lifetime could pay for a new Lexus SUV, a durably practical vehicle that might last you just as long. That's not all: the millions of available pet extras—like sessions with a pet clairvoyant or other high-end pet luxuries—cost, well, extra.[2]

A willingness to open our wallets for animal companions has fueled tens of thousands of pet businesses of every imaginable size, type, and configuration across the continent. New pet technologies, for example, are flourishing in a gadget-hungry marketplace. "Toletta" is one. It's a kitty litter box that monitors a cat's health by, first, recognizing individual cats using facial recognition software and, then, tracking weight, urine volume, and frequency of litter-box use. The machine then offers diagnostic suggestions and connects the data to an app on your smartphone. "DOGTV" is another. It's a subscription television service that offers "scientifically developed sights and sounds" to relax and entertain your dog while you're away. "Dig" is "the dog person's dating app."

"SpotOn.Pet" is an Uber-like driving service that guarantees its drivers will take pets; car-seat covers and dog- or cat-harness seat belts are included.[3]

According to the US Bureau of Labor Statistics, American families spent more on their pets in 2011 than they did on alcohol ($456), landline phones ($381), or men and boys' clothing ($404). The household cash that went to pet food alone was more than spending on candy ($87), bread ($107), chicken ($124), cereal ($175), or reading materials ($115). During the 2008–2009 economic funk, while many Americans frequently felt they couldn't justify a restaurant night out, money for pet food didn't dip at all. "People like to spend on their pets," says Crossman, shrugging a small, of-course-they-do shrug. Pets are family, and when emotional stakes are high, some proportional capital investment is only natural: we love animals; we're willing to pay.[4]

We'll pay, that is, as long as they're *our* animals living in *our* homes. Billions of wild creatures—many of them nearing oblivion in the world's shrinking wildernesses—aren't quite so lucky.

Americans spent almost *45 times* more on their pets in 2014 than all US federal and state governments paid to help the almost 1,500 US species listed as threatened or in imminent danger of extinction. In Canada, pet owners shelled out close to C$7.7 billion (US$5.9 billion) for pet care and lavishments in 2016, while the federal government parted with barely C$95 million (US$72.3 million) that 2015/16 fiscal year for all spending on its species-at-risk program across the country. Altogether, around the planet, pet people are estimated to spend more than four times as much on their dogs, cats, birds, and other pets as the combined amount paid by most of the world's nations to save our Earth's wondrous and irreplaceable variety of life. With the continued existence of perhaps a million species hanging in the balance, wild birds, mammals, reptiles, amphibians, and fish are the desperately poor cousins to our moneyed, comfortable, and frequently overweight pets. No wonder US dog and cat numbers have soared by as much as 60 percent in the last three decades, while global populations of noninsect wild animals have taken a nosedive and the overall risk of species extinctions has climbed during the same period.[5]

"I don't know if there's a single obvious fact" to explain our reluctance to pay more for wildlife conservation, says biologist Anthony Waldron. "We know it's inadequate." Maybe we're consciously avoiding the issue or simply don't think about it. Nothing suggests that the money spent on pets comes at the expense of dollars for wildlife. Instead, pets are near to us and have the power to demand our attention—and gifts of affection. They look at us, pleading and adorable, square in the face every day. Wild animals, on the other hand, tend to be out of sight and out of mind. That's especially true for those creatures whose scarcity is becoming worse. It's not really pet animals versus wild ones. It's not even about balancing human material wants against the natural world's needs. It is, instead, mainly about us—some people in tune with their biophilia; others not so much.

"A lot of people have this misconception that, essentially, there's this weird battle between man and nature," Waldron tells me, speaking by Skype from his home in Cambridge, United Kingdom. "And in fact, a more accurate characterization would be it's a battle between men who want to conserve nature and men who don't. It's definitely a human conflict. And nature has no voice in it in a strange way."

Waldron is a thoughtful, tousle-haired Brit with an elfin grin and a chalk-dry sense of humor. Over the past several years, the biologist has become known as a world expert on the economics and finance of biodiversity conservation. He's affiliated with Cambridge University but does most of his work as an independent consultant. His main job right now is with the Wyss Foundation–funded "Campaign for Nature," a multi-stakeholder partnership that's helping the UN Convention for

Biodiversity map a way to protect 30 percent of the planet's wildlands and oceans by 2030. (Right now, protected areas cover 15 percent of land and freshwater and 7 percent of the marine world.) Waldron leads a team trying to figure out what it might cost to preserve a wild third (or so) of the earth. They want to have an idea before the convention's 15th Conference of the Parties in Kunming, China, in late 2020. "It's a massive challenge," he says, "not least because nobody actually knows where they want the protected areas to be."[6]

Waldron is a finance and numbers guy in the difficult-to-enumerate world of living things. He has, he admits, come some distance from his early university days digesting Mallory's legends of King Arthur and the metered brilliance of Shakespeare. He was an English major first, he says, with a particular interest in medieval literature. He graduated with an English degree, and like many English majors, he wondered what next. Serendipity intervened. "For a bunch of strange reasons," he says, vaguely, "I ended up as a forest guide in the Amazon." Everything changed. The deep green, the flowers, the birds, and the biology of the place got under his skin. He returned to school to do a master's in biology. It was a big leap, but it was made more so by his program's inclusion of economics training. It was a long way from George Bernard Shaw, but it was the grounding he needed to head back to the tropics. He joined a nongovernmental organization helping cocoa farmers find ways to remain profitable while conserving as much nature as possible. The cocoa industry is now considered a model for sustainable farming and, importantly, marketplace transformation through environmental certification schemes.

"That's where I learned that biology will not save the planet," Waldron says, "that we need to consider the wider picture, and I've been sort of considering the wider picture ever since." In 2013, Waldron and a team from the University of Georgia published a first thorough look at "the wider picture" for global conservation funding. The study, published in the journal *Proceedings of the National Academy of Sciences*, created a massive database to track the complex meandering of money streams destined for the protection of nature. It was complicated, painstaking work, he describes, involving complicated mathematics and sophisticated forensic accounting. The result is a previously unseen glimpse of who is spending what and where on conservation. It's a picture that reveals much about how conservation-related financial decisions are made and, importantly, where the spending for nature really ought to be going instead.[7]

Conservation spending by the entire world was $21.5 billion per year, on average, between 2001 and 2008, according to the research. That is, the money humans pay to stop the greatest loss of life's diversity since the end of the dinosaurs is about half of what Americans pay for their daily cups of coffee every year. It's a gloom-inducing, piddling amount. But Waldron insists the news is actually good in at least one important respect: the study was able to identify underfunded areas with a lot of biodiversity where just a little conservation money could make a big difference. That is, we may not have to break the bank to improve things for a lot of wildlife.[8]

"There's been a lot of work on how human activity makes things worse for nature," Waldron explains. "And, almost completely separately, there's this new field of, you know, optimistic conservation, where you're looking at the effectiveness of conservation, what impact is it having—which is also a good way of making it work better, if you look for the most impactful places. It's called evidence-based conservation." Forty countries with the most sorely underfunded conservation efforts are also home to almost one-third of all threatened mammal species and belong to some of the most species-rich regions on Earth, the research found. After figuring in the relative impact of government effectiveness and national stability (most countries at war also have a greater variety of wildlife and more wildlife threats), the database offers important guidance for deciding where conservation dollars should go. Since much of the conservation funding for developing nations comes from international donors (developed countries usually pay for their own conservation), the picture drawn by the numbers is an important road map for directing conservation dollars.

It's also a somewhat unflattering portrait of relative conservation spending by many rich countries, like the United States and Canada. Between 2001 and 2008, the United States was in the bottom half of all the 199 nations ranked according to the conservation spending that should be expected of them (given their country size and economic and political circumstances). Canada was not much better. Compared with their economic peers, both countries spent less on conservation than average. France was ranked the 35th worst conservation cheapskate, while the United Kingdom and Australia were also in the top third of nations that underfund conservation.[9]

"Essentially, the voices shouting for economic development—not even economic development but just economic benefits—from the exploitation of land and sea have generally been louder," says Waldron. "And that's partly because of this externality problem: these people are getting economic benefits from nature, and it's free. And so, they don't take them into account. And as far as they're concerned, in short-term thinking, you just keep taking more and more." Even countries whose conservation spending is above average (relative to what's expected) are probably not providing adequate support for troubled wildlife. Most scientists and conservationists agree that there simply isn't enough conservation money to go around. Keeping more species from vanishing is necessarily costly, and so far it hasn't been a priority for many people. Part of the problem, says Waldron, is that few can agree on just how much conservation investment is enough. While estimates exist, a consensus seems a long way off.

Some say $80 billion might do it. A group of British conservationists came up with that figure a few years ago as the cost for appreciably improving the lot for all the world's at-risk species listed by the International Union for Conservation of Nature. The researchers—led by conservation economist Donal McCarthy with the Royal Society for the Protection of Birds—wondered what it would take to shift the status of species by at least one conservation category. That is, what's the price tag to "downlist" wildlife from critically endangered to endangered, from endangered to vulnerable, and so on. Writing in the leading journal *Science*, they arrived at an answer: about $4 billion a year is required to help wildlife directly, they said, and another $76 billion or so to protect habitat. The paper was among the first to ballpark an overall, worldwide cost for protecting biodiversity, and it's been cited scores of times since.[10]

For some, however, the figure still looks a lot like a guess. McCarthy and his coauthors began their calculations with speculative estimates by bird experts of the money needed to help each of 211 threatened bird species (about one-fifth of global birds at risk). Then, they used those estimates to extrapolate costs for other threatened birds and wildlife. "Like in the north of England," says Waldron, "this is equivalent to going up to a farmer and saying, what do you think? And he'll suck in his teeth and say, 'Oh, well, I'd say about double.' It's the equivalent to going up to 211 farmers, and they suck their teeth. That's a little unfair, of course. These were highly recognized conservation experts in birds, but you can see some of the pitfalls involved in extrapolating from 211 birds to saving the planet."

Another estimate might be closer—say, between $150 billion and $440 billion. In 2014, a high-level panel with the UN Convention on Biological Diversity named that staggeringly wide range as the likely price for meeting the convention's world biodiversity goals by 2020. The goals—known as the Aichi Biodiversity Targets—were agreed to by the convention's signatory countries in Aichi, Japan, in 2010. They include improving or maintaining the status of all threatened species around the planet and protecting 17 percent of all land and 10 percent of oceans. In its report summary, the authors acknowledge—sheepishly, I imagine—the oversized margin of error: "The Panel acknowledged a range of uncertainties and recognised that further research is vital to help refine these estimates," they write. The word "refine" lends some wonderfully crafted understatement. The research team goes on: "[A] variety of factors would affect the magnitude of the funding requirements." The admission has a ring of exasperation. According to Waldron, it shouldn't be a surprise. "There's no single right answer," he says, "because it depends on how you balance out the way you address conservation."[11]

Nothing's simple. You could spend all your money in places with the most threatened wildlife only to find those same places are too poor, too corrupt, or too troubled to see the contribution have an impact. Alternatively, you could spend it in a stable country with less wildlife and less conservation need, but where the dollars get to where they're needed. Some of the balancing involves resolving differences in conservation aims. Some want funds concentrated where the most species are found. ("Biodiversity hot spots," biologists call them). Others want money distributed so wildlife from all different regions remains represented. These decisions, of course, affect conservation costs. Coming up with a useful cost forecast often means making hard choices first. "Essentially, it's about politics," Waldron declares. "And that includes conservation politics."

That's a problem: uncertainty's most debilitating symptom is paralysis. Those with conservation money tighten their purse strings when they fear dollars might go wasted or misspent. Nobody wants to pay millions to save a rhino to find that paltry thousands actually make it to help the beast. If there's no telling what good—if any—is done by investing in wildlife, few will put their cash on the line. "For example," says Waldron, "I've been talking to consultants who work in environment with business, and they're saying big businesses are just queued up to do something about biodiversity in the same way that they queued up to do something about climate change. They just say, 'Tell us what to do.' We just haven't yet been able to define a set of actions and goals and targets that they can then buy in on."

Waldron's solution is to look back before trying to look forward. In a landmark 2017 paper in the journal *Nature*, the biologist and his colleagues explored past conservation contributions over 13 years (between 1996 and 2008) in 109 countries. It was another colossal accounting challenge. The researchers took stock of not only the conservation money shelled out in each case but also the local economic, agricultural, and population pressures that were (essentially) working against conservation at the same time. They compared these figures together with what they learned about the fate of wildlife in these places. "If you want to actually quantify conservation effort," says Waldron, "we know that the amount that you invest corrected for local cost is one of the fundamental drivers of what you achieve. So, let's put those all together. Let's put the pressures and the positive effort quantified as the spending into a single model and see if it actually explains the global changes in biodiversity over this period of about 13 years. And they did—almost exactly."[12]

The first key lesson is that conservation spending works. Wild creatures are better off when funds are there to help them. That may sound obvious, but a lack of clarity around what's really being achieved in conservation has been creating a sense of futility in the field. ("It's much simpler for donors just to say we don't want to invest in country *x* because it seems to have high levels of corruption," says Waldron.) The study offers reassurance: across the 109 countries, dollars spent on conservation reduced the worsening of species' conservation status by almost one-third (on average). In seven countries, wildlife actually improved. "The more adequate the funding is, usually the more people you're employing and the bigger the area you're guarding. So, there's a fairly intuitive correlation."

The second lesson is this: the amount needed to rescue the world's imperiled species isn't a number; it's more like an equation. Changed values on one side can be offset by balancing numbers on the other. Waldron describes a kind of grade 11 physics problem: conservation funders are pushing a car uphill from behind, while the many forces of human development are at the front, pushing back. Adding more force to one end or the other determines where your efforts to save nature wind up. "The whole thing ends up as a sort of tug of war between what I was describing earlier as the two sides of human endeavor: those who want to conserve nature, and those who want to carry out actions that are detrimental to it. And essentially it balances out and leads to quite a simple equation: when you put it all together, given these pressures, this is the amount of funding you would need to keep the car standing where it is—the car being the world's species."

The equation, while based on the past, allows researchers to anticipate the future. In particular, they can ask what happens to the variety of life as human development gathers steam—which it continues to do—and what conservation efforts can do to balance it. The push-me-pull-you model allows researchers to explore scenarios that trade forces from one side (e.g., economic interests) for forces on the other (e.g., dollars to prevent extinctions). "It's a forecasting model that's developed by using conservationist spending and human pressures that have been shown to affect biodiversity in the past," the scientist explains. "I have to run scenarios saying if you want to look at it this way, this is where you will go; if you want to look that way, that's where you would go.

"Some of the scenarios involve political and economic realities. I have to essentially balance those needs against what the biologists are saying. So, because of that, it comes down to the power politics of who can get their voice heard, who has the influence, who has the power. That's what politics is."

Science alone, in other words, doesn't have straight answers. Estimating costs of conservation requires Waldron's wider view, incorporating all the things people think are important. Things like business and economic growth. ("And the reason I'm saying this is because the amount of money spent on economic development dwarfs the amount of money spent on biodiversity conservation," he says.) Things like jobs and comfort. Even things like the other animals we love—our pet creatures at home.

Unfortunately, right now, most thinking is heavily skewed toward putting our very human concerns—and our pets—first. And many people are yet to understand or accept the idea that nature and its services are important to many of these human concerns as well. Meanwhile, nature is being shortchanged. A 2017 report by the Arizona-based nonprofit Center for Biological Diversity, for example, calculates that the US Fish and Wildlife Service makes a lot of promises to recover populations of species at risk of extinction, but it spends only $82 million each year to achieve them. The real price tag for keeping the pledges, says the group, is about $2.3 billion annually—about 28 times more. "Everything we do choose to conserve, we don't fund it properly."[13]

Back at the Toronto Christmas Pet Show—not far from where Grant Crossman casually manages fair operations from his information booth —a woman is holding a brilliant yellow-orange sun parakeet on her finger. It has a tiny sombrero on its head and is dressed in a luridly colorful poncho. The bird's name is Koa, and he's a willing, easygoing model.

The clothes, of course, are a goofy gag. Everyone thinks he's cute. Few get the cultural appropriation part of the joke: sun parakeets—called "sun conures" in the pet world—don't live in Mexico. They barely live in their small, native region of northeastern South America anymore. Most have been caught and sold to the pet trade. While captive breeding tries to keep up with bird-lover demand, the International Union for Conservation of Nature says trapping for the wild birds continues. Wild sun parakeet numbers are still falling. Many believe the species is gone altogether from its once-parakeet-packed home in southern Guyana. It's considered endangered throughout the rest of its range. Like Mexico's beloved axolotl, more sun parakeets now live in people's homes around the world than live and thrive in the wild.

Koa, however, isn't at the show to draw attention to the plight of his wild brethren or even to his sartorial sense of humor; he's here as a professional artist. He's "internationally renowned," boasts owner Gina Keller, for creating and selling paintings. Remarkably, it appears to be true: some of the artwork is propped for display on tiny easels. It resembles—vaguely—desperate marks made by a blindfolded calligrapher. Five Canadian dollars will get you a small sample. Some canvases can sell for C$100. People will pay: the works are, after all, a rare glimpse of creative expression from the frontier of birdy genius. And Koa's style is, well, distinctive. (Even Jackson Pollock endured accusations of monotony.) It's made him a celebrity, says Keller, cheerily: "He has thousands of Instagram followers."

Fame. Appreciation. Monetary reward. Few painters of the human kind could wish for more. Art, after all, succeeds when it makes connections. Painters yearn to overcome their solitude, to share their expressed sensibilities in a way that others recognize. Koa and Keller's artistic enterprise works like that, too. Koa's paintings are just one bird's attempt to bridge the great human–animal divide, to step over the barriers between our biologically (creatively?) different worlds. Why not? Linking ourselves to our pets—searching to gratify our biophilia—is what drives most of the rest of the massive, multibillion-dollar pet industry. It's certainly at the root of most of what's on offer here at this enormous Toronto pet show: A chance to buy material goods and treats as a means to communicate our affection for our pets, to acknowledge and fortify our mutual connection. The hundreds of vendors here, Crossman tells me, all begin with the same idea.

"You could say any business owner in here starts off with the passion for the pet," he says as he busily types out a cell phone text. He pauses and looks up. "Right?"

None has a direct line to pets that's quite as literal as the one belonging to Meghan Vickell: "In terms of my purpose," she says, "it's really to connect the animal kingdom with humanity and to help bridge that gap. . . . But what I want to make clear here—and what's really beautiful—is I always give the pets open forum at the end. I ask them, is there anything you would like to communicate. . . . Often, they want to talk about their feelings. And that's the big switcheroo. Here, this person came to talk about their animal, and, by the end of it, we're helping the human more."

Sure, the pets are happy to tell their owners what they want—"that they want more treats, or that they want this or that"—but often, says Vickell, the animals want to weigh in with advice for their humans, too. After silently watching their owners interact with other humans, pets sometimes have pointed opinions about what they've seen. Once, recalls Vickell, a woman's dogs revealed to the communicator that their owner ought to stay away from her daughter-in-law. The younger woman was just "bad energy," the animals declared through Vickell: "Do not go there."

Connecting to other creatures can reveal the unexpected. Or—more tellingly—it can show that spending money is easy. Getting value is hard. Perhaps it's just not possible to buy our way to a better understanding of animals. Maybe lavishing pets with gifts isn't a route to a greater mutual appreciation and intimacy. Other nonhuman creatures inhabit "a world older and more complete" than ours, wrote the naturalist-author Henry Beston, "gifted with extensions of the senses we have lost or never attained, living by voices we shall never hear." The currency creatures use to measure fondness and comprehension is unlikely to resemble our money and presents. As much as we may want to, we can't spend our way to a greater connection to other life.

What money can do, however, is help conservation. More spending to save biodiversity works; investing in species helps them battle back against threats overall. Dollars can make a difference in our relationship with animals, but not necessarily at home. Buying wild animals a more hopeful future is valuing the existence of life and wonder around us. Money can't buy love, but it can help keep the loneliness of a world without biodiversity at bay.[14]

The key financial question for Vickell, however, may not be as complicated: I ask her whether she thinks working as an animal clairvoyant—as a conduit connecting our two sentient realms—can translate into a good living for a young urban professional. "I believe it can. Absolutely," she tells me, grinning radiantly. "My mentor, just for 15 minutes, she's getting $400—or something crazy."

CHAPTER 9
Guardian Dogs and Animal Emissaries

Pete Coppolillo, the ardent conservationist, likes dogs. In truth, he can hardly stop marveling at them. "These dogs are incredible," he says, almost beaming. Coppolillo is sitting across a table at the Motel 6 in Shelby, Montana, pushed back comfortably in a metal chair. He's rugged looking and fit with his head shaved clean and a cropped, salt-and-pepper beard. His face, with bright brown eyes under heavy eyebrows, is unusually expressive. Right now, it's flooded with warmth—for the dogs, for these pets. He sips his beer. "I mean, they're really good," he smiles.

Coppolillo has been around conservation for a long time and in a lot of places. He's worked with the Wildlife Conservation Society, a leading New York–based conservation group, in Africa, Asia, and South America. He's no stranger to the harm domestic dogs can do to wildlife. They are—not to put too fine a point on it—a terror. Only cats and rodents have arguably done more lasting damage to wild creatures around the planet. Dogs have played a role in the known extinctions of 11 bird, reptile, and mammal species so far and threaten nearly 200 others. Coppolillo has seen the dangers up close. He's studied wildlife on Tanzania's Serengeti Plain. He knows the tragedy of the dog-transmitted canine distemper that ravaged the great lion prides there. He's worked in the region where the pet-borne disease and others, such as rabies, obliterated the African wild dogs from the area. The domestic dogs are fed in villages and homes, but they still roam in packs. They chase wildlife. They spread sickness. In their coddled innocence, the animal companions are amok on the landscape. They're our pets, and they can be a nightmare for the wild world.[1]

Coppolillo, of course, knows all this. Few know it better. But he also knows another side of the story. Understanding it is critical, he says, if we're going to get the conservation of nature right. Pets don't have to be four-legged versions of people at our worst; they can partner with our better angels instead. As animals, our creature companions are uniquely equipped as emissaries to the wild world, to connect us to nature in a real sense and to help us to protect it. Coppolillo has seen this utopian relationship firsthand. He's the executive director of a Montana-based organization that trains and uses dogs to sniff out clues to help conservationists save beleaguered wildlife. The group is called Working Dogs for Conservation, and it is perhaps the largest of a handful of similar dog-employing wildlife protection groups at work around the globe.

"So, I suppose our story is part of the exception to the rule with dogs," says Coppolillo, "because in a lot of cases you've got dogs chasing wildlife, bringing down a lot of wildlife and stuff like that. This is different. These are detection dogs." He looks up. "They help. That's what they do."

Shelby is a little town, but Montana is vast. It's like a big, wild holdout of a place. The oversized sweep and ruggedness is conspicuous and impressive. To the east, grassy plains reach to the horizon across low hills and long-ago-carved riverbeds. Overhead, the sky is massive and bright. To the west, the monumental Rocky Mountains touch a few distant clouds. The sheer scale of nature here seems like something from the past. It's a frontier of sorts, and perhaps one of America's last. It belongs to "the idea of wilderness" imagined by Wallace Stegner, a favorite writer of the American West who lived in Montana as a boy; the untrammeled wild of these places, he famously wrote, is "the geography of hope." Montana cleaves proudly to the image—even as it gets harder and harder to keep the wider world from intruding.

"We've been lucky so far," Zach Crete tells me when we meet in the morning. Crete is an invasive species program coordinator with the Montana Department of Fish, Wildlife, and Parks. He's a typical-looking field biologist—earnest and slightly rumpled with a ball cap and beard. He's easy in conversation and cheerful; we're talking and waiting in the lobby of a Shelby hotel for others in our group, including Coppolillo's colleague Aimee Hurt. Hurt is a cofounder of Working Dogs for Conservation and among the lead trainers and handlers.

Crete has invited Hurt and her conservation dogs on a hunt for invasive aquatic zebra mussels. Invasive species can devastate native wildlife and ecosystems, but so far, Montana's relative remoteness has spared it some of the worst. The mussels, however, seem to be always closing in. In 2016, for instance, a routine sample taken from the Tibor Reservoir (also known as Lake Elwell), about an hour east of Shelby, sounded the alarm: near-microscopic mussel larvae—called veligers—were discovered drifting in the water. In the same year, another sample from nearby Canyon Ferry Reservoir also showed possible-but-inconclusive evidence of the mollusks. Montana officials shuddered; estimates suggest a full-fledged invasion could cost the state more than $230 million annually in tourism losses and damage. Since then, repeated searches have failed to uncover more signs of the animal's arrival, but Crete's job is to make sure. That's where the dogs come in. "Let's see if we can find something," he says after we all load our cars and drive an hour east to the breezy shore of the Tibor Reservoir. "Hopefully not."[2]

The dogs are what I've come to see. "The dogs make life way easier for us, and fast," says Crete, standing by the waterside. "We can sample the water. We can check for veligers and other signs. But it's a big lake. It takes time. That's time here at the lake and the time in the lab checking through samples."

Mussels can be cryptic and hard to encounter until, suddenly, they're everywhere and all too common. By that time, they're as noticeable as they are impossible to stop. Zebra mussels (and their close cousin, quagga mussels) are small mollusks that arrived in North America from their native home in eastern Europe decades ago. Within a short time, the species established itself in the Great Lakes and quickly transformed ecosystems in these and other waters across half the continent. They're notorious for colonizing water pipes in thick, dense layers, choking public water supplies and clogging hydro-plant intakes. They also filter massive amounts of plankton and nutrients, literally sucking the life out of water and away from native organisms that normally feed on these plankton. Montana has remained mussel-free so far, but the 2016 detections were a wake-up call. "The mussels are a large part of our focus right now," says Crete.

The remarkable canine sense of smell helps balance the equation: early detection makes eradication more likely. "Prior to dogs, the method was looking for the thing personally, with your eyes," says Hurt, who is gathering gear at her vehicle. She opens the door and an eager blond Labrador retriever named Lily is the first to tumble out. Two other labs, Atlas and Wicket, follow clumsily. Within seconds, the dogs are sniffing the cars, grass, people, everything. Their eagerness is frenetic. They push past, and Hurt continues: "Suddenly, you've switched the paradigm to looking for it by scent, and that makes an incredible difference."

Today's job belongs to Lily. The other dogs are along only for the ride. Atlas, a young male that joined the team in 2015 with a great nose but failing eyes, is still learning his way. Wicket, a female, spent 12 years working for the organization before being retired in 2017. She's the closest thing the group has to a rock star; she spent those 12 years as one of the most accomplished conservation detection dogs ever. While some dogs are difficult to retrain to switch from one target scent to another, Wicket had a genius for understanding the goal of a search and zeroing in on a new smell with ease. She's hunted for everything from plants to animals to animal poop in seven countries and 18 states. She's traveled—as Hurt proudly boasts—more than 161,000 kilometers (100,000 miles) for the sake of wildlife, including some of it by bush plane, kayak, and elephant. These days, she's simply an old and trusted companion. She lives with Hurt and still likes to get out in the truck. After a few minutes, she and Atlas are returned to the vehicle. Lily will work solo today.

Lily seems to settle as soon as Hurt dresses her in a red dog vest. The uniform is a signal to shift gears; she's still busily smelling the ground, but she's in a different, more-focused mode: all business. Hurt leads her to the water's edge, and the pair begin walking the beach. Lily moves ahead of her handler, almost shuddering with excitement but diligently resisting any urge to rush. Her nose swings busily from side to side, combing the coarse sand where it's lapped at by the lake. The tall grass nearby—stretching to the distance in all directions—bends with the chilling wind. A few loons, in autumn plumage, float far out. Crete and I watch from the bank along with Pam Taylor, an officer with the Department of Fish and Wildlife from the neighboring state of Washington. She's here to learn about the dogs too. It's an impressive sight. Nothing about Lily's earlier behavior suggests her familiarity with self-restraint, but here, at work, she's a surprise: she's intense, seemingly careful, and—in her frenetic way—methodical. Dog and handler walk a narrow strip of the shore. Hardly five minutes pass before Lily abruptly sits, fidgety and expectant, at the water's edge. She looks around.

"Oh," Crete says to me, a little grimly. A sitting dog is the signal: just as pointers and other hunting dogs learn to freeze, pointing their nose at a discovered scent, the conservation detection dogs are taught to sit tight by the source of a suspect smell. Crete sighs: "We've got some action already."

The use of pets for wildlife conservation is far from new. Neither is the irony. The practice—along with the apparent paradox—has been around for more than a century. As early as the 1890s, for example, companion canines were used to find flightless New Zealand kiwis and the nation's ground-dwelling parrot, the kakapo, in efforts to protect these fast-disappearing birds from the jaws of . . . well, marauding dogs. Populations of the creatures were plummeting fast. (The kakapo remains critically endangered even now.) New Zealand's five species of nocturnal kiwis and the nocturnal kakapo had lived most of their evolutionary history without any ground predators. Then, about 800 years ago, humans arrived with their pets and pests. Domestic dogs—along with rats, cats, and other copassengers on the human journey—soon roamed and ravaged the countryside, devastating many of the small and flightless animals living on the islands. Before the turn of the nineteenth century, biologists were spurred to act. They turned to the perpetrators—the dogs themselves—to help sniff out the struggling creatures so efforts could be made to save them. Dogs are still used in kiwi conservation today—even as more than three-quarters of adult kiwi deaths in popular holiday regions of the country are still caused by off-leash dogs.[3]

Saving birds continued to be the focus of conservation-dog work for the next century. Many dogs have been bred for bird hunting, so finding feathered conservation targets was a natural fit. In other contexts, however, the greater potential of sniffer dogs was expanding. Beginning with World War II, for instance, dogs became experts at detecting bombs and land mines or for finding missing people. Later, their sniffing skills became a tool for discovering drugs and other contraband. More recently, dogs and their noses have become potential early detection systems for cancer, identifying the disease's telltale odor from patients. The use of detection dogs in wildlife conservation, however, began to expand its role and gather momentum beginning in the 1980s and 1990s. As Hurt tells it, a Wyoming ranch dog may have had a hand in it.[4]

One September day in 1981, somewhere near the prairie town of Meeteetse, Wyoming, Lucille and John Hogg discovered their dog, Shep, with a weird weasellike creature in its mouth. Shep appeared to have killed the animal as it boldly approached his food bowl. When Lucille Hogg took the attractive, masked creature to be stuffed and mounted, the puzzled taxidermist called wildlife officials. It was, as it turned out, a black-footed ferret. None had been seen in the wild for the previous seven years. Most biologists considered the ferret extinct in its natural home on the American plains—a victim (mainly) of rancher control of the prairie dogs, which ferrets eat. Conservationists were surprised and delighted, and they scrambled to the animal's rescue.[5]

"So they trapped the rest of the population they could find on that ranch and made a captive breeding facility," says Hurt. "And when they were trapping them, they were using dogs." The dogs were trained to sniff out the live ferrets.

In the decades since, feces—rather than ferrets—have made the work of detection dogs ever more essential to conservation efforts, says Coppolillo: "What really catalyzed it was the advent of, or the possibility of, fecal DNA—being able to recover DNA from feces or a species' scat. When the molecular techniques got good enough to do that, it really opened up a huge number of doors, because it made it possible to not only identify a species noninvasively—so you don't have to catch them, you don't have to harass them, you don't even have to see them—but as the techniques have improved, now we can know individuals."

The detection dogs, in other words, can uncover a trove of biological and behavioral data simply by sniffing out the poop of rare and endangered animals. And as the molecular technology has developed, says Coppolillo, the amount conservationists can learn by sampling the poop has expanded almost exponentially. "We also now get stress hormones and reproductive hormones and, you know, diet information and all sorts of stuff like that from scats," he says. "So the joke I always make is that the value of turd just keeps going up and up."

These days, beyond simply finding live wildlife, conservation dogs sniff for information-rich feces, find dead birds and bats around wind turbines, and discover signs of disease or other telltale biological clues in water and across landscapes. Research shows that, in many cases, the dogs are far better than other survey methods for measuring the presence and relative numbers of plants and other wildlife. For finding scat alone, the dogs are at least five times as effective as human collectors. Apart from the fieldwork, the dogs also play a vital and global role helping to intercept smuggled wildlife—sniffing out illegal ivory, rhino horn, tiger parts, and live animals for the pet trade—and checking boats, cargo, and other gear that might be inadvertently bringing nonnative beasts and plants to places they don't belong.[6]

Over the last 20 years or so, says Coppolillo, business has been booming. Working Dogs for Conservation—a not-for-profit charitable organization—is among the most established in the field, operating since 2000. Conservation Canines, a more research-focused group at the University of Washington's Center for Conservation Biology, is also an early pioneer in the field, beginning in 1997. (The founders of both organizations began developing their techniques together with help from Barbara Davenport, a leading narcotics dog trainer with the Washington State Department of Corrections.) Other outfits—such as Midwest Conservation Dogs in Wisconsin, the Conservation K9 Consultancy in the United Kingdom, Detection Dogs for Conservation in Australia, and Green Dogs Conservation in South Africa—have emerged elsewhere around the planet.

Coppolillo's group—eight staff and 30 dogs—now works with governments, universities, and nongovernment conservation organizations in 19 countries. They have dogs permanently stationed in six. In the wildlife hot spot of Zambia's Luangwa Valley, for instance, Working Dogs for Conservation has trained a team of detection and tracking dogs to battle poaching and wildlife-product smuggling, including the illegal trade in elephant tusk, rhino horns, and animal skins. The organization's pets do similar work on the celebrated Serengeti Plain of Tanzania and in Kazakhstan and the Kyrgyz Republic of central Asia. A new pilot project is starting in the Falkland Islands, using the dogs to keep shipborne rats and mice from reaching seabird colonies there. Closer to home, the canine conservationists are uncovering the movements of grizzly bears, black bears, mountain lions, and wolves across the Centennial Mountains range of Montana and Idaho, and they're keeping tabs on endangered San Joaquin kit foxes in California. Along with their mussel detection work—they sniff boats and boat trailers at highway inspection stops—the group's dogs have also proved invaluable in finding the alien plant, Dyer's woad, that's threatening to overwhelm prairie pastureland. More recently, the remarkable ability of the dogs to find and discriminate scents in moving water means they may soon track invading brook trout in rushing western mountain streams.

The conservation dogs, of course, are pets. They're Labradors. They're border collies. They're mixed-breed shepherds. They're the same as all the canine confederates descended through the ages from generations of companionable mutts. They're like millions of lovable dogs—curled by the fire or snoring on the carpet—except, says Coppolillo, that they're not. Not really. "The cool thing is that the dogs we are looking for are the dogs that don't make good pets," he explains. "These are high-drive, very high-energy, very focused individuals who have a super high interest in playing with a toy."

It's another twist to the conservation dog story: bad dogs are best. These obsessive, busy pet partners come to Coppolillo's group from animal shelters across the country. All are rescues. After 9/11 and the wars in Iraq and Afghanistan, the detection dog of choice, Belgian shepherds, became hard to come by. The conservation group began searching humane society kennels and other pet rescue facilities. What they discovered—not surprisingly—is that these places for unwanted dogs were an ideal source of the super-charged, obnoxious variety. "Those are the kinds of dogs we look for," Coppolillo explains.

The best conservation champions, it seems, may be the most uncompanionable of animal companions, but that doesn't make them any less compelling to watch. Coppolillo says the organization's dogs often attract attention. People seem to love to watch the animals at work. It's another advantage: conservation dogs garner notice that raises the profile of both the work they do and of conservation more generally. Consider, for instance, Oddball the sheepdog.

Oddball was an enthusiastically determined Maremma sheepdog in southern Australia who, along with a succession of other Maremma sheepdogs after him, helped expand the role of conservation pets to include direct wildlife protection. The idea of "guardian dogs" to keep wild predators from livestock has been around for about as long as there's been livestock, but using them to guard vulnerable wild animals is relatively new. In the Australian coastal town of Warrnambool, a local farmer Allan "Swampy" Marsh was using the dogs on his farm to guard his free-range chickens from the jaws of predators. In 2005, when fox attacks on a colony of little penguins on nearby Middle Island cut the number of those birds to fewer than 10 (from more than 500 a few years earlier), Marsh was convinced dogs could help. Oddball became the island's first dog sentinel in 2006, and the penguins—whose numbers have climbed back to more than 100—have been guarded by Maremma sheepdogs during the breeding season since. The achievement inspired a popular 2015 family film, *Oddball*, and made the dog and his groundbreaking conservation story famous.[7]

After Oddball, other conservation causes took notice. Zoos Victoria, a zoo-based conservation organization also based in Australia, launched a similar guardian dog program to protect battered populations of eastern barred bandicoots—considered "vulnerable" to extinction by the International Union for Conservation of Nature. The bandicoots, once widespread in southern Australia, are effectively extinct on the continent's mainland thanks to foxes and feral domestic cats. Now, only about 400 individuals survive in two sites where the animals have been reintroduced. (Another eastern barred bandicoot subspecies lives in slightly more robust numbers in Tasmania.) Efforts to guard the breeding bandicoots with fences have had limited success. Conservationists hope the dogs will be more effective, repeating the results of their penguin work.[8]

In a twist on the "guardian" pet idea, some dogs—and even cats—have been set free on islands less as protectors and more as aggressors. Conservationists have found that releasing pets onto islands can be effective in ridding them of other invasive species such as rats and rabbits. The scheme has proven effective in improving the success of some native animals, say scientists, including seabirds whose eggs were being eaten by the alien rodents. Using invaders to battle invasions has its obvious problems, and the subsequent need to rid these places of the ecologically troublesome feral pets comes with its own challenges in need of creative solutions. In New Zealand, for instance, conservation detection dogs are being used to find feral cats to help rid them from the countryside.[9]

In South Africa, meanwhile, one of the most troubling of that nation's conservation concerns is the plight of its big, charismatic wild cats. There, and in many other sub-Saharan African countries, cattle ranchers and other herdsmen often kill cheetahs, leopards, lions, and other cats to protect livestock. For many of these people, goats and cattle are their bread and butter and the only hope of a livelihood; defending the farm animals is essential. Meanwhile, in Africa and elsewhere around the world, large carnivores are among the planet's most imperiled wildlife: of the globe's 31 largest carnivores—big cats, wolves and jackals, wolverines, bears, hyenas, and the like—almost two-thirds are threatened with extinction, according to the International Union for the Conservation of Nature. Populations for more than three out of four of these species are dwindling—some are falling fast—and more than half have seen their ranges shrink by as much as 99 percent from historic sizes. Many of these magnificent animals, say scientists, appear destined to vanish from the wild altogether.[10]

Conservationists hope guardian dogs can help turn the trend around. Unlike Oddball and his fellow dogs trained to protect wild animals directly, the guardian dogs in Africa (and elsewhere) are simply encouraged to do what they've been bred to do over thousands of years— defend livestock from predators, including the big cats. Researchers say that by encouraging farmers to use guardian dogs more often than guns, snares, or poison, they can keep both cattle and the endangered predators safe. The fiercely territorial dogs—raised and bonded with the herds they protect—bark and menace any prowling animals that venture near and eventually frighten them away. Studies of the dogs' effectiveness found livestock deaths due to predators were reduced by 91 percent on South African ranches when canine protectors were on the scene. That translates into more than $3,000 per year per farm in the pockets of ranchers through savings from reduced animal losses. The researchers also found that ranchers were noticeably more at ease with prowling carnivores living on their rangeland. They became more tolerant of big cats—presumably because they trusted the dogs to protect the cattle and goats. More cheetahs and other predators are seen on these guardian-dog-defended ranches than on farmland of those with none.[11]

The Namibia-based Cheetah Conservation Fund has been supporting this pet-protection approach for the past 25 years. In 1994, the group began supplying Anatolian shepherds (donated by an American kennel at the time) to Namibian ranchers who used them to keep cheetahs, lions, and leopards at bay without killing the big feline predators. Since then, according to the organization, the program has trained and placed over 650 livestock guardian dogs—both Anatolian shepherds and Kangal dogs—in Namibia, South Africa, and Tanzania. The result has been a transformation of local attitudes toward the declining populations of cheetahs as well as other predators, the group says. It's an important milestone for the cheetah, whose small populations (totaling fewer than 7,000 individuals across just 10 percent or so of its historic range) have plummeted until some scientists consider them already endangered.[12]

Populations of yellow-crested cockatoos—the wild ones, not the caged pets—have already fallen to that endangered status, and they've continued right past it toward the brink of extinction: in their only native homeland on Sulawesi and the Lesser Sunda Islands in Indonesia, the well-known parrot is now considered "critically endangered." Although the trade in pet parrots is considered the main reason the natural wild population is now fewer than 3,000 birds, the cockatoos have added a strange twist to the pets-as-conservation-helpmates story: through happenstance and inadvertence, the consequences of cockatoo pet keeping may help to save the day in the end.

Cockatoos are beautiful, sociable, and remarkably intelligent birds. Although protected by international and Indonesian law, the parrots are so popular that ignoring these rules is often too lucrative for trappers to resist; one yellow-crested cockatoo can fetch as much money as four months of an Indonesian's average salary. The wild parrots have few powers to slow their descent: they're slow breeders—laying just two or three eggs a year—and have little capacity to bounce back. In Hong

Kong, however, a wild population of the yellow-crested cockatoos is doing rather well. While the big, commercial island city isn't a place the birds naturally occur, as many as 200 of them now live as invasive aliens there, descendants of escaped pets likely going back all the way to the nineteenth century. Some of the parrot ancestors may have been intentionally released from a large aviary during World War II. Whatever the case, the cockatoos' kin all arrived in Hong Kong as caged birds and feathered companions. Now, they're living wild and quite happily in the territory's trees, eating and breeding with a level of success that's the envy of Indonesian officials trying restore the birds in their native homeland.[13]

Conservationists in Vietnam and China may have similar feelings about the wattle-necked soft-shelled turtle. The endangered reptile has been hunted almost to extinction in its native range in the two Asian nations. Locals catch and eat it as a traditional delicacy and use it as a source of medicine. The Turtle Conservation Fund describes the animal as one of the 48 most endangered turtle species on the planet. Yet, while native populations continue to suffer, invasive wattle-necked soft-shelled turtles in Hawaii appear to be doing just fine. Chinese laborers are thought to have introduced the species to the archipelago in the 1800s, and the turtle has since established itself on the island of Kauai (with sightings of other individuals on nearby Oahu and Maui).[14]

In 2017, biologist Luke Gibson of the University of Hong Kong and Ding Li Yong of the Australian National University took stock of how many animals around the world share the strange inverted circumstances of Hong Kong's cockatoos or Hawaii's turtles. The pair compared records of established invasive species against lists of animals considered at risk in their native ranges (e.g., the International Union for Conservation Red List of Threatened Species). They found 49 birds, mammals, and reptiles around the world are simultaneously in danger of extinction at home but living successfully as invaders elsewhere.

Among them is the Philippine deer, now disappearing in the Philippines but established as newcomers to Guam and the Mariana Islands, and the banteng, a wild cow hunted almost to oblivion in its native Southeast Asia but flourishing as an introduced species in Australia. Even the Burmese pythons, now vexingly common as pet descendants in Florida's Everglades, are listed by the international conservation body as in danger of vanishing from their native homeland in Asia (where their skin is used in traditional medicines).[15]

To Gibson and Yong, these bizarre, upside-down scenarios are a potential conservation windfall: the escaped exotic pets and their heirs, wild in new environments and far from the pressures that imperil them at home, may be their species' saving grace. By chance and almost certainly with help from irresponsible humans, they've become another example of how pets can actually help wildlife in trouble. In their paper, the authors suggest that the introduced alien populations could be a source of individuals for reintroduction, translocated back to their native ranges to reinforce imperiled populations there. In some cases, invasive "substitutes" could offset demand for their natural wild-caught counterparts. Researchers could also study the wild aliens as surrogates to learn about the species without disrupting the delicately poised few left in their native wild. "Such creative conservation strategies could help stem the continuing worldwide degradation of biodiversity," the authors write.[16]

Others take a more sobering view. Hong Kong's yellow-crested cockatoos, for example, are having an impact on native birds and wildlife in the city, even if it appears relatively benign so far. Invasive wattle-necked soft-shelled turtles, meanwhile, are transforming the freshwater lakes and streams of Kauai, because no native turtles or other large aquatic predators live on the island. The endangered-at-home-but-happy-in-Hawaii turtle is being blamed for a decline in native Hawaiian fish on the island and for eating another endangered species, Newcomb's snail—a kind of air-breathing water snail found only in six of Kauai's mountain streams. The success of Florida's Burmese pythons is another good example; the big snakes are barely scraping by in Asia, but in the Sunshine State they're flourishing—even as they're considered public enemy number one in Everglades conservation.[17]

Part good and part bad, these invasive pet descendants are examples of what some scientists describe as a troubling "conservation paradox." On the face of it, it's better that an animal should survive as an alien away from its native range than not to survive at all. Total extinction has no road back. Yet, if the transplanted creature is causing havoc and putting other native species at risk, the issue quickly becomes ethically and philosophically complex. The conservation responses, argue researchers in a 2016 essay in the journal *Conservation Biology*, may suddenly require balancing the value of one species over others. It's a balancing act, in other words, that can seem anathema to the idea of conservation itself. What's worse, say the researchers, is that the paradox isn't always easy to see; the impacts of invasive aliens can take time to reveal themselves. "[T]he devil," they write, "hides in the details. . . ."[18]

Of course, exotic pets don't have to live as potentially destructive wild aliens to help their native wild brethren; they can be good for conservation even as they remain in our care, lazing in their cages or drifting in aquariums. At least, that's what some pet keepers, scientists, and even conservationists believe. The rationale belongs to a kind of "Noah's Ark" way of thinking. It's the same as the scientific and conservation reasons often given in defense of zoos: beyond mere entertainment, exotic animals in captivity can help preserve species that are about to blink out of existence in nature; they can inspire and nurture interest in wildlife among people who see and interact with them; they can be a source of animals for research; and they can encourage techniques and expertise among pet keepers that can be put to use by conservationists in the field. It may not always work out that way, but scientists Frank Pasmans and

An Martel believe pet keeping's benefits—at least where reptiles and amphibians are concerned—can be worth it overall.[19]

Pasmans and Martel, are the veterinary pathologists from Belgium's Ghent University who—along with doctoral student Annemarieke Spitzen-van der Sluijs—were the first to describe the salamander-killing fungus known as *Batrachochytrium salamandrivorans*, or Bsal. They've also studied its frog-decimating cousin, *B. dendrobatidis*, or Bd, for years. Both diseases, which have been blamed for amphibian declines and extinctions around the world, have traveled the world literally on the backs of pets, and the two researchers are no strangers to the conservation consequences of exotic pet keeping. Yet, not long ago, the pair joined other scientists to pen an appeal in the journal *Veterinary Record* arguing in favor of reptile and amphibian pet keeping.[20]

The authors claim that, despite the risks, exotic pets are a source of scientific inspiration. The writers name several celebrated European herpetologists—reptile and amphibian scientists—who began their love of the animals as kids, keeping the scaly or slimy creatures as childhood companions. People who keep and breed exotic pets frequently become a trove of expertise. When conservation efforts need intimate understanding of an animal's behavior and biology, pet owners can be an immense help. Meanwhile, captive exotic animals are often invaluable subjects for critical conservation-relevant research—as the Bd and Bsal studies by Pasmans and Martel show. While an argument against many of these claims was published by the same journal a few weeks later, the case—even if a little less glorifying than expressed in the commentary— remains an important one. The conservation values of pet keeping can't be strictly overlooked.[21]

Lily and the conservation dogs, of course, are a different story. Furry and responsive, linked to us by thousands of years of dependency and domestication, they are perhaps the more practical animal insiders as partners in conservation. By the shore of Montana's Tibor Reservoir, moments after Lily's discovery of suspected zebra mussel scent, the dog and her handler are playing ecstatically with a toy. (They're not celebrating the potentially grim news for Montana's waterways; the toy-play is Lily's reward for a job well done.) Crete and I reach the spot and find a small mat of aquatic weed washed up on the sand. Crete pulls it apart, examining it carefully. "There," he says, finally. On the tip of his finger, the biologist reveals a ragged shard of a shell, no bigger than a lentil. He examines it carefully and appears at once relieved. "Pea clam."

Despite its tiny size, the piece is enough to inspire Crete with reasonable confidence that the shell's former owner is not likely an invading mussel but a benign and common species often found in the state. (Tests and a water sample taken at the site later confirm that the reservoir continues to be mussel free.) Pea clams are a family of miniature freshwater clams with a number of native Montana species in the clan. Similar in a few respects to their mussel cousins, the pea clam piece could easily have an odor profile capable of fooling the dog, Crete tells me. What's more remarkable to me is that such an impossibly small particle within a clump of waterside weeds could have attracted Lily's notice at all.

"She has to be close, a couple of inches," Hurt explains when she joins us. "The scent of something really small won't travel over a couple of feet. It becomes dependent on the wind. . . . But she can find tiny shells, veligers, tiny stuff that no person would ever see." To pull it off requires covering a lot of ground closely. It means working systematically, thoroughly, and, with any luck, efficiently. At the same time, Hurt says, any effort at too much control over these dogs risks cramping their exuberance and wild enthusiasm. These latter characteristics may be annoying in a typical house pet, but they're essential to the drive these conservation dogs need. The balance is the trick. To a certain extent, it requires a new kind of connection between the pet and its handler. The dogs, says Hurt, have to be allowed to be dogs—and to pursue their natural dog rambunctious curiosity and passion for play—while understanding, in the back of their minds, the inherent joy of connecting with their humans.

"Them being tuned into 'here's a human calling all the shots,' that makes them more responsive, for sure," she says as Lily, at her side, continues to pull at her toy. "But we aren't trying to make them super-focused on us. . . . This work has a certain degree of intelligent disobedience involved with it."

The magic comes from rethinking the relationship between pet and pet owner. Between companion animal and companion. Dogs that are allowed to be dogs—rather than fashionable props or compliant drudges—seem to thrive in the world for which they were, in essence, designed. It's a place that straddles the wild world's natural, unregulated intensity and the human world's often paradoxical obsession with both control and wonder. A new connection emerges that may not be new at all; it may be closer to our former bond with animals back when we slept on the ground and called their wilderness our home. Without always imposing our terms on our relationship with pets, we can be close in the way we were once close to other animals—and vice versa. A conservation dog, explains Hurt, can be a creature first and, at the same time, an emissary in our human relationship with the plurality of all life. Feeling close to the dog can be like taking a step closer to nature.

CHAPTER 10
The Pet-Keeper Conservationist

Edward O. Wilson wasn't yet a conservation hero and giant among biologists when he met Methuselah in the Sierra de Trinidad near Cuba's southern coast. The year was 1953, and the future author of the concept of biophilia was still a Harvard graduate student. The trip to Cuba was his first to the tropics. It was, he recalls, a childhood dream fulfilled. He had grown up in various towns across Alabama, tracking insects, snakes, and frogs through lush, local marshes. But from his boyhood and beyond, Wilson longed to witness the diversity of tropical life. There, myriad creatures and plants promised a banquet of new species, complexity, and enchantment. His yearning was fed by exhilarating accounts he'd read by equatorial biologist-writers, like explorer and naturalist William Beebe. "The tropics I nurtured in my heart were the untamed centers of Creation," Wilson writes in his memoir *Naturalist*. The journey to Cuba—the first of Wilson's many to the globe's teeming and sultry midlatitudes—turned up remarkable ant species for his graduate work and many other strange creatures besides. Methuselah was among them.[1]

Methuselah was a lizard brought to Wilson's attention while he tramped in the isolated mountains. It was captured by the plant scientists with whom he was traveling. The animal was almost a foot long—far larger than most of the local anole lizards around—with rough-looking, folded gray skin and sly, rotating eyes. A crescent-shaped ridge rose from the back of its head. The young biologist had never seen anything like it. It resembled, he thought, the chameleons of Africa. He later learned that the species, found only in Cuba, is actually an oversized member of the anole lizard group—it's now commonly known as the short-bearded anole—but it shares, astonishingly, many characteristics and habits of its far-distant chameleon relatives. "I named the lizard Methuselah for its craggy features and gray wrinkled skin," Wilson recounts, "and kept it as a pet for the rest of my summer's travels."[2]

Methuselah, the Biblical character, is best known as the oldest person in the scripture (969 when he died, says the book) and, ultimately, as the grandfather of Noah, another celebrated rescuer of life's diversity. Methuselah, the pet, accompanied Wilson from Cuba to Mexico's Yucatan Peninsula. Wilson continued on to Mexico City and to the pine woods of the surrounding plateau. He traveled beyond and down to the lush, rich rainforests near Veracruz and up the slopes of Pica de Orizaba, a volcanic mountain close to the city of Orizaba. Methuselah remained Wilson's companion throughout his season-long tropical expedition. The lizard was a coadventurer in the scientist's first exhilarating experience with exotic tropical diversity. In the end, the pair—Wilson in rapturous awe and the lizard likely just dazed—flew home together to Harvard. Methuselah stayed with the biologist into the school year in eastern Massachusetts. From the windows, as the ivy climbed their stately quarters, they watched autumn arrive. The leaves of maples turned crimson and then gold, and the cool of the temperate mornings grew sharper.

Long before, Wilson had collected snakes, lizards, and insects through-out his boyhood. He filled cages and bottles. He begins his book-length account of his chronic fever for biology with a seaside remembrance from age seven. He recalls spotting jellyfish and rays at Florida's Para-dise Beach and catching a toadfish and keeping it in a jar. The context of these experiences was the disintegration of his family. He, an only child, had been sent to the coast to stay with people whose names he can't recall while his mother and father navigated their divorce. Wilson turned to natural history, he admits later, for solace. "A nomadic exis-tence made Nature my companion of choice," he explains, "because the outdoors was the one part of my world I perceived to hold rock steady. Animals and plants I could count on; human relationships were more difficult."[3]

The approach was apparently effective. While other hardships and tragedies continued to hammer him into early adulthood—blindness in one eye from a spiny fish, a partial loss of hearing as a teen, persistent poverty, relocations from town to town and school to school, frequent loneliness and brutal bullying, and his father's alcoholism and eventual suicide by gunshot at the side of the road—Wilson writes with endur-ing, almost unfathomable buoyancy. Heartbreak is one thing, but joy found in the fantastic insects, snakes, and amphibians along Florida's shore or at an Alabama pond edge is something else. You don't have to be familiar with natural life to find salvation in its company: "Hands-on experience at the critical time, not systematic knowledge, is what counts in the making of a naturalist," he declaims.

Although Wilson had previously kept wild animals at his home growing up, Methuselah is the first in his memoir to be described as "a pet." By this time, he is a young man. He declares his fondness for the lizard. It's a wholly human sentiment. The biologist in him is there too; as he spends time with Methuselah, his curiosity is piqued by the animal's chameleonlike behavior closely, and he publishes a scientific paper about it in an academic journal. (He also reflects with certain self-recrimination that, considering Cuba's short-bearded anoles may be threatened with extinction, taking one from the wild probably wasn't the wisest thing he could have done.)

Yet, Wilson's relationship with Methuselah as a pet seems to me important. Keeping animals found in nature is something I did as a kid. I kept company with turtles, salamanders, and an American toad named Rudyard for years. I greeted them when I returned from classes. I fed them with mealworms and other larvae and watched, mesmerized, as they stalked the crawling food in terraria on my bookshelf. I wanted to be familiar with them in a way I couldn't be—or so I imagined—in the field. In this sense, they were pets; I was in it to increase my chances of a connection and of some more-intimate understanding. My father, who became a fisheries ecologist, kept snakes and other creatures in the same way when he was young. Other budding biologists going back centuries have done so as well. For some, it takes only catching the animal, holding it in hand, and releasing it again. The goal is a moment of closeness—however terrifying—and a glimpse of a latticework span bridging our species, one that might not otherwise come into view. A sense of a nature lover's rite of passage is in it—even as the motivation may seem paradoxical and difficult to make out.

"I have cast back, trying to retrieve my emotions to understand why I explored swamps and hunted snakes with such dedication and reck- lessness," Wilson writes after recounting his near-death effort to cap- ture—unsuccessfully—a deadly, five-foot cottonmouth moccasin when he was 15. "The activities gave me little or no heightened status among my peers; I never told anyone most of what I did. Pearl [Wilson's step- mother] and my father were tolerant but not especially interested or encouraging; in any case I didn't say much to them either, for fear they would make me stay closer to home.

"My reasons were mixed. They were partly exhilaration at my entry into a beautiful and complex new world. And partly possessiveness; I had a place that no one else knew. And vanity; I believed that no one, anywhere, was better at exploring woods and finding snakes. And ambition; I dreamed I was training myself someday to be a professional field biologist. And finally, an undeciphered residue, a yearning remaining deep within me that I have never understood, nor wish to, for fear that if named it might vanish."[4]

Conservationists want to get their hands on animals. They want, for some reason, to be close. They want to have pets. Not all of them, but many. The urge is there. Wilson kept Methuselah as his pet reptile, and years later—as he was gathering his ideas about biophilia into his 1984 book—he had a lively cocker spaniel to entertain him. (The dog interrupts him around page 127, launching into a territorial barking fit as a jogger runs past.) Undoubtedly, in his more than 90 years, the groundbreaking biologist had other pets as well. Many conservationists have them and love them. The flip side is perhaps less often true: not many pet owners think consciously of conservation. For many—as the research described in this book makes clear—the planet's shrinking diversity often doesn't warrant as much consideration as do animal companions. Yet, few among these same pet owners aren't moved by the sights and sounds of wildlife when they have a chance to encounter it. Appreciating other sentient life—as something, perhaps, essential to human meaning and spirit—is common to both pet people and the devoted defenders of nature. The groups are not two; they belong to the same tribe.

To some extent, science bears this out. Several years ago, Norwegian psychologist Tore Bjerke and his colleagues found what they considered a link between owning pets and a more general interest in wildlife. They surveyed more than 680 residents of Trondheim, Norway, and found pet owners reported "liking" more of 24 common species of local wild animals—creatures such as hedgehogs, squirrels, small birds, badgers, bats, and bumblebees—than did their petless neighbors. (Mosquitos, rats, snails, and insects were among the exceptions; noisome creatures found few fans in either group.) The other thing about Trondheim's pet people, the researchers discovered, is that they're more likely to engage with nature—whether feeding wildlife, watching birds, or settling into a nature program on television. "These results indicate that pet ownership is associated with people's attitudes toward wildlife *in general*, and not only their attitudes toward *specific* pet species," the authors write.[5]

Other scientists were impressed. They tested the idea elsewhere. Survey results from almost 400 Canadian university students in Windsor, Ontario, for example, showed pet owners score higher than nonowners on a scale of positive attitudes toward all living creatures. Another study found pet owners in the United Kingdom—along with people who otherwise feel good about pets—are more likely to oppose plans that put human needs before the needs of wildlife and to stand behind efforts to stop species extinctions. Interestingly, they were also more inclined to resist conservation strategies that compromised a single species for the sake of biodiversity overall. That is, pet owners appear to think of individual animals, in and of themselves, to be intrinsically and morally valuable; abstract, big-picture notions such as biodiversity—no matter how worthy—have trouble competing.[6]

The difference is subtle enough to be hardly a difference at all. In the same English pet owner study, researcher Cameron Shuttlewood and colleagues suggest the natural, animal-focused inclinations of pet owners comprise, in many respects, the same stuff conservationists are made of: pet people, like those concerned about nature, like to think of protecting animals as much as or more than larger economic interests. People already cuddling with a pet at home are primed, it seems, to consider the welfare of other animals elsewhere. It makes sense. Just as conservationists like Wilson can be pet people, the animal sympathies of pet owners are fertile ground for cultivating conservation. Targeted efforts to help pet lovers understand the troubles facing wildlife—and not simply those directly relevant to pets or the pet industry—could help recruit from among their millions new legions of advocates in the ongoing fight for life's diversity. "One practical application," writes Shuttlewood and his coauthors, "would be for conservation planners to liaise with pet-based groups early in the planning stages of wildlife management to attempt to foster support within the broader community."[7]

There's more to it, of course. For a lot of pet lovers, the happy, wild-things-are-great-too feeling has limits: they're unimpressed, for example, when conservation concerns don't jive well with the lifestyles of their cherished animal companions. In Australia, most dogs—80 to 90 percent—walk the nation's beaches off leash, despite their known habit of running freely over the nests, eggs, and young of breeding shorebirds. (South Australia's hooded plover is among them and considered vulnerable to extinction across its range there.) Kathryn Williams, a professor in environmental psychology at the University of Melbourne, and her colleagues asked almost 400 beach dog walkers about the practice. About a third strongly agreed that dogs on the beach should always be leashed—a figure curiously at odds with the actual number of tethered dogs—while another third thought dogs should run free. (Others had no position on the issue, which likely means . . .) Interestingly, while more than half of pet walkers agreed that dogs, in general, harm beach birds, most considered their own dog to be a blameless, wildlife-friendly exception.[8]

Accounts by cat owners often appear even more dissonant. Researchers in England tallied the wild prey brought home by cats in two English villages and compared the numbers against their owners' views of the pets' impact on native animals. The results were puzzling. Altogether, the 86 cats tracked during the four-month study returned 325 small mammals, birds, and reptiles. Cat owners correctly predicted that their pet was likely to bring home some wild prey during the period. Most, however, had no prior idea of the sheer size of the final tally. What's more, owners who discovered during the study that their cats were actually prodigious wildlife killers were no more likely to think of cats as a wildlife problem than owners of cats that returned few prey. In fact, two-thirds of all cat people didn't consider cats harmful to the wild whether their cats were fearsome hunters or not. The pets, they suggested, are only doing what comes naturally. Almost all (98 percent) said keeping cats inside wouldn't solve anything. "These results . . . emphasize the strong differences in objectives between conservationists and cat owners," the authors conclude, highlighting what's become an entrenched and perhaps unhelpful cliché. The findings "further suggest that some cat owners may have distorted views regarding their cats' place in the environment."[9]

Cat owners, simply put, may love their pets more than wildlife—or perhaps *as* wildlife. And love, as they say, isn't known for seeing things very clearly. It's a problem, but animal affection is animal affection—biophilia, perhaps—even if it's a fondness that falls first on creatures near to hand. There, of course, is the nub of the matter: seeing only the harm from pet keeping and ignoring the essential goodwill toward animals behind it risks alienating those whose feelings reflect the core of conservation. In their study, Shuttlewood and colleagues note that British pet owners—fiercely opposed to limits on their own pet's liberty to roam outside—were similarly adamant that wild creatures should wander free as well, unrestricted and unbothered in nature. Their attitudes toward pets and toward wildlife were parallel. These same pet-positive people also supported finding new ways to keep track of wild animals and ecosystem health. Their hearts, in other words, appear to be in the right spot.

Competing interests in some respects don't necessarily diminish what pet owners and conservationists have in common—a mutual hope for life on earth shared with other beings.[10]

"Pet owners are thinking more about the environment," says Chris Bentley by phone from his home in Boulder, Colorado. "That's why a lot of pet businesses want to be seen by pet owners as thinking more about the environment too."

Bentley is a thoughtful, soft-spoken man with a remarkable, decades-long career as a pet-business entrepreneur. In the late 1970s, recruited by a wealthy client from his job as a guesthouse ranch hand, he helped launch Aspen Pet Products—now a top supplier of pet toys, leashes, collars, and other pet paraphernalia around the world. Later, he was instrumental in starting the popular natural pet food company known as "I and Love and You." But he was—and is, he says—an impassioned environmentalist first. That's key. It's what brought him to Colorado in the first place; in the 1970s and early 1980s, the state was something of an environmental hotbed. "John Denver was up there and [sustainable energy pioneers] Amory Lovins and Hunter Lovins," says Bentley. "I really wanted to be part of the environmental movement, and I have been ever since.

"I went to Paris for the climate talks. I've been at marches all over the country. I've taken busloads of students. I guest lecture at the University of Colorado on sustainability and entrepreneurship and green jobs. So, I wouldn't say I'm an expert, but I've been at the forefront for a long time."

In 2010, Bentley decided his concern for the troubled planet needed more of his time. He stepped back from the business development front lines for a bit and decided to marry his passions: he began asking other pet-business leaders to come together to find ways for improving the industry's environmental and social impact. He formed the Pet

Sustainability Coalition a couple of years later. After approaching 30 to 40 companies to join, Bentley found initial support from 8. Among them was Petco, the second-largest pet retailer in North America. Hunter Lovins, a well-known environmentalist and author who is also the president of the nonprofit organization Natural Capitalism Solutions, helped the group get off the ground.

The Pet Sustainability Coalition encourages member companies—now numbering more than 85 in North America and, more recently, several in Europe—to sign on by first answering a questionnaire about their current sustainability and work practices. The test—designed in partnership with B Lab, the nonprofit group that recognizes socially and environmentally responsible certified B Corporations, or B Corps—is a benchmark against which pet companies measure their progress. Pet Sustainability Coalition staff offer direction, tools, and seminars to help them improve. "The biggest thing is that people need a road map," Bentley explains. "They know they need to do stuff, but they aren't sure how."

The Pet Sustainability Coalition offers acknowledgment when companies make positive changes, but it stops short of administering a strict environmental certification program. It doesn't, for instance, provide ecolabels for pet products to alert buyers of the environmental and social attitudes of member companies. (Members are, however, given a coalition "communications kit" and encouraged to post the group's logo on their Web site.) The coalition—less than a decade old and still developing—simply doesn't have the resources to keep up with a more rigorous assessment program, says Bentley. The task of always updating standards and independently tracking member performance would be overwhelming. It would also be difficult to police. "You would need to know who's greenwashing and who's not," he says, describing the corporate use of superficial and cosmetic environmental practices to hide a business's more harmful impacts.

For Bentley and Pet Sustainability Coalition, sustainability really means urging businesses to do what they can in the fight against climate change. Global warming is the thing. Bentley's goal is to convince pet industry players to use less energy, reduce some of their waste, and shrink the sector's greenhouse gases as much as they can. In many cases, the suggestions the group offers can actually help companies to become more efficient and improve profits, he says. There's often not much of a downside. Many businesses are glad to hear it—though, suggests Bentley, pet products companies are generally more responsive to the new way of thinking than those in pet foods.

The only problem is that wildlife conservation isn't really part of the Pet Sustainability Coalition game plan. At least, not right now. While the group sometimes touches on environmental issues beyond climate and energy in seminars or materials—such as discussions of pet food protein sources or the wild harvest of aquarium fish—its number one target is the warming world. The group's "sustainability" assessment test, for example, focuses on waste and carbon emissions. The reason is simple, says Bentley: climate change "is a global crisis. It's going to kill us all if we don't wake up right now. So, yeah, establishing a sustainability coalition is just one way me and a bunch of other like-minded people in Boulder here and other places are trying to do our part. . . . I could give you a detailed description about what we're doing for biodiversity, but I'd be kind of jerking your chain, if you know what I mean." Bentley considers for a moment. "Let's just say that there were more pressing issues. What we face and what I'm doing is dealing with global warming."

Climate change is a crisis. But when considering the environmental impact of the pet industry, it simply may not be as pressing as the global loss of biodiversity. In truth, the pet business's more lasting damage to the natural world so far has come not from its greenhouse gases but from its devastating impacts on the variety and richness of life. Pets have already contributed to more than 160 known and presumed wildlife extinctions and to hundreds of other wild animal declines and dwindling ranges around the world. (By comparison, climate change—while expected to profoundly affect biodiversity in the future—has yet to be tied directly to the global extinction of many species so far.) Pet invaders are especially prodigious killers. Pet industry demand, meanwhile, takes other rare and endangered creatures directly from the wild until they risk vanishing altogether. The global reach of the trade in animals plays its sinister part by delivering new wildlife diseases to creatures unprepared to resist them. And the pet food industry's hunt for protein is hammering forage fish and fueling the ongoing sacrifice of species and rainforest for the sake of pastureland to grow meat.[11]

The Pet Sustainability Coalition's approach may aim at the lesser of two important green targets, but there's promising lessons in it. The group has tapped into a willingness by a small-but-growing number of pet companies to add at least some environmental considerations to their business models. It's a start, even if increasing efficiency and reducing a company's carbon footprint are probably an easier sell than the kinds of systemic changes needed to protect wildlife. Bentley says his group intentionally targets "low-hanging fruit" first. Conservation issues simply aren't as well known in the industry. "I think biodiversity would be low on the average person's plate now," he says.

Over the past few decades, nonprofit environmental certification or assessment schemes—some with strict rules and others, like the Pet Sustainability Coalition, with more gently instructive benchmarks—have helped transform the world of environmental regulation. Once the near-exclusive sphere of governments, the creation of standards that push corporations to care about where products come from and how they're made is now frequently the job of consumers (along with concerned citizens) and industries together. As more buyers demand environmentally friendly products, more companies are listening or even teaming up with them to find a competitive edge in the new field of sustainability. These days, environmental standards and product labels apply to coffee, tea, cocoa, flowers, spices, soy, fish, timber, sugar, beef, and scores of other products. Many of the systems are well known—such as the Forest Stewardship Council's global forest management certification or the UTZ certification for sustainably farmed coffee—while others are not so much. Many are seen as absolutely central to environmental protection and social equity, preserving forests, bolstering the climate, and improving lives for millions of farmers and producers. When the standards work, they work well; the marketplace changes: environmental impact, for example, joins other considerations—such as price and quality—to drive buyer behavior and influence company practices. But it's not usually quite so simple.[12]

Lorne Johnson knows the challenges as well as anyone. Johnson is a Canadian conservationist who has spent a large part of his career leading or working with organizations to help create voluntary sustainability standards for industry. He led the Canadian chapter of the Forest Stewardship Council Canada for a time and, later, the Cornerstone Standards Council, a group administering environmental guidelines for the digging work of cement and gravel companies. For a brief-but-frenetic period, he helped lead the Canadian Boreal Forest Agreement, a massive cooperative accord between major forest companies and top environmental groups. These days, he's an adviser for two large environmental philanthropic foundations in Canada, helping to support programs in biodiversity conservation and sustainable energy. He's also a longtime friend of mine.

"It's funny," Johnson tells me, speaking by phone. "At first, I thought 'what the hell is he talking about, certification in the pet industry.' And then the more I thought about it, I thought it's the perfect sector. It's ripe for it."

Ripe, that is, for change. Consumer and citizen frustration is key. Most industries won't simply acknowledge responsibility for environmental harm on their own accord. Most prefer to avoid the responsibility and costs of doing something about it. Most, explains Johnson, have to be urged. They're coaxed by frustrated consumers and concerned citizens who first become aware of serious environmental or ethical problems with the marketplace. These people—appalled to find that governments are doing little about it—use their protest and buying power to take matters into their own hands. "They're not getting solutions," he says.

It's this groundswell of vexed awareness that's the spark. In Lucas Simons's *Changing the Food Game*—a book-length portrait of how shifts to sustainability can transform markets—persistent attention to problems builds the pressure for change. The attention comes when people who care convince other people to care. Simons uses sustainability efforts in the cocoa industry and similar examples underway in palm oil, timber, and sugarcane production to make his case: "change agents" and campaigners have to keep the pressure on, he suggests, until companies respond to protect their brand and reputation. These companies might move slowly at first, with token, showpiece efforts, but eventually meaningful transformation happens. "Pretty much any certification system around the world that I've ever seen has always been born out of frustration and opportunism," says Johnson.[13]

Industry has to notice, of course. It has to feel it. To make pet companies responsive to conservation consequences, pet people who care about animals—the sector's consumers—have to vote with their wallets. They have to reward companies who act responsibly and pressure laggards to come aboard. These pet-owner conservationists are cat and dog people, too, and everyone else with a stake in the game. Pet owners may differ on some conservation issues—on the question of outdoor pets, for example—but it's a no-brainer for animal lovers to insist that the pet industry take more responsibility for its impacts on wildlife. Our mutual affection for all creatures should demand an industry certification system that tracks every pet company's commitment to biodiversity conservation (a standard already in place in the certificate program of the Association of Zoos and Aquariums, for example) from the start of the supply chain—the forest or the sea, say—to the store. Coming together is crucial.

"So much of it is about personal relationships and people starting to think about themselves differently and the kind of transformation that comes through that," Johnson explains. "And when you're in different silos and different tents, when you've discussed the exclusive 'we're awesome tent' and then the 'everybody else sucks' tent, things don't change, right?"

Cat-versus-bird battles don't help. Conservation messages that challenge the legitimacy of biophilia belonging to pet ownership aren't useful either. Our mutual goals are more important. A greater awareness of nature's plight and a remedial transformation of the pet marketplace are both aims on which all animal lovers can agree. Knowing the issues and sharing information are essential: almost 300 years after Swedish physician and biologist Carl Linnaeus invented his naming system for life on earth, just 1.7 million animals, plants, fungi, and microscopic protists have been given scientific names. The actual number of species on the planet is at least four to five times that number—including an estimated 8.1 million mostly not-yet-known animals and plants alone. Only an infinitesimal fraction of these are familiar to us as pets. From among the named species, meanwhile, only 105,000 have been studied enough to assess how well they're coping in this crowded, changing world, and from among these about 27 percent are known to be in danger of extinction. In 2019, the Intergovernmental Science-Policy Platform on Biodiversity and Ecosystem Services used these estimates to conclude that the known and unknown species currently at risk of vanishing—most without our awareness that they exist at all—likely exceeds one million. The sheer scale of the destruction is sobering—but the scope of our ignorance is perhaps more alarming still.[14]

Knowing is crucial. Pet owners and conservationists strengthen their collective influence by being informed. Some targets for our attention are clear. For instance, with combined consumer power to bring the pet industry onside, pet owners and others could push governments for wildlife protections beyond the current, often-inadequate international pet trade regulations in place now, such as the Convention on International Trade in Endangered Species of Wild Fauna and Flora. In particular, efforts are needed to close a regulatory gap that exists for animals illegally exported from their country of origin into US or European markets. Researchers say these stateless animals find few rules apply to protect them. Similarly, lax scrutiny and policing in some countries are contributing to the "laundering" of wild-caught creatures as animals bred in captivity. For many exotic animals, the cost and difficulty of captive breeding are prohibitive compared with simply trapping creatures from the wild. Studies of some exotic pet species—such as green pythons from Indonesia—that have compared the capacity of legitimate breeding facilities with the numbers of animals available on the market suggest the volumes of so-called captive-bred pets sold around the world are implausible.[15]

Another focus could be the role of pets and the pet trade as a leading cause of invasions by alien species. Here, deliberate releases and accidental escapes by pet owners share the blame, but a lack of awareness may be the real culprit. In many instances, pet owners believe they're doing what's best for an animal they're no longer willing or able to care for; exotic wild creatures appear to belong in the wild, any wild. Pet lovers may not understand the harm or, in some cases, may have been misinformed by organizations that continue to suggest feral pets are part of the natural landscape. Awareness campaigns, particularly through participating pet and pet food companies, could offset these troubling campaigns and urge prevention. Exotic pet sellers could require buyers to have completed minor training that equips them with care and handling skills as well as conservation education. Pet food sellers could include labels on packaging to remind people of the conservation dangers of escaped, released, and unsupervised pets. The industry could also encourage better sanitary measures—quarantine protocols or entry controls—to stop strange, pet-borne diseases arriving from distant lands and devastating local wildlife.[16]

Raising awareness of pet owners and others can have other benefits as well: as more pet owners learn about the scale and seriousness of pet-related conservation issues, chances improve that more animal-loving pet people will do what they can to help. They might grow more insistent, for example, about knowing where a pet animal comes from. They might hesitate before releasing a live pet into a habitat where it doesn't belong, or they might think twice about dumping aquarium water outdoors and possibly contaminating local environments with disease. They might even become more vigilant concerning the impacts of free-roaming cats, dogs, and other pets on wildlife across the countryside.

Conservationists, however, need to consider that challenging pet owners about particular practices may not be as important as encouraging concern for animals beyond those at home. Many people already keep their pets indoors or under strict control—that is, leashed—or carefully watched when outdoors. Encouraging better awareness of pet impacts on other animals may convince more pet owners of this wisdom. At the same time, encouraging pet owners to merely be more mindful of wildlife consequences from off-leash animals can be important too. Inspiring them to do what they can in their own way to reduce the harm is an important step. That pets can hurt wildlife even when they're not hunting for them isn't widely known, for instance. A pet that's seen as a predator can paralyze wild animals with fear and disrupt efforts to breed and raise young. Backyard cats, for example, cause birds to call in alarm, which, in turn, attracts other nest predators, such as crows. Research models in the United Kingdom suggest that even small increases in bird "fear" from the presence of more cats can see bird populations plummet. Barking dogs are known to affect nesting behavior in coots, a marsh bird, and the whereabouts of a threatened species of deer. Sometimes pet poop is enough: cat feces and urine has even been linked to less feeding by both mountain beavers and house finches as well as signs of anxiety in rodents. Armed with information, pet owners can do a lot to curb these unexpected impacts.[17]

Awareness has other benefits. Exotic pet collectors, for instance, might resist their attraction to increasingly difficult-to-acquire species. In the bird and exotic pet trade, some animals become more widely sought after and traded when they're known to be uncommon or threatened with extinction. Rarity is the appeal. Some are so little known that reliable information or estimates of their natural populations don't exist. Some have appeared in the pet market—varieties of monitor lizards, for example—before they've even been described by science. Better information could encourage other small changes in pet ownership habits too, such as making any outdoor time an after-dinner ritual; research suggests dogs and cats kill less if they're well fed before being allowed outside. (Some cats, however, are known to continue to hunt even with a full belly.) Studies also suggest keeping pets indoors at night—at least—can cut the number of mice, voles, and other small mammals they catch (but appears to increase the number of reptiles and amphibians they kill). Animal grooming that includes clipping claws can help handicap a pet's hunting ability and cut its take of wild prey. Ensuring pets are vaccinated and picking up after them when they defecate can also reduce the chances of unleashing disease.[18]

Pet owners with better information might consider using bells, bibs, or sonar devices on the collars of pets that are allowed to roam freely. Researchers tracking cats with and without bells in New Zealand found the simple jingling device reduced the number of successful bird kills by half and the number of killed rodents by almost two-thirds. Similar reductions of wildlife deaths have also been reported in Britain. (The bells may be less effective at saving reptiles, amphibians, and insects.) Another device, a brightly colored cloth cover for cat collars that makes the pets visually conspicuous, has also been shown to cut the number of cat-killed Australian wildlife by about half among animals with good color vision, such as birds and reptiles. (Mice and rodents with lousy color vision didn't fare as well). A newer product known as a CatBib may be even more effective. The cloth bib hangs loosely over a cat's chest and is designed to interfere with the animal's ability to pounce on prey (but not its climbing, jumping, or running skills). Researchers found pet owners who used the device cut the bird hunting success of their cats by more than 80 percent.[19]

What's clear is that life's diversity needs pet owners on its side—whatever that takes. Our wildlife has a far better chance if it has the blessing of those who already believe that other beings on earth are essential to our experience here. These biophilia-inspired conservationists number in the billions, and, importantly, they wield clout over a massive industry with the power to change wildlife fortunes around the world.

More than 35 years ago, when E. O. Wilson was writing *Biophilia* and crystalizing his notion that other beings are essential to human fulfillment, the biologist probably had only a dim idea about the wildlife damage done by pets and the pet industry. Tallies of pet-related extinctions and wild animal declines hadn't yet come in. Back then, the scale of the problem simply wasn't as huge; US dog and cat numbers, for instance, were about half of what they are now. Some biologists were aware of the issue, of course. Its size and seriousness, however, would take years to find wider notice among scientists and the general public. As Wilson mapped out his biophilia argument, he believed conservation's true enemies lurked elsewhere. Habitat loss was his prime culprit. (His book blames Cuba's government, for instance, for clearing much of the irreplaceable wilderness he had visited on his affecting first tropical journey in 1953: "Now it has come down to this," he writes, "in a negligible interval of evolutionary time, within the lifespan of Fidel Castro and one unheroic entomologist of approximately the same age visiting a nonstrategic part of the island, much of the woodland and hence a large part of Cuba's history have vanished.")

Pets were on the side of the good guys. Animal companions are described by Wilson, fondly, as an important reflection of our human kinship with other creatures—a particularly emotion-laden incarnation of our deeper biophilia. "Dogs are especially popular because they live by human-like rituals of greeting and subservience," he writes. "The family to whom they belong is part of their pack. They treat us like giant dogs, automatically alpha in rank, and clamor to be near us. We in turn respond to their joyous greetings, tail wagging, slavering grins, dropped ears, groveling, bristling fur, and noisy indignation at territorial trespass."[20]

Wilson's reaction to pets—mirroring earlier feelings for his own creature companion, Methuselah—is similar to his wonder for animal life more generally. He describes meeting a "pet" bonobo that was being raised by researchers at the Language Research Center of Georgia State University. Bonobos, small cousins to the chimpanzee, are listed as endangered in their limited wild range within the Democratic Republic of Congo. This particular primate—named Kanzi, and now somewhat famous for his remarkable language skills—approached Wilson as it entered the room and, after some preliminary reticence, climbed into his lap. When the biologist offered Kanzi grape juice, the bonobo contently drank it down and embraced him. "The episode was unnerving. . . . I realized that I had responded to him almost exactly as I would to a two-year-old child—same initial anxieties, same urge to communicate and please, same gestures and food sharing ritual."[21]

Recognizing that an advanced primate raised in close proximity to people may offer an exaggerated illustration of pet-keeping's promise of a human–animal bond, Wilson nevertheless describes companion animals, generally, in similarly positive and affecting terms. Pets and the humanlike intimacy of our reaction to them reveal a biological connectedness that, for Wilson, only strengthens his case for biophilia. It's a case that, in turn, makes the conservation of other, more distant wild animals seem obvious as well. "We are literally kin to other organisms," he explains. "The phylogenetic continuity of life with humanity seems an adequate reason by itself to tolerate the continued existence of apes and other organisms."[22]

It's a logic train that most pet owners, as animal lovers, are happy to climb aboard. Most conservationists would happily join them: creatures—whether in our homes or in our forests—are not simply fellow beings on this hurtling, spinning planet, they're kindred descendants of our same ancient family. We're blood, in a manner of speaking. Pet people have long been those most likely to intuit this relationship. Experience with pets prepares the ground for the seeds of conservation. The wildlife threats created by pet keeping are undeniable, but the importance of a human–pet connection for generating the will to right these wrongs is critical too. A love of animals as our relatives—if not our housemates—could be their salvation. "Thus," Wilson writes of pets, "we favor certain animals because they fill the superficial role of surrogate kin. It is the most disarming reason for nurturing other forms of life. Only a churl could find fault."[23]

Afterword

An extinction crisis is underway, and it's robbing the only living planet of the greatest biological diversity our solar system has ever known. Our love of pets—a modern incarnation of biophilia's ancient urge—is its ironic accomplice: as wildlife numbers drop and a million wild species risk vanishing forever, our pet animals accelerate the losses while more than doubling their own numbers in the last half century. More than 400 million of them—more pets than people—are now at home in the United States and Canada, and perhaps as many as 1.7 *billion* dogs and cats live around the globe. We let them roam free. They prey on nature—killing perhaps tens of billions of wild animals every year. We take pets from the wild directly, depleting natural populations. We carelessly set them free again in landscapes where they don't belong. We move their diseases around the world, spreading deadly contagions to every wild corner. We clear habitat to raise cattle or pull tons of fish from the sea for kibble and pet chow. And, while we spend more on the pet industry than most nations earn in a year, we're not paying nearly enough to stem the tide of disappearing wild species.[1]

The cost to life's richness has been high—and it's an accounting that seems to have escaped much attention: cats and dogs (now the most abundant carnivores alive) are the chief culprits in the extinction of at least 74 species of wild birds, mice, lizards, and other animals that will never be seen on earth again. Another 600 wildlife species are being threatened by these pets (along with other invading predators) and risk the same bleak fate. Trappers supplying the pet trade have obliterated races from at least three bird species from the wild while another sought-after 13 species teeter very close to the brink. Pet-industry-targeted snakes, lizards, and turtles are five times more likely to be threatened with extinction than reptiles that are not targeted, and one in every four parrot species on earth may soon live only as pets with no counterparts left in the wild. The aquarium trade is hammering exotic fish populations too, but nobody knows by how much. Pet-borne diseases are behind the presumed extinction of 90 frog species and have ravaged other animals, including lions, wild dogs, and sea mammals. And pet-food-eating US pets swallow one-third as much meat (i.e., animal-derived calories) as their human counterparts, supporting a livestock industry that's leveling habitat and has fueled a sixth of all extinctions in modern times. Meanwhile, scientists conservatively estimate that almost 500 species of birds, mammals, fish, reptiles, and amphibians may have blinked out of existence in the wild over the past century and a bit.[2]

Blame biophilia. Blame an otherwise inexplicable human yearning to link with life beyond our own. Blame whatever it was those tens of millennia ago that inclined us to bring home a wolf and fashion a dog. Inexorably—perhaps even genetically—we've been driven to connect with the earth's other inhabitants. But instead of reaching out, we've brought some of them in. We've insisted on animal partnerships within our orbit rather than meeting them in theirs. It's had consequences: pet animals behave as we do. Uncontained and unrestrained, they share our recklessness; naturally unconscious to what they're doing, they've become us—or at least our henchmen—in the thoughtless, continuing harm of nature.

In biologist Edward O. Wilson's hopeful view, our biophilia is supposed to rally us to save these fellow creatures and the other life to which we're so inherently attached. Yet, pets appear to be taking over as all the "other life" we need. Our biophilia doesn't discriminate. Pets as much as wildlife attract our evolutionary inclination to want them around. The difference is they have an edge: they're closer to us than their wild cousins—closer in proximity and (often) temperament, in their (usually exaggerated) promise of solace and health, and in their (real or imagined) emotional connection. Through no effort of their own, pets are subverting our inborn fondness for all living things and turning it to their particular advantage.

And we pet owners blithely oblige: pets satisfy our biophilia's insistent urge, and we never need leave home. We win, and our pets win. Wildlife, on the other hand, isn't so lucky. As numbers of companion animals soar, wild animals aren't merely being sidelined; they're being clobbered—by pets. Our household creatures and the industry that supports them are driving many less-companionable wild animals off oblivion's cliff edge. Our fondness for pets and our attraction to wildlife increasingly resembles a zero-sum game: more creatures in our living rooms seems to mean fewer animals and species in the wild. These losses of biological diversity, in turn, are diminishing the power of natural ecosystems; they're sapping strength from the same living world that all animals—including humans—need to survive. The paradox is clear: the people most inclined to share our planet with other beings are the same among us who keep the pets that risk our common future.

They are the same among us, too, who can turn the situation around. In small but increasing numbers, pets are being recruited as conservation allies instead of wildlife enemies. They help with conservation research and protect wild creatures on almost every continent. People who keep pets, meanwhile, are revealed as the most likely conservationists. They have the most interest in nature and tend to put wildlife needs ahead of our human-centric scheming. Most important in the battle to stop extinctions, pet people—rather than the petless—are more likely to champion the fight.[3]

Pet owners number in the billions. People in two-thirds of American households are among them. If a better awareness of pet-keeping's wildlife harm marshals support from even a fraction of these animal lovers, a legion of new conservationists would transform our wild world. With the buying power equivalent of a midsize country, these pet-owner conservationists can affect badly needed change in a multibillion-dollar pet industry and generate support for conservation causes. A push for environmental certification that puts wildlife needs first could coax pet companies to fund species-at-risk and wilderness protection programs, encourage better pet-ownership practices, and ensure their pets and pet products come from sustainable sources. Awareness might shift the habits and attitudes of more pet people too, encouraging vigilance about the ways their love of animals can hurt nature. The trick is bringing us all together—the pet owners, the conservationists, and the others in biophilia's thrall—for a common, life-affirming cause. So far, evidence shows that conservation works. Combined efforts by people and organizations have slowed losses to biodiversity by as much as one-fifth. But it's not enough: our planet's magnificent-but-shrinking wildlife array needs all the help it can get.

Maggie, my dog, is back. She has arrived from another room as a welcome relief from writing's isolation. Her delicacy is uncanny: she slips into the room and lies down unnoticed, then she looks up regularly until I acknowledge her. She can wait a long time; she has all the patience in the world for me. She's pleased when I give her a nod. She wags her tail.

During the writing of this book, Maggie became ill. Something she had eaten or some other unknown cause sent her into a spiral of listlessness with no appetite and blood from her bowels. Excellent veterinary care quickly set her right, but I had some time to reflect on the little dog's importance. The vet's sizeable bill soon monetized my thinking; the amount was far more than I've ever donated to a conservation cause in a year. It's a meaningless comparison, I realize; the cost for my pet's care wasn't ever a question. Maggie is part of my days; I'd have one less tether to my world without her.

Our connection with other animals moors us, too, even when we're unfamiliar with them. In an essay for the *Economist* magazine a few years ago, Edward O. Wilson reflects on the dimming luster of life's gleaming variety. He wonders how to handle the problem when most species remain unknown to us and large numbers simply vanish before science can ever discover them. In the riddle is the answer. Biophilia, as Wilson earlier explains, is not our connection to animals; it's our *desire* to connect. It's the urge to affiliate with life, not the affiliation itself. If a connection is there, we'll seek a deeper one still. It's the *striving* to comprehend—an imperative possibly built-in by its evolutionary staying power—that we're after; happiness is in the yearning curiosity, not in what we already know. Our wonder and enchantment with animals and other life arises from this constant coaxing—biophilia's limbic tug—and it takes the chill out of the sometimes-abject solitude that comes with being so singularly human.[4]

Our love of sharing life with pets might have something to do with this. We like to imagine the fathomless depths our bond might someday reveal. The wild world—still mostly unknown—offers an even more limitless source of this comforting mystery. Animal companions are good and perhaps even necessary company. An enigmatic multitude of species is vital, too, promising billions of wondrous, yet-uncontemplated nonhuman ways to exist. To sacrifice one for the other—pets for wildlife or vice versa—is to consign ourselves to one or another kind of tedious isolation. Pet lovers and conservationists alike understand this clearly.

In his essay, Wilson laments a problem with the word "Anthropocene"—the increasingly common label for the current human-focused era in Earth's history. The term reflects the contemporary period in which our planet is essentially remade and remodeled for our one species alone. It reflects that our human impact is everywhere. For Wilson, however, the term Anthropocene sounds too much like a hopeful triumph, assigning nature and all animals to the background for good. There is nothing encouraging about a world with little room left for nature. The label Anthropocene is far too cheerful for such a barren state. "I prefer to call it the Eremocene," the biologist suggests instead. His explanation of the word has a somber finality: "the Age of Loneliness," he writes. The choices we make now are that stark. The predictable presence of our unnatural companions will not be enough. If we lose our connection to the grandeur and variety of other sentient life—if our biophilia finds less and less of the living mystery for which it yearns—our own solace-seeking species may find this newest epoch the most desolate and distressing yet.[5]

Acknowledgments

A seemingly common characteristic of thoughtful, tirelessly curious people is generosity; restless minds seem to like to share what they turn up. For this project, many enthusiastic, knowledgeable people lent me their time, expertise, and patience. They were welcoming when I visited or tagged along in the field, and they were cheerful when I kept pressing my questions until my understanding was clear. Their passion for the work—and for the animals—was infectious.

Among those who graciously spoke to me for this book, agreed to visits or interviews, or otherwise took me along for the ride are the following: Alejandro Martinez in Mexico City; biologists Luis Zambrano and Gerardo Ceballos at the National Autonomous University of Mexico; Ottawa media relations consultant Paddy Moore; Ann Lambert (with Chara), child-life specialist Michèle Taché, as well as Rachel and Xavier at the Children's Hospital of Eastern Ontario in Ottawa; Alan Beck, director of the Center for the Human–Animal Bond at Purdue University's College of Veterinary Medicine; University of Michigan professor Bradley Cardinale; Cornwall city council candidate Mary Jane Proulx; Maarten McDougald; Robert Prowse; Chris Rogers of the City of Cornwall; Pete Marra of the Migratory Bird Center at the Smithsonian Institution; Swamp Apes founder Tom Rahill (I'm thankful for his time taking me into the Everglades and, importantly, for the brilliant jury-rigging of his suddenly broken clutch to finally get us out again); *Swamp People* executive producer Brian Catalina, Troy Landry, and the *Swamp People* crew; Michael Kirkland of the South Florida Water Management District; University College London professor Tim Blackburn; Marc Bekoff, emeritus professor at the University of Colorado; biologist John Urquhart (who originally spoke to me for *ON Nature* magazine); Annemarieke Spitzen-van der Sluijs; Craig Stephen of the Canadian Wildlife Health Cooperative; Samuel Iverson with Environment and Climate Change Canada; Global Exotic Pets owner Rob Conrad; Université de Montréal professor Stéphane Roy (whose comments appeared in an earlier story I did for *Maclean's* magazine); David Pharo and Eva Lara of the South Florida office of the US Fish and Wildlife Service; biologist Bert Harris; Sheldon Jordan of Canada's Wildlife Enforcement Directorate; and Tim Harrison of Outreach for Animals.

Thanks to Scott Sobel of Media and Communications Strategies in Washington, DC, for arranging my tour of the Champion Petfoods facility in Morinville, Alberta, and to Jeff Johnston, senior vice president for Research, Innovation, and Product Development, and Leigh Newton, the company's business development manager, for helping with the visit. I'm also very grateful to the following for agreeing to be interviewed or for answering my questions: Champion Petfoods' president and CEO Frank Burdzy; Marion Nestle of New York University; Gregory Okin at the University of California, Los Angeles; University of Washington biologist Tim Essington; Clean Label Project executive director Jackie Bowen; pet clairvoyant Meghan Vickell; Toronto Christmas Pet Show organizer Grant Crossman; biologist Anthony Waldron; Gina Keller; Pete Coppolillo and Aimee Hurt of Working Dogs for Conservation;

Zach Crete with the Montana Department of Fish, Wildlife, and Parks; Pet Sustainability Coalition founder Chris Bentley; and Lorne Johnson.

Erin Johnson deserves my praise and immense gratitude as the warm and patient editor who recognized the importance of this story, endured my regular interruptions, and coaxed the manuscript into its final form. Many thanks also to Chris Bucci and my friend Ian Malcolm for their tremendous help and direction at the front end of this endeavor.

Finally, I want to thank my family—Priscilla Ferrazzi, our girls Hannah and Laura, and (of course) Maggie—for their tireless support and encouragement. This book is for my kids.

Notes

Prologue

1. Rebecca Kessler, "Talon Hunt," *Natural History* 118 (2009): 34–39.
2. Skoglund et al., "Ancient Wolf Genome" (see Selected Bibliography); Ed Yong, "A New Origin Story for Dogs," *Atlantic,* 2016, https://www.theatlan tic.com/science/archive/2016/06/the-origin-of-dogs/484976/; Tim Flannery, "Raised by Wolves," *New York Review of Books,* April 5, 2018, https://www .nybooks.com/articles/2018/04/05/raised-by-wolves/.
3. Yong, "A New Origin Story"; American Pet Products Association (APPA), *Pet Industry Market Size & Ownership Statistics* (APPA, 2018), https://www .americanpetproducts.org/press_industrytrends.asp.
4. Wilson, *Biophilia,* 1 (see Selected Bibliography); Wilson, *Biophilia,* 2.

Chapter 1

1. Vance, "Axolotl Paradox" (see Selected Bibliography); "Day of the Sala-mander Proposed by Senator," *Mexico News Daily,* March 1 2018, https:// mexiconewsdaily.com/news/senator-urges-feb-1-be-day-of-the-salamander/.
2. Voss, Woodcock, and Zambrano, "A Tale" (see Selected Bibliography).
3. Voss, Woodcock, and Zambrano, "A Tale."
4. Vance, "Axolotl Paradox."

5. Ambystoma Genetic Stock Center, *History of the Ambystoma Genetic Stock Center*, 2019, https://ambystoma.uky.edu/genetic-stock-center/history.php.

6. Philip Hoare, "More Tigers Live in US Back Yards than in the Wild. Is This a Catastrophe?" *Guardian*, June 20, 2018, https://www.theguardian.com /environment/shortcuts/2018/jun/20/more-tigers-live-in-us-back-yards -than-in-the-wild-is-this-a-catastrophe; Nijman et al., "Wildlife Trade" (see Selected Bibliography).

7. APPA, *Pet Industry Market Size*; Canadian Animal Health Institute, *Latest Canadian Pet Population Figures Released*, 2017, https://www.canadianveter inarians.net/documents/canadian-pet-population-figures-cahi-2017; "Es-timated Pet Population in the United Kingdom (UK) from 2009 to 2018 (in Millions)," Statistica, 2019, https://www.statista.com/statistics/308229/esti mated-pet-population-in-the-united-kingdom-uk/; "A Guide to Worldwide Pet Ownership," Petsecure, 2017, https://www.petsecure.com.au/pet-care/a -guide-to-worldwide-pet-ownership/.

8. All monetary amounts are in US dollars unless otherwise specified. The Harris Poll, *Pets Really Are Members of the Family*, June 2011, https://the harrispoll.com/americans-have-always-had-interesting-relationships-with -their-pets-whether-that-pet-is-a-cat-dog-parakeet-or-something-else -the-pet-industry-is-thriving-and-for-good-reason-more-than-three-in-f/; APPA, *Pet Industry Market Size*; Coate and Knight, "Pet Overpopula-tion" (see Selected Bibliography); "Pet Owner Survey," American Animal Hospital Association, 2004, https://faunalytics.org/wp-content/uploads /2015/05/Citation1058.pdf2004; Bradshaw, *The Animals among Us*, 128 (see Selected Bibliography).

9. Cavanaugh, Leonard, and Scammon, "Tail of Two Personalities" (see Se-lected Bibliography).

10. Wilson, "Biophilia and the Conservation Ethic" (see Selected Bibliogra-phy).

11. Wilson, *Biophilia*, 1.

12. "Venomous Snakes," Centers for Disease Control and Prevention, 2018, https://www.cdc.gov/niosh/topics/snakes/default.html.

13. Cook and Mineka, "Selective Associations" (see Selected Bibliography); Hoehl et al., "Itsy Bitsy Spider" (see Selected Bibliography).

14. Wilson, *Biophilia*, 2.

15. Ulrich, "Biophilia, Biophobia, and Natural Landscapes" (see Selected Bibliography); Beatley, *Biophilic Cities* (see Selected Bibliography).
16. Wilson, *Biophilia*, 115.
17. Wilson, *Biophilia*, 145.
18. Ceballos, Ehrlich, and Dirzo, "Biological Annihilation" (see Selected Bibliography); Rosenberg et al., "Decline of the North American Avifauna" (see Selected Bibliography).
19. Ceballos et al., "Accelerated Modern Human-Induced Species Losses" (see Selected Bibliography).
20. Intergovernmental Science-Policy Platform on Biodiversity and Ecosystem Services (IPBES), *The Global Assessment Report* (see Selected Bibliography); Hoffmann et al., "Impact of Conservation" (see Selected Bibliography); Larsen et al., "Inordinate Fondness Multiplied and Redistributed" (see Selected Bibliography); Stork, "How Many Species of Insects" (see Selected Bibliography).
21. Brodie et al., "Secondary Extinctions of Biodiversity" (see Selected Bibliography); Barnosky et al., "Has the Earth's Sixth Mass Extinction Already Arrived?" (see Selected Bibliography).
22. Smil, "Harvesting the Biosphere" (see Selected Bibliography).
23. Watson et al., "Protect the Last of the Wild" (see Selected Bibliography); Maxwell et al., "Ravages of Guns, Nets and Bulldozers" (see Selected Bibliography); Davidson et al., "Geography of Current and Future Global Mammal Extinction Risk" (see Selected Bibliography).
24. World Wildlife Fund (WWF), *Living Planet Report* (see Selected Bibliography), 75; Rowan, "Companion Animal Statistics" (see Selected Bibliography); Gillett, "Pet Overpopulation" (see Selected Bibliography).
25. United Nations, *World's Population Increasingly Urban* (see Selected Bibliography).
26. Waldron et al., "Reductions in Global Biodiversity Loss" (see Selected Bibliography).
27. Doherty et al., "Invasive Predators" (see Selected Bibliography).
28. Hooper et al., "A Global Synthesis" (see Selected Bibliography); Duffy, Godwin, and Cardinale, "Biodiversity Effects in the Wild Are Common" (see Selected Bibliography); Bjerke, Østdahl, and Kleiven, "Attitudes and Activities Related to Urban Wildlife" (see Selected Bibliography); Daly and Morton, "Empathic Differences" (see Selected Bibliography).

Chapter 2

1. Benjamin Zhang, "Emotional-Support Animals Are Becoming a Big Problem on Planes, and Airlines Want Them to Go Away," *Business Insider*, June 29, 2018, https://www.businessinsider.com/emotional-support-animals -big-problem-airlines-want-to-stop-them-2018-6.

2. Farah Stockman, "People Are Taking Emotional Support Animals Everywhere. States Are Cracking Down.," *New York Times*, June 18, 2019, https://www.nytimes.com/2019/06/18/us/emotional-support-animal .html; "Family Physician Survey: Pets and Health," The Human–Animal Bond Research Institute (HABRI), 2014, https://habri.org/2014-physician -survey.

3. Bradshaw, *Animals among Us*, 76.

4. Friedmann and Thomas, "Animal Companions" (see Selected Bibliography).

5. Bradshaw, *Animals among Us*, 79; Friedmann and Thomas, "Animal Companions."

6. Parker et al., "Survival Following an Acute Coronary Syndrome" (see Selected Bibliography).

7. Jones, "Early Drug Discovery" (see Selected Bibliography); Miller and Tran, "More Mysteries of Opium Reveal'd" (see Selected Bibliography); Sneader, *Drug Discovery*, 1 (see Selected Bibliography).

8. Pierotti and Fogg, *The First Domestication*, 326 (see Selected Bibliography); Tim Flannery, "Raised by Wolves," *New York Review of Books*, April 5, 2018, https://www.nybooks.com/articles/2018/04/05/raised-by-wolves/.

9. Bradshaw, *Animals among Us*, 41; Holland Cotter, "Its Reign Was Long, with Nine Lives to Start," *New York Times*, July 25, 2013, https://www .nytimes.com/2013/07/26/arts/design/divine-felines-cats-of-ancient-egypt -at-the-brooklyn-museum.html.

10. Bradshaw, *Animals among Us*, 48.

11. Carter and Porges, "Neural Mechanisms" (see Selected Bibliography); Nagasawa et al., "Oxytocin-Gaze Positive Loop" (see Selected Bibliography).

12. Stoeckel et al., "Patterns of Brain Activation" (see Selected Bibliography); Kurdek, "Pet Dogs as Attachment Figures" (see Selected Bibliography); Bradshaw, *Animals among Us*, 127–150.

13. Bradshaw, *Animals among Us*, 124; Saunders et al., "Exploring the Differences" (see Selected Bibliography); Bradshaw, *Animals among Us*, 86.

14. Batty et al., "Associations of Pet Ownership" (see Selected Bibliography); Batty and Bell, "Animal Companionship and Risk of Suicide" (see Selected Bibliography).

15. Louv, *Last Child in the Woods,* 323 (see Selected Bibliography); Palomino et al., "Online Dissemination of Nature–Health Concepts" (see Selected Bibliography); Kuo, "Nature-Deficit Disorder" (see Selected Bibliography); Tomita et al., "Green Environment and Incident Depression" (see Selected Bibliography).

16. United Nations, *The World's Cities* (see Selected Bibliography); Bradshaw, *Animals among Us.*

17. Cardinale, Palmer, and Collins, "Species Diversity Enhances Ecosystem Functioning" (see Selected Bibliography).

18. Worm et al., "Impacts of Biodiversity Loss" (see Selected Bibliography).

19. Hooper et al., "A Global Synthesis"; Hoffmann et al., "Impact of Conservation."

20. Bradshaw, *Animals among Us,* 225.

21. Bradshaw, *Animals among Us,* 159–164.

Chapter 3

1. Chris Rogers, *A New Cat Control By-Law as Part of a City/Community Cat Population Control Partnership Strategy (Interim Report)* (City of Cornwall, Planning Development and Recreation, May 2018), 6.

2. Loss, Will, and Marra, "Impact of Free-Ranging Domestic Cats" (see Selected Bibliography); Marra and Santella, *Cat Wars,* 212 (see Selected Bibliography).

3. Loss, Will, and Marra, "Impact of Free-Ranging Domestic Cats"; Rosenberg et al., "Decline of the North American Avifauna."

4. Coleman and Temple, "Effects of Free-Ranging Cats" (see Selected Bibliography); Coleman and Temple, "Rural Residents' Free-Ranging Domestic Cats" (see Selected Bibliography); Blancher, "Estimated Number of Birds Killed" (see Selected Bibliography); Woinarski, Burbidge, and Harrison, "Ongoing Unraveling of a Continental Fauna" (see Selected Bibliography); Lowe et al., *100 of the World's Worst Invasive Alien Species,* 11 (see Selected Bibliography).

5. Tim Doherty et al., "The Bark Side: Domestic Dogs Threaten Endangered

Species Worldwide," Conversation, 2017, https://theconversation.com/the
-bark-side-domestic-dogs-threaten-endangered-species-worldwide-76782;
Doherty et al., "Global Impacts of Domestic Dogs" (see Selected Bibliography).

6. Doherty et al., "Global Impacts of Domestic Dogs"; Terrence McCoy, "The Dog Is One of the World's Most Destructive Mammals. Brazil Proves It.," *Washington Post*, August 20, 2019, https://www.washingtonpost.com/world/the_americas/the-dog-is-one-of-the-worlds-most-destructive-mammals-brazil-proves-it/2019/08/19/c37a1250-a8da-11e9-8733-48c87235f396_story.html.

7. Ruiz-Izaguirre et al., "Roaming Characteristics" (see Selected Bibliography).

8. Doherty et al., "The Bark Side."

9. Doherty et al., "Invasive Predators"; Twardek et al., "Fido, Fluffy, and Wildlife Conservation" (see Selected Bibliography).

10. Marra and Santella, *Cat Wars*, 152–153.

11. Natalie Angier, "That Cuddly Kitty Is Deadlier Than You Think," *New York Times*, January 29, 2013; "About Alley Cat Allies," Alley Cat Allies, https://www.alleycat.org/about/.

12. Jessica Gall Myrick, "Study Shows the Paw-sitive Effects of Watching Cat Videos," Conversation, August 7, 2018, https://theconversation.com/study-shows-the-paw-sitive-effects-of-watching-cat-videos-43454.

13. Driscoll et al., "Taming of the Cat" (see Selected Bibliography); Hu et al., "Earliest Evidence" (see Selected Bibliography).

14. Driscoll et al., "Taming of the Cat."

15. Driscoll et al., "Taming of the Cat."

16. Loss and Marra, "Merchants of Doubt" (see Selected Bibliography).

17. Alley Cat Allies, https://www.alleycat.org; Jessica Pressler, "Must Cats Die So Birds Can Live?" *New York Magazine*, June 9, 2013.

18. Alley Cat Allies, https://www.alleycat.org.

19. Elizabeth Holtz, *Trap-Neuter-Return Ordinances and Policies in the United States: The Future of Animal Control, Law & Policy Brief* (Bethesda, MD: Alley Cat Allies, January 2013), 14; Loss et al., "Responding to Misinformation" (see Selected Bibliography).

20. IPBES, *Global Assessment Report*; Riesen, "Pet Overpopulation Crisis" (see Selected Bibliography); Stephanie Fellenstein, "New York City Veteri-

narian Takes on Pet Overpopulation," *DVM360 magazine* (2011), https: //veterinarynews.dvm360.com/new-york-city-veterinarian-takes-pet-over population?pageID=1.

21. "Pet Statistics" American Society for the Prevention of Cruelty to Animals (ASPCA), https://www.aspca.org/animal-homelessness/shelter-intake -and-surrender/pet-statistics; "Why You Should Spay/Neuter Your Pet," Humane Society of the United States (HSUS), https://www.humaneso ciety.org/resources/why-you-should-spayneuter-your-pet; Canadian Federation of Humane Societies, *Cats in Canada: A Report on the Cat Overpopulation Crisis*, 2017, https://d3n8a8pro7vhmx.cloudfront.net/cfhs /pages/1782/attachments/original/1524169616/Cats_In_Canada_2017 -FINAL-EN-LRs.pdf?1524169616; Kay et al., "A Scoping Review" (see Selected Bibliography).

22. Weiss et al., "Goodbye to a Good Friend" (see Selected Bibliography); see, e.g., Flockhart, Norris, and Coe, "Predicting Free-Roaming Cat Population Densities" (see Selected Bibliography); Gunther, Raz, and Klement, "Association of Neutering with Health" (see Selected Bibliography).

23. Carver, *Birding in the United States,* (see Selected Bibliography).

24. GCat Rescue, https://www.gcatrescue.com/; David Streitfeld, "As Google Feeds Cats Owl Lovers Cry Foul," *New York Times*, May 26, 2018, "The Plight of Burrowing Owls at Shoreline Park," Santa Clara Valley Audubon Society, http://www.scvas.org/page.php?page_id=6810.

25. American Bird Conservancy, "Feral Cats Relocated from Jones Beach State Park," YubaNet.com, January 8, 2019, https://yubanet.com/life/feral-cats -relocated-from-jones-beach-state-park/.

26. Lisa Gray, "The Nine Lives of Jim Stevenson," *Houston Chronicle*, December 12, 2007, https://www.chron.com/entertainment/article/The-nine -lives-of-Jim-Stevenson-1800994.php.

27. John Carey, "Cat Fight," *Conservation*, March 9, 2012, https://www.con servationmagazine.org/2012/03/cat-fight/; Cat Defender, "Nico Dauphiné Is Let Off with an Insultingly Lenient $100 Fine in a Show Trial That Was Fixed from the Very Beginning," *Cat Defender* (blog), 2012, http://cat defender.blogspot.com/2012/01/.

28. Hall et al., "Community Attitudes and Practices" (see Selected Bibliography).

29. Royal Society for the Protection of Birds (RSPB), "Are Cats Causing

Bird Declines?" RSPB, 2019, https://www.rspb.org.uk/birds-and-wildlife /advice/gardening-for-wildlife/animal-deterrents/cats-and-garden-birds /are-cats-causing-bird-declines/#P47LfUfb9J1FrS5m.99; Hall et al., "Community Attitudes."

30. Julie Power, "War on Feral Cats: Australia Aims to Cull 2 Million," *Sydney Morning Herald*, February 17, 2017, https://www.smh.com.au/national/war -on-feral-cats-australia-aims-to-cull-2-million-20170214-gucp4o.html.

31. Kelly-Leigh Cooper, "Why a Village in New Zealand Is Trying to Ban All Cats," *BBC News*, August 29, 2018, https://www.bbc.com/news/world -asia-45347136.

Chapter 4

1. Pimentel, Zuniga, and Morrison, "Update" (see Selected Bibliography).

2. Lance Richardson, "Python Wars: The Snake Epidemic Eating Away at Florida," *Guardian*, August 22, 2019, https://www.theguardian.com/envi ronment/2019/aug/22/florida-python-action-team-snake-epidemic; Seet-erama, Engel, and Mozumder, "Implications of a Valuation Study" (see Selected Bibliography).

3. Card et al., "Novel Ecological and Climatic Conditions" (see Selected Bibliography).

4. IPBES, *Global Assessment Report.*

5. Bellard, Cassey, and Blackburn, "Alien Species as a Driver of Recent Extinctions" (see Selected Bibliography); Blackburn, Bellard, and Ricciardi, "Alien Versus Native Species" (see Selected Bibliography).

6. Wodzicki and Wright, "Introduced Birds and Mammals" (see Selected Bibliography); International Union for Conservation of Nature (IUCN), "Threatened Species in Each Country (Totals by Taxonomic Group)," IUCN, 2018, file:///C:/Users/User/Downloads/2018_2_RL_Stats_Table_5.pdf; Robertson et al., *Conservation Status of New Zealand Birds*, 23 (see Selected Bibliography).

7. Wodzicki and Wright, "Introduced Birds and Mammals"; Robertson et al., *Conservation Status of New Zealand Birds*; Bellard, Cassey, and Blackburn, "Alien Species as a Driver."

8. Evans, Kumschick, and Blackburn, "Application of the Environmental Impact Classification for Alien Taxa" (see Selected Bibliography); Bellard, Cassey, and Blackburn, "Alien Species as a Driver."

9. Holmes et al., "Globally Important Islands" (see Selected Bibliography); Blackburn, Bellard, and Ricciardi, "Alien Versus Native Species."
10. Dyer et al., "Global Distribution and Drivers" (see Selected Bibliography); Sarah Zielinski, "The Invasive Species We Can Blame on Shakespeare," Smithsonian.com, 2011, https://www.smithsonianmag.com/science-nature/the-invasive-species-we-can-blame-on-shakespeare-95506437/#mXI16kRHzJi0GdVX.99.
11. Jerry Dennis, "A History of Captive Birds," *Michigan Quarterly Review* 53 (Summer 2014): http://hdl.handle.net/2027/spo.act2080.0053.301.
12. Dennis, "A History of Captive Birds"; Rachel Nuwer, "A Buddhist Ritual Gets an Ecologically Correct Update," *Audubon,* January–February 2014, https://www.audubon.org/magazine/january-february-2014/a-buddhist-ritual-gets-ecologically.
13. Saul et al., "Assessing Patterns in Introduction Pathways" (see Selected Bibliography); Stringham and Lockwood, "Pet Problems" (see Selected Bibliography); Bomford et al., "Predicting Establishment Success" (see Selected Bibliography).
14. Holmes et al., "Globally Important Islands"; Owens, "Big Cull" (see Selected Bibliography); "Strategic Plan 2016–2022," Australia Invasive Species Council, 2016, https://invasives.org.au/wp-content/uploads/2015/02/Strategic-Plan-2016-2022-summary.pdf.
15. Wallach et al., "Summoning Compassion" (see Selected Bibliography).
16. Ted Williams, "Recovery: The Salvation of Desecheo National Wildlife Refuge," *Nature Conservancy* (blog), November 2017, https://blog.nature.org/science/2017/11/06/recovery-the-salvation-of-desecheo-national-wildlife-refuge/.
17. Pearce, *The New Wild* (see Selected Bibliography); Ricciardi and Ryan, "Exponential Growth of Invasive Species Denialism" (see Selected Bibliography); Russell and Blackburn, "Rise of Invasive Species Denialism" (see Selected Bibliography).

Chapter 5
1. AmphibiaWeb (Web site), 2019, https://amphibiaweb.org.
2. "Summary Statistics," IUCN, 2019, https://www.iucnredlist.org/resources/summary-statistics#Summary%20Tables; Scheele et al., "Amphibian Fungal Panzootic" (see Selected Bibliography).

3. Yap et al., "Averting a North American Biodiversity Crisis" (see Selected Bibliography).
4. US Fish and Wildlife Service (USFWS), *Injurious Wildlife Species; Listing Salamanders Due to Risk of Salamander Chytrid Fungus* (USFWS, 2014), https://www.fws.gov/injuriouswildlife/pdf_files/Econ-RFA-Draft_12-28 -15.pdf.
5. Scheele et al., "Amphibian Fungal Panzootic."
6. O'Hanlon et al., "Recent Asian Origin of Chytrid Fungi" (see Selected Bibliography); Scheele et al., "Amphibian Fungal Panzootic."
7. Scheele et al., "Amphibian Fungal Panzootic."
8. Spitzen-van der Sluijs et al., "Rapid Enigmatic Decline" (see Selected Bibliography); Martel et al., "*Batrachochytrium salamandrivorans*" (see Selected Bibliography).
9. Martel et al., "Recent Introduction of a Chytrid Fungus" (see Selected Bibliography).
10. Martel et al., "Recent Introduction of a Chytrid Fungus."
11. Feldmeier et al., "Exploring the Distribution" (see Selected Bibliography).
12. Normile, "Driven to Extinction" (see Selected Bibliography).
13. Chomel, Belotto, and Meslin, "Wildlife, Exotic Pets, and Emerging Zoonoses" (see Selected Bibliography).
14. Tompkins et al., "Emerging Infectious Diseases of Wildlife" (see Selected Bibliography); MacPhee and Greenwood, "Infectious Disease, Endangerment, and Extinction" (see Selected Bibliography); Daszak, Cunningham, and Hyatt, "Emerging Infectious Diseases of Wildlife" (see Selected Bibliography).
15. Daszak et al., "Emerging Infectious Diseases."
16. Roelke-Parker et al., "Canine Distemper Virus Epidemic" (see Selected Bibliography).
17. Vianaa et al., "Dynamics of a Morbillivirus" (see Selected Bibliography); Almberg et al., "Parasite Invasion Following Host Reintroduction" (see Selected Bibliography).
18. Macdonald, "Dangerous Liaisons and Disease" (see Selected Bibliography).
19. Meli et al., "Feline Leukemia Virus and Other Pathogens" (see Selected Bibliography); Chiu et al., "Multiple Introductions" (see Selected Bibliography).

20. "Hawaii: Paradise for Some—But an Ongoing Extinction Crisis for Birds," American Bird Conservancy, 2019, https://abcbirds.org/program/hawaii/.

21. Scott, Conant, and Van Riper, eds., "Evolution, Ecology, Conservation, and Management of Hawaiian Birds" (see Selected Bibliography).

22. LaPointe, Atkinson, and Samuel, "Ecology and Conservation Biology of Avian Malaria" (see Selected Bibliography); Foster and Robinson, "Introduced Birds and the Fate of Hawaiian Rainforests" (see Selected Bibliography).

23. Daszak et al., "Emerging Infectious Diseases."

24. Shapiro et al., "Type X Strains of *Toxoplasma gondii*" (see Selected Bibliography).

25. MacPhee and Greenwood, "Infectious Disease, Endangerment, and Extinction" (see Selected Bibliography).

26. Carl Zimmer, "U.S. Restricts Movement of Salamanders, for Their Own Good," *New York Times*, January 12, 2016, https://www.nytimes.com/2016/01/13/science/us-restricts-movement-of-salamanders-for-their-own-good.html.

27. Douglas Main, "Salamander Trade Ban Draws Praise and Frustration," *Newsweek*, January 26, 2016, http://www.newsweek.com/salamander-trade-ban-draws-praise-and-frustration-419853; USFWS, *Injurious Wildlife Species; Listing Salamanders Due to Risk of Salamander Chytrid Fungus* (USFWS, 2015), https://www.fws.gov/injuriouswildlife/pdf_files/Econ-RFA-Draft_12-28-15.pdf.

28. Richgels et al., "Spatial Variation in Risk and Consequence" (see Selected Bibliography).

Chapter 6

1. Rene Ebersole, "Meet the Undercover Crime Unit Battling Miami's Black Market of Birds," *Audubon*, Fall 2018, https://www.audubon.org/magazine/fall-2018/meet-undercover-crime-unit-battling-miamis-black.

2. Harris et al., "Measuring the Impact" (see Selected Bibliography); Eaton et al., "Trade-Driven Extinctions" (see Selected Bibliography); "Summary Statistics," IUCN, 2019, https://www.iucnredlist.org/resources/summary-statistics#Summary%20Tables.

3. Eaton et al., "Trade-Driven Extinctions"; Nijman et al., "Wildlife Trade."

4. Harris et al., "Measuring the Impact of the Pet Trade."

5. Nijman et al., "Wildlife Trade."

6. Nijman et al., "Wildlife Trade."

7. Nijman and Nekaris, "Harry Potter Effect" (see Selected Bibliography).

8. Frank and Wilcove, "Long Delays in Banning Trade" (see Selected Bibliography); Smith et al., "Summarizing US Wildlife Trade" (see Selected Bibliography); Ashley et al., "Morbidity and Mortality" (see Selected Bibliography).

9. Bush, Baker, and Macdonald, "Global Trade in Exotic Pets" (see Selected Bibliography); Commission for Environmental Cooperation (CEC), *Sustainable Trade in Parrots*, 52 (see Selected Bibliography).

10. TRAFFIC, *Reducing Demand for Illegal Wildlife Products* (TRAFFIC, 2018), https://www.traffic.org/site/assets/files/11081/demand_reduction _research_report.pdf.

11. Tejeda, "Science and Sleuthing" (see Selected Bibliography); Bush, Baker, and Macdonald, "Global Trade in Exotic Pets"; Frank and Wilcove "Long Delays in Banning Trade"; Auliya et al., "Trade in Live Reptiles" (see Selected Bibliography).

12. Defenders of Wildlife, *Combating Wildlife Trafficking from Latin America to the United States* (Defenders of Wildlife, 2015), https://defenders.org /publication/combating-wildlife-trafficking-latin-america-united-states.

13. Wright et al., "Nest Poaching in Neotropical Parrots" (see Selected Bibliography); Olah et al., "Ecological and Socio-Economic Factors" (see Selected Bibliography); David Shukman and Sam Piranty, "The Secret Trade in Baby Chimps," BBC News, January 30, 2017, https://www.bbc.co.uk /news/resources/idt-5e8c4bac-c236-4cd9-bacc-db96d733f6cf; Brian Hare, "The Science behind Why Chimpanzees Are Not Pets," *ScienceBlogs*, 2009, https://scienceblogs.com/intersection/2009/03/04/the-science-behind -why-chimpan.

14. Bush, Baker, and Macdonald, "Global Trade in Exotic Pets"; Anvar Ali, Rajeev Raghavan, and Neelesh Dahanukar, "*Sahyadria denisonii*. The IUCN Red List of Threatened Species," IUCN, 2015, http://dx.doi.org/10.2305 /IUCN.UK.2015-1.RLTS.T169662A70082469.en.

15. Raghavan et al., "Effect of Unmanaged Harvests" (see Selected Bibliography);

Dee et al., "Assessing Vulnerability of Fish" (see Selected Bibliography); Rhyne et al., "Expanding Our Understanding" (see Selected Bibliography).

16. Rhyne et al., "Expanding Our Understanding"; Bush, Baker, and Macdonald, "Global Trade in Exotic Pets."

17. "Birds Involved in Trafficking Scheme Released by Officials," NBC Miami News, April 14, 2018, https://www.nbcmiami.com/news/local/Birds -Involved-in-Trafficking-Scheme-Released-by-Officials-479790403 .html.

18. Defenders of Wildlife, *Combating Wildlife Trafficking.*

Chapter 7

1. Agriculture and Agri-Food Canada, *Pathfinder—Global Dog and Cat Food Trends* (Ottawa: Government of Canada, September 2018), http://www .agr.gc.ca/eng/industry-markets-and-trade/international-agri-food-market -intelligence/reports/pathfinder-global-dog-and-cat-food-trends /?id=1535032183174#i; Ben Dummett, Dana Mattioli, and Dana Cimilluca, "Nestlé in Talks to Buy Pet-Food Maker for $2 Billion," *Wall Street Journal,* July 2, 2018, https://www.wsj.com/articles/nestle-in-talks-to-buy -pet-food-maker-for-2-billion-1530531553.

2. Kim et al., "Evaluation of Arsenic" (see Selected Bibliography).

3. Tim Wall, "US Natural Pet Food Market Sales Top US$8.2 Billion," Pet foodIndustry.com, March 17, 2017, https://www.petfoodindustry.com/arti cles/6299-us-natural-pet-food-market-sales-top-us82-billion?v=preview.

4. Okin, "Environmental Impacts" (see Selected Bibliography).

5. Stoll-Kleemann and O'Riordan, "Sustainability Challenges" (see Selected Bibliography); Machovina, Feeley, and Ripple, "Biodiversity Conservation" (see Selected Bibliography).

6. Stoll-Kleemann and O'Riordan, "Sustainability Challenges"; Maxwell et al., "Ravages of Guns, Nets and Bulldozers."

7. Maxwell et al., "Ravages of Guns, Nets and Bulldozers"; Machovina, Feeley, and Ripple, "Biodiversity Conservation"; Stoll-Kleemann and O'Riordan, "Sustainability Challenges"; IPBES, *Global Assessment Report.*

8. Vale and Vale, *Time to Eat the Dog* (see Selected Bibliography).

9. Okin, "Environmental Impacts."

10. Stoll-Kleemann and O'Riordan, "Sustainability Challenges."

11. Essington et al., "Fishing Amplifies Forage Fish Population Collapses" (see Selected Bibliography).
12. DeSilva and Turchini, "Towards Understanding the Impacts" (see Selected Bibliography); Twardek et al., "Fido, Fluffy, and Wildlife Conservation."
13. Essington et al., "Fishing Amplifies Forage Fish Population Collapses."
14. Pauly and Zeller, eds., *Global Atlas of Marine Fisheries* (see Selected Bibliography); Sarah Zielinski, "Seven Endangered Seabirds Around the World," Smithsonian.com, June 1, 2010, https://www.smithsonianmag.com/science-nature/seven-endangered-seabirds-around-the-world-29320343/; Gremillet et al., "Persisting Worldwide Seabird-Fishery Competition" (see Selected Bibliography).
15. Gremillet et al., "Persisting Worldwide Seabird-Fishery Competition"; Pikitch et al., *Little Fish, Big Impact,* 108 (see Selected Bibliography); Sydemana et al., "Best Practices for Assessing" (see Selected Bibliography).
16. Cury et al., "Global Seabird Response" (see Selected Bibliography).
17. Worm and Branch, "Future of Fish" (see Selected Bibliography); Worm et al., "Impacts of Biodiversity Loss"; Worm et al., "Rebuilding Global Fisheries" (see Selected Bibliography); Costello et al., "Global Fishery Prospects" (see Selected Bibliography); UN Food and Agricultural Organization (FAO), "Oceans Crucial for Our Climate, Food and Nutrition," FAO, 2014, http://www.fao.org/news/story/en/item/248479/icode/.
18. Kim et al., "Evaluation of Arsenic"; Sara Chodosh, "Freaking Out about Heavy Metals in Your Food? Here's What You Should Know," *Popular Science*, August 17, 2018, https://www.popsci.com/heavy-metals-baby-food#page-2.

Chapter 8

1. APPA, *Pet Industry Market Size*; Euromonitor International, *State of Global Pet Care: Trends and Growth Opportunities*, Euromonitor International, 2017, https://go.euromonitor.com/EV-NA2017-PIJAC-LP.html?utm_campaign=EV-NA2017-PIJAC&utm_medium=Blog&utm_source=Blog&utm_content=PIJAC&utm_term=; World Population in Review (2019), http://worldpopulationreview.com/countries/countries-by-gdp/.
2. US Bureau of Labor Statistics (USBLS), *Spending on Pets: 'Tails' from the Consumer Expenditure Survey* (USBLS, 2013), https://www.bls.gov/opub/btn

/volume-2/pdf/spending-on-pets.pdf; "How Much Is That Doggy?" Ontario Veterinary Medical Association (OVMA), 2018, https://www.ovma.org/assets/1/6/Cost_of_Care_2018_DOG.pdf; "How Much Is That Kitty?" OVMA, 2018, https://www.ovma.org/assets/1/6/Cost_of_Care_2018_CAT.pdf.

3. Richard Kestenbaum, "The Biggest Trends in the Pet Industry," *Forbes,* 2018, https://www.forbes.com/sites/richardkestenbaum/2018/11/27/the-biggest-trends-in-the-pet-industry/#6635ba1df099.

4. USBLS, "Spending on Pets."

5. USFWS, *Federal and State Endangered and Threatened Species Expenditures* (Washington, DC: USFWS, 2014), 415; Compares APPA 2014 pet spending ($58.04 billion) to USFWS 2014 spending ($1.3 billion) for total species; Statistics Canada, *Detailed Household Final Consumption Expenditure* (Statistics Canada, 2019), https://www150.statcan.gc.ca/t1/tbl1/en/tv.action?pid=3610022501; Environment and Climate Change Canada, *Horizontal Evaluation of the Species at Risk Program* (Environment and Climate Change Canada, 2018), http://publications.gc.ca/collections/collection_2018/eccc/En4-345-2018-eng.pdf; Euromonitor International, *State of Global Pet Care: Trends and Growth Opportunities,* pet industry spending figure for 2017 $116.6 billion (corrected to $92.9 billion in 2005 dollars) compared with global conservation spending estimates of $21.5 billion (in corrected 2005 dollars): 4.3 times more; IPBES, *Global Assessment Report.*

6. IPBES, *Global Assessment Report.*

7. Waldron et al., "Targeting Global Conservation Funding" (see Selected Bibliography).

8. Waldron et al., "Targeting Global Conservation Funding."

9. Waldron et al., "Targeting Global Conservation Funding."

10. McCarthy et al., "Financial Costs" (see Selected Bibliography).

11. Convention on Biological Diversity (CBD) High-Level Panel, *Resourcing the Aichi Biodiversity Targets: An Assessment of Benefits, Investments and Resource Needs for Implementing the Strategic Plan for Biodiversity 2011–2020,* (Montreal, Canada: UN CBD, 2014): 122.

12. Waldron et al., "Reductions in Global Biodiversity Loss."

13. Greenwald et al., *Shortchanged,* 11 (see Selected Bibliography).

14. Beston, *The Outermost House* (see Selected Bibliography).

Chapter 9

1. Doherty et al., "Global Impacts of Domestic Dogs."
2. "Mussel Infestation Could Cost Montana $234 Million Annually," Montana Department of Natural Resources and Conservation, 2019, http://dnrc.mt.gov/mussel-infestation-could-cost-montana-234-million-annually.
3. Beebe, Howell, and Bennett, "Using Scent Detection Dogs" (see Selected Bibliography).
4. Fischer-Tenhagen et al., "Odor Perception by Dogs" (see Selected Bibliography).
5. David Weinberg, "Decline and Fall of the Black-Footed Ferret," *Natural History* 95 (1986): 63–77.
6. Beebe, Howell, and Bennett, "Using Scent Detection Dogs"; Wasser et al., "Scent-Matching Dogs" (see Selected Bibliography).
7. Austin Ramzy, "Australia Deploys Sheepdogs to Save a Penguin Colony," *New York Times*, November 3, 2015, https://www.nytimes.com/2015/11/05/world/australia/australia-penguins-sheepdogs-foxes-swampy-marsh-farmer-middle-island.html.
8. Oliver Milman, "Victoria Zoos Train Maremma Bodyguards in Bid to Save Bandicoots," *Guardian*, August 8, 2014, https://www.theguardian.com/world/2014/aug/08/zoos-victoria-trains-maremma-bodyguards-save-bandicoots.
9. Twardek et al., "Fido, Fluffy, and Wildlife Conservation"; Glen et al., "Wildlife Detector Dogs and Camera Traps" (see Selected Bibliography).
10. Ripple et al., "Status and Ecological Effects" (see Selected Bibliography).
11. Rust, Whitehouse-Tedd, and Macmillan, "Perceived Efficacy of Livestock-Guarding Dogs, (see Selected Bibliography).
12. Laurie Marker, "The Year of the Livestock Guarding Dog," Cheetah Conservation Fund, 2019, https://cheetah.org/ccf-blog/livestock-guarding-dogs/the-year-of-the-livestock-guarding-dog/; Weise et al., "Distribution and Numbers of Cheetah" (see Selected Bibliography).
13. John R. Platt, "Illegal Pet Trade Wiping Out Yellow-Crested Cockatoos," *Scientific American*, 2003, https://blogs.scientificamerican.com/extinction-countdown/illegal-pet-trade-yellow-crested-cockatoos/; Wang, Ho, and Chu, "Diet and Feeding Behavior" (see Selected Bibliography).
14. Marchetti and Engstrom, "Conservation Paradox" (see Selected Bibliography).

15. Gibson and Yong, "Saving Two Birds with One Stone" (see Selected Bibliography).

16. Gibson and Yong, "Saving Two Birds with One Stone."

17. Wang, Ho, and Chu, "Diet and Feeding Behavior."

18. Marchetti and Engstrom, "Conservation Paradox," 437.

19. Pasmans et al., "Future of Keeping Pet Reptiles and Amphibians" (see Selected Bibliography).

20. Pasmans et al., "Future of Keeping Pet Reptiles and Amphibians."

21. Pasmans et al., "Future of Keeping Pet Reptiles and Amphibians"; Warwick et al., "Future of Keeping Pet Reptiles and Amphibians" (see Selected Bibliography).

Chapter 10

1. Wilson, *Naturalist*, 416 (see Selected Bibliography).

2. Wilson, *Naturalist*, 151.

3. Wilson, *Naturalist*, 52.

4. Wilson, *Naturalist*, 91.

5. Bjerke, Østdahl, and Kleiven, "Attitudes and Activities Related to Urban Wildlife."

6. Daly and Morton, "Empathic Differences"; Shuttlewood, Greenwell, and Montrose, "Pet Ownership" (see Selected Bibliography).

7. Shuttlewood, Greenwell, and Montrose, "Pet Ownership."

8. Williams et al., "Birds and Beaches, Dogs and Leashes" (see Selected Bibliography).

9. McDonald et al., "Reconciling" (see Selected Bibliography).

10. Shuttlewood, Greenwell, and Montrose, "Pet Ownership."

11. Sixty-three extinctions attributed to cats, 11 to dogs, and 90 to the pet-borne spread of Bsal; Doherty et al., "Global Impacts of Domestic Dogs"; IPBES, *Global Assessment Report.*

12. Simons, *Changing the Food Game*, 268 (see Selected Bibliography).

13. Simons, *Changing the Food Game.*

14. The IUCN Red List of Threatened Species (Web site), 2019, https://www.iucnredlist.org/; IPBES, *Global Assessment Report.*

15. Bush, Baker, and Macdonald, "Global Trade in Exotic Pets"; Lyons and Natusch, "Wildlife Laundering through Breeding Farms" (see Selected

Bibliography); Nijman and Shepherd, *Wildlife Trade from ASEAN to the EU* (see Selected Bibliography).

16. Pasmans et al., "Future of Keeping Pet Reptiles and Amphibians"; Loss and Marra, "Merchants of Doubt"; Twardek et al., "Fido, Fluffy, and Wildlife Conservation."

17. Twardek et al., "Fido, Fluffy, and Wildlife Conservation."

18. Bush, Baker, and Macdonald, "Global Trade in Exotic Pets"; Pasmans et al., "Future of Keeping Pet Reptiles and Amphibians."

19. Twardek et al., "Fido, Fluffy, and Wildlife Conservation"; Gordon, Matthaei, and Van Heezik, "Belled Collars Reduce Catch" (see Selected Bibliography).

20. Wilson, *Biophilia,* 126.

21. Wilson, *Biophilia,* 129.

22. Wilson, *Biophilia,* 130.

23. Wilson, *Biophilia,* 126.

Afterword

1. IPBES, *Global Assessment Report;* APPA, *Pet Industry Market Size;* Twardek et al., "Fido, Fluffy, and Wildlife Conservation."

2. Doherty et al., "Invasive Predators and Global Biodiversity Loss"; Eaton et al., "Trade-Driven Extinctions"; CEC, *Sustainable Trade in Parrots;* Bush, Baker, and Macdonald, "Global Trade in Exotic Pets"; Dee et al., "Assessing Vulnerability of Fish"; Scheele et al., "Amphibian Fungal Panzootic"; Stoll-Kleemann and O'Riordan, "Sustainability Challenges"; Ceballos, Ehrlich, and Dirzo, "Biological Annihilation."

3. Shuttlewood, Greenwell, and Montrose, "Pet Ownership"; Bjerke, Østdahl, and Kleiven, "Attitudes and Activities Related to Urban Wildlife."

4. Edward O. Wilson, "Beware the Age of Loneliness," *Economist,* November 18, 2013, https://www.economist.com/news/2013/11/18/beware-the-age-of-loneliness.

5. Wilson, "Beware the Age of Loneliness."

Selected Bibliography

Bibliography selections include books, scientific articles, and reports relied upon in writing this book. Popular press articles and Web site content were also used to inform the work, and their references can be found in Notes.

Almberg, Emily S., Paul C. Cross, Andrew P. Dobson, Douglas W. Smith, and Peter J. Hudson. "Parasite Invasion Following Host Reintroduction: A Case Study of Yellowstone's Wolves." *Philosophic Transactions of the Royal Society B* 367 (2012): 2840–2851.

Ashley, Shawn, Susan Brown, Joel Ledford, Janet Martin, Ann-Elizabeth Nash, et al. "Morbidity and Mortality of Invertebrates, Amphibians, Reptiles, and Mammals at a Major Exotic Companion Animal Wholesaler." *Journal of Applied Animal Welfare Science* 17 (2014): 308–321.

Auliya, Mark, Sandra Altherr, Daniel Ariano-Sanchez, Ernst H. Baard, Carl Brown, et al. "Trade in Live Reptiles, Its Impact on Wild Populations, and the Role of the European Market." *Biological Conservation* 204 (2016): 103–119.

Barnosky, Anthony D., Nicholas Matzke, Susumu Tomiya, Guinevere O. U. Wogan, Brian Swartz, et al. "Has the Earth's Sixth Mass Extinction Already Arrived?" *Nature* 471 (March 2011): 51–57.

Batty, G. David, and Steven Bell. "Animal Companionship and Risk of Suicide." *Epidemiology* 29, no. 4 (July 2018): e25–e26.

Batty, G. David, Paola Zaninotto, Richard G. Watt, and Steven Bell. "Associations of Pet Ownership with Biomarkers of Ageing: Population Based Cohort Study." *BMJ* 359 (2017): https://doi.org/10.1136/bmj.j5558.

Beatley, Timothy. *Biophilic Cities: Integrating Nature into Urban Design and Planning* (Washington, DC: Island Press, 2011): 208.

Beebe, Sarah C., Tiffani J. Howell, and Pauleen C. Bennett. "Using Scent Detection Dogs in Conservation Settings: A Review of Scientific Literature Regarding Their Selection." *Frontiers of Veterinary Science* 3 (2016): https://doi.org/10.3389/fvets.2016.00096.

Bellard, Céline, Phillip Cassey, and Tim M. Blackburn. "Alien Species as a Driver of Recent Extinctions." *Biology Letters* 12 (2016): https://doi.org/10.1098/rsbl.2015.0623.

Beston, Henry. *The Outermost House: A Year of Life on the Great Beach of Cape Cod.* New York: Holt Paperbacks, reprint edition, 2003.

Bjerke, Tore, Torbjørn Østdahl, and Jo Kleiven. "Attitudes and Activities Related to Urban Wildlife: Pet Owners and Non-Owners." *Anthrozoös* 16 (2003): 252–262.

Blackburn, Tim M., Céline Bellard, and Anthony Ricciardi. "Alien Versus Native Species as Drivers of Recent Extinctions." *Frontiers in Ecology and the Environment* (2019): https://doi.org/10.1002/fee.2020.

Blancher, Peter P. "Estimated Number of Birds Killed by House Cats (*Felis catus*) in Canada." *Avian Conservation and Ecology* 8 (2013): 3.

Bomford, Mary, Fred Kraus, Simon C. Barry, and Emma Lawrence. "Predicting Establishment Success for Alien Reptiles and Amphibians: A Role for Climate Matching." *Biological Invasions* (2009) 11: 713. https://doi.org/10.1007/s10530-008-9285-3.

Bradshaw, John. *The Animals among Us: The New Science of Anthrozoology.* London: Penguin Random House, 2017.

Brodie, Jedediah F., Clare E. Aslan, Haldre S. Rogers, Kent H. Redford, John L. Maron, et al. "Secondary Extinctions of Biodiversity." *Trends in Ecology & Evolution* 29 (2014): 664–671.

Bush, Emma R., Sandra E. Baker, and David W. Macdonald. "Global Trade in Exotic Pets 2006–2012." *Conservation Biology* 28 (2014): 663–676.

Campbell Grant, Evan H., Erin Muths, Rachel A. Katz, Stefano Canessa, Michael J. Adams, et al. "Using Decision Analysis to Support Proactive Management of Emerging Infectious Wildlife Diseases." *Frontiers in Ecology and the Environment* (2017): https://doi.org/10.1002/fee.1481.

Card, Daren C., Blair W. Perry, Richard H. Adams, Drew R. Schield, Acacia S. Young, et al. "Novel Ecological and Climatic Conditions Drive Rapid Adaptation in Invasive Florida Burmese Pythons." *Molecular Ecology* 27 (2018): 4744–4757.

Cardinale, Bradley J., Margaret A. Palmer, and Scott L. Collins. "Species Diversity Enhances Ecosystem Functioning through Interspecific Facilitation." *Nature* 415 (January 2002): 426–429.

Carter, C. Sue, and Stephen W. Porges. "Neural Mechanisms Underlying Human–Animal Interaction: An Evolutionary Perspective." In *The Social Neuroscience of Human–Animal Interaction*, edited by L. S. Freund, S. McCune, L. Esposito, N. R. Gee, and P. McCardle, 89–105. Washington, DC: American Psychological Association, 2016.

Carver, Erin. *Birding in the United States: A Demographic and Economic Analysis.* Washington, DC: US Fish and Wildlife Service, 2013.

Cavanaugh, Lisa A., Hillary Leonard, and Debra Scammon. "A Tail of Two Personalities: How Canine Companions Shape Relationships and Well-Being." *Journal of Business Research* 61 (2008): 469–479.

Ceballos, Gerardo, Paul R. Ehrlich, Anthony D. Barnosky, Andrés García, Robert M. Pringle, et al. "Accelerated Modern Human–Induced Species Losses: Entering the Sixth Mass Extinction." *Science Advances* 1 (2015): https://doi.org/10.1126/sciadv.1400253.

Ceballos, Gerardo, Paul R. Ehrlich, and Rodolfo Dirzo. "Biological Annihilation via the Ongoing Sixth Mass Extinction Signaled by Vertebrate Population Losses and Declines." *PNAS* 114 (2017): https://doi.org/10.1073/pnas.1704949114.

Chiu, Elliott S., Simona Kraberger, Mark Cunningham, Lara Cusack, Melody Roelke, et al. "Multiple Introductions of Domestic Cat Feline Leukemia Virus in Endangered Florida Panthers." *Emerging Infectious Diseases* 25 (2019): 92–101.

Chomel, Bruno B., Albino Belotto, and François-Xavier Meslin. "Wildlife, Exotic Pets, and Emerging Zoonoses." *Emerging Infectious Diseases* 13 (2007): 6–11.

Coate, Stephen, and Brian Knight. "Pet Overpopulation: An Economic Analysis." *B.E. Journal of Economic Analysis & Policy* 10 (2010): https://doi.org/10.2202/1935-1682.2574.

Coleman, John S., and Stanley A. Temple. "Effects of Free-Ranging Cats on Wildlife: A Progress Report." In *Proceedings of the Fourth Eastern Wildlife Damage Control Conference*, edited by Scott R. Craven, 7, 1989, http://digitalcommons.unl.edu/ewdcc4/7.

Coleman, John S., and Stanley A. Temple. "Rural Residents' Free-Ranging Domestic Cats: A Survey." *Wildlife Society Bulletin* 21 (1993): 381–390.

Commission for Environmental Cooperation (CEC). *Sustainable Trade in Parrots: Action Plan for North America.* Montreal, Canada: CEC, 2017.

Cook, Michael, and Susan Mineka. "Selective Associations in the Observational Conditioning of Fear in Rhesus Monkeys." *Journal of Experimental Psychology: Animal Behavior Processes* 16 (1990): 72–89.

Costello, Christopher, Daniel Ovando, Tyler Clavelle, C. Kent Strauss, Ray Hilborn, et al. "Global Fishery Prospects under Contrasting Management Regimes." *PNAS* 113, no. 18 (2016): 5124–5129.

Cury, Philippe M., Ian L. Boyd, Sylvain Bonhommeau, Tycho Anker-Nilssen, Robert J. M. Crawford, et al. "Global Seabird Response to Forage Fish Depletion—One-Third for the Birds." *Science* 334 (2011): 1703–1706.

Daly, Beth, and Larry L. Morton. "Empathic Differences in Adults as a Function of Childhood and Adult Pet Ownership and Pet Type." *Anthrozoös* 24 (2009): 371–382.

Daszak, Peter, Andrew Cunningham, and Alex Hyatt. "Emerging Infectious Diseases of Wildlife: Threats to Biodiversity and Human Health." *Science* 287 (2000): 443–449.

Davidson, Ana D., Kevin T. Shoemaker, Ben Weinstein, Gabriel C. Costa, Thomas M. Brooks, et al. "Geography of Current and Future Global Mammal Extinction Risk." *PLOS ONE* 12 (2016): https://doi.org/10.1371/journal.pone.0186934.

Dee, Laura E., Kendra Anne Karr, Celia J. Landesberg, and Daniel J. Thornhill. "Assessing Vulnerability of Fish in the U.S. Marine Aquarium Trade." *Frontiers in Marine Science* 5 (2019): 527.

Dennis, Jerry. "A History of Captive Birds." *Michigan Quarterly Review* 53 (2014): http://hdl.handle.net/2027/spo.act2080.0053.301.

DeSilva, Sena S., and Giovanni M. Turchini. "Towards Understanding the Impacts of the Pet Food Industry on World Fish and Seafood Supplies." *Journal of Agricultural and Environmental Ethics* 21 (2008): 459–467.

Doherty, Tim S., Chris R. Dickman, Alistair S. Glen, Thomas M. Newsome, Dale G. Nimmo, et al. "The Global Impacts of Domestic Dogs on Threatened Vertebrates." *Biological Conservation* 210 (2017): 56–59.

Doherty, Tim S., Alistair S. Glen, Dale G. Nimmo, Euan G. Ritchie, and Chris R. Dickman. "Invasive Predators and Global Biodiversity Loss." *PNAS* 113 (2016): 11261–11265.

Driscoll, Carlos A., Juliet Clutton-Brock, Andrew C. Kitchener, and Stephen J. O'Brien. "The Taming of the Cat." *Scientific American* 300 (2009): 68–75.

Duffy, J. Emmett, Casey M. Godwin, and Bradley J. Cardinale. "Biodiversity Effects in the Wild Are Common and as Strong as Key Drivers of Productivity." *Nature* 549 (2017): 261–264.

Dyer, Ellie E., Phillip Cassey, David W. Redding, Ben Collen, Victoria Franks, et al. "The Global Distribution and Drivers of Alien Bird Species Richness." *PLOS Biology* 15 (2017): e2000942.

Eaton, James A., Chris R. Shepherd, Frank E. Rheindt, J. Berton C. Harris, S. Bas van Balen, et al. "Trade-Driven Extinctions and Near-Extinctions of Avian Taxa in Sundaic Indonesia." *Forktail* 31 (2015): 1–12.

Essington, Timothy E., Pamela E. Moriarty, Halley E. Froehlich, Emma E. Hodgson, Laura E. Koehn, et al. "Fishing Amplifies Forage Fish Population Collapses." *PNAS* 112 (2015): 6648–6652.

Evans, Thomas, Sabrina Kumschick, and Tim M. Blackburn. "Application of the Environmental Impact Classification for Alien Taxa (EICAT) to a Global Assessment of Alien Bird Impacts." *Diversity and Distributions* (2016): 1–13.

Feldmeier, Stephan, Lukas Schefczyk, Norman Wagner, Gunther Heinemann, Michael Veith, et al. "Exploring the Distribution of the Spreading Lethal Salamander Chytrid Fungus in Its Invasive Range in Europe: A Macroecological Approach." *PLOS ONE* (2016): https://doi.org/10.1371/journal.pone.0165682.

Fischer-Tenhagen, Carola, Dorothea Johnen, Wolfgang Heuwieser, Roland Becker, Kristin Schallschmidt, et al. "Odor Perception by Dogs: Evaluating Two Training Approaches for Odor Learning of Sniffer Dogs." *Chemical Senses* 42 (2017): 435–441.

Flockhart, D. Tyler, D. Ryan Norris, and Jason B. Coe. "Predicting Free-Roaming Cat Population Densities in Urban Areas." *Animal Conservation* 19 (2016): 472.

Foster, Jeffrey T., and Scott K. Robinson. "Introduced Birds and the Fate of Hawaiian Rainforests." *Conservation Biology* 21 (2007): 1248–1257.

Frank, Eyal G., and David S. Wilcove. "Long Delays in Banning Trade in Threatened Species." *Science* 363 (2019): 686–688.

Friedmann, Erika, and Sue A. Thomas. "Animal Companions and One Year Survival after Discharge from a Coronary Care Unit." *Public Health Reports* 95 (1980): 307–312.

Gibson, Luke, and Ding Li Yong. "Saving Two Birds with One Stone: Solving the Quandary of Introduced, Threatened Species." *Frontiers in Ecology and the Environment* 15 (2017): 35–41.

Gillett, Tracy. "Pet Overpopulation: A Global Crisis." *International Animal Health Journal* 1 (2014): 38–42.

Glen, Alistair S., Dean Anderson, Clare J. Veltman, Patrick M. Garvey, and Margaret Nichols. "Wildlife Detector Dogs and Camera Traps: Comparison of Techniques for Detecting Feral Cats." *New Zealand Journal of Zoology* 43 (2016): 127–137.

Gordon, J. K., C. Matthaei, and Y. Van Heezik. "Belled Collars Reduce Catch of Domestic Cats in New Zealand by Half." *Wildlife Research* 37 (2010): 372–378.

Greenwald, Noah, Brett Hartl, Loyal Mehrhoff, and Jamie Pang. *Shortchanged: Funding Needed to Save America's Most Endangered Species.* Tucson, AZ: Center for Biological Diversity, 2016.

Gremillet, David, Aurore Ponchon, Michelle Paleczny, Maria-Lourdes D. Palomares, Vasiliki Karpouzi, et al. "Persisting Worldwide Seabird-Fishery Competition Despite Seabird Community Decline." *Current Biology* 28 (2018): 4009–4013.

Gunther, I., T. Raz, and E. Klement. "Association of Neutering with Health and Welfare of Urban Free-Roaming Cat Population in Israel, during 2012–2014." *Preventive Veterinary Medicine* 157 (2018): 26–33.

Hall, Catherine M., Nigel A. Adams, J. Stuart Bradley, Kate A. Bryant, Alisa A. Davis, et al. "Community Attitudes and Practices of Urban Residents Regarding Predation by Pet Cats on Wildlife: An International Comparison." *PLOS ONE* 11 (2016): e0151962.

Harris, J. Berton C., Morgan W. Tingley, Fangyuan Hua, Ding Li Yong, J. Marion Adeney, et al. "Measuring the Impact of the Pet Trade on Indonesian Birds." *Conservation Biology* 31 (2017): 394–405.

Hoehl, Stefanie, Kahl Hellmer, Maria Johansson, and Gustaf Gredebäck. "Itsy Bitsy Spider . . . : Infants React with Increased Arousal to Spiders and Snakes." *Frontiers in Psychology* (2017): https://doi.org/10.3389/fpsyg .2017.01710.

Hoffmann, Michael, Craig Hilton-Taylor, Ariadne Angulo, Monika Böhm, Thomas M. Brooks, et al. "The Impact of Conservation on the Status of the World's Vertebrates." *Science* 330 (2010): 1503–1509.

Holmes, Nick D., Dena R. Spatz, Steffen Oppel, Bernie Tershy, Donald A. Croll, et al. "Globally Important Islands Where Eradicating Invasive Mammals Will Benefit Highly Threatened Vertebrates." *PLOS ONE* 14 (2019): e0212128.

Hooper, David U., E. Carol Adair, Bradley J. Cardinale, Jarrett E. K. Byrnes, Bruce A. Hungate, et al. "A Global Synthesis Reveals Biodiversity Loss as a Major Driver of Ecosystem Change." *Nature* 486 (2012): 105–109.

Hu, Yaowu, Songmei Hu, Weilin Wang, Xiaohong Wu, Fiona B. Marshall, et al. "Earliest Evidence for Commensal Processes of Cat Domestication." *PNAS* 111 (2014): 116–120.

Intergovernmental Science-Policy Platform on Biodiversity and Ecosystem Services (IPBES). *The Global Assessment Report on Biodiversity and Ecosystem Services of the Intergovernmental Science-Policy Platform on Biodiversity and Ecosystem Services.* Bonn, Germany: IPBES secretariat, 2019.

Jones, Alan Wayne. "Early Drug Discovery and the Rise of Pharmaceutical Chemistry." *Drug Test and Analysis* 3 (2011): 337–344.

Kay, Aileigh, Jason B. Coe, David Pearl, and Ian Young. "A Scoping Review of Published Research on the Population Dynamics and Control Practices of Companion Animals." *Preventive Veterinary Medicine* 144 (2017): 40–52.

Kellert, Stephen R., and Edward O. Wilson, eds. *The Biophilia Hypothesis.* Washington, DC: Island Press, 1993.

Kim, Hyun-Tae, John P. Loftus, Sabine Mann, and Joseph J. Wakshlag. "Evaluation of Arsenic, Cadmium, Lead and Mercury Contamination in Over-the-Counter Available Dry Dog Foods with Different Animal Ingredients (Red Meat, Poultry, and Fish). *Frontiers in Veterinary Science* 5 (2018): https://doi.org/10.3389/fvets.2018.00264.

Kuo, Ming. "Nature-Deficit Disorder: Evidence, Dosage, and Treatment." *Journal of Policy Research in Tourism, Leisure and Events* 5 (2013) 172–186.

Kurdek, Lawrence A. "Pet Dogs as Attachment Figures for Adult Owners." *Journal of Family Psychology* 23 (2009): 439–446.

LaPointe, Dennis A., Carter T. Atkinson, and Michael D. Samuel. "Ecology and Conservation Biology of Avian Malaria." *Annals of the New York Academy of Sciences* 1249 (2012): 211–226.

Larsen, Brendan B., Elizabeth C. Miller, Matthew K. Rhodes, and John J. Wiens. "Inordinate Fondness Multiplied and Redistributed: The Number of Species on Earth and the New Pie of Life." *The Quarterly Review of Biology* 92 (2017): 229–265.

Loss, Scott R., and Peter P. Marra. "Merchants of Doubt in the Free-Ranging Cat Conflict." *Conservation Biology* 32 (2018): 265–266.

Loss, Scott R., Tom Will, Travis Longcore, and Peter P. Marra. "Responding to Misinformation and Criticisms Regarding United States Cat Predation Estimates." *Biological Invasions* (2018): https://doi.org/10.1007/s10530-018 -1796-y.

Loss, Scott R., Tom Will, and Peter P. Marra. "The Impact of Free-Ranging Domestic Cats on Wildlife of the United States." *Nature Communications* 4 (2013): 1396–1403.

Louv, Richard. *Last Child in the Woods: Saving Our Children from Nature-Deficit Disorder.* Chapel Hill, North Carolina: Algonquin Books of Chapel Hill, 2005.

Lowe, Sarah, Michael Browne, Souad Boudjelas, and Maj De Poorter. *100 of the World's Worst Invasive Alien Species: A Selection from The Global Invasive Species Database.* Auckland: Invasive Species Specialist Group, International Union for Conservation of Nature, 2000.

Lyons, Jessica A., and Daniel J. D. Natusch. "Wildlife Laundering through Breeding Farms: Illegal Harvest, Population Declines and a Means of Regulating the Trade of Green Pythons (*Morelia viridis*) from Indonesia." *Biological Conservation* 144 (2011): 3073–3081.

Macdonald, David W. "Dangerous Liaisons and Disease." *Nature* 379 (1996): 400–401.

Machovina, Brian, Kenneth J. Feeley, and William J. Ripple. "Biodiversity Conservation: The Key is Reducing Meat Consumption." *Science of the Total Environment* 536 (2015): 419–431.

MacPhee, Ross D. E., and Alex D. Greenwood. "Infectious Disease, Endangerment, and Extinction." *International Journal of Evolutionary Biology,* (2013): https://doi.org/10.1155/2013/571939.

Marchetti, Michael P., and Tag Engstrom. "The Conservation Paradox of Endangered and Invasive Species." *Conservation Biology* 30 (2016): 434–437.

Marra, Peter P., and Chris Santella. *Cat Wars: The Devastating Consequences of a Cuddly Killer.* Princeton, NJ: Princeton University Press, 2016.

Martel, An, Mark Blooi, Connie Adriaensen, Pascale Van Rooij, Wouter Beukema, et al. "Recent Introduction of a Chytrid Fungus Endangers Western Palearctic Salamanders." *Science* 346 (2014): 630–631.

Martel, An, Annemarieke Spitzen-van der Sluijs, Mark Blooi, Wim Bert, Richard Ducatelle, et al. "*Batrachochytrium salamandrivorans* sp. nov. Causes Lethal Chytridiomycosis in Amphibians." *PNAS* 110 (2013): 15325–15329.

Maxwell, Sean L., Richard A. Fuller, Thomas M. Brooks, and James E. M. Watson. "The Ravages of Guns, Nets and Bulldozers." *Nature* 536 (2016): 143–145.

McCarthy, Donal P., Paul F. Donald, Jörn P. W. Scharlemann, Graeme M. Buchanan, Andrew Balmford, et al. "Financial Costs of Meeting Global Biodiversity Conservation Targets: Current Spending and Unmet Needs." *Science* 338 (2012): 946–949.

McDonald, Jennifer L., Mairead Maclean, Matthew R. Evans, and Dave J. Hodgson. "Reconciling Actual and Perceived Rates of Predation by Domestic Cats." *Ecology and Evolution* 5 (2015): 2745–2753.

Meli, Marina L., Valentino Cattori, Fernando Martinez, Guillermo Lopez, Astrid Vargas, et al. "Feline Leukemia Virus and Other Pathogens as Important Threats to the Survival of the Critically Endangered Iberian Lynx (*Lynx pardinus*)." *PLOS ONE* 4 (2009): e4744.

Miller, Richard J., and Phuong B. Tran. "More Mysteries of Opium Reveal'd: 300 Years of Opiates." *TiPS* 21 (2000): 299–304.

Nagasawa, Miho, Shouhei Mitsui, Shiori En, Nobuyo Ohtani, Mitsuaki Ohta, et al. "Oxytocin-Gaze Positive Loop and the Coevolution of Human-Dog Bonds." *Science* 348 (2015): 333–336.

Nijman, Vincent, and K. Anne-Isola Nekaris. "The Harry Potter Effect: The Rise in Trade of Owls as Pets in Java and Bali, Indonesia." *Global Ecology and Conservation* 11 (2017): 84e94.

Nijman, Vincent, Abdullah Langgeng, Hélène Birot, Muhammad Ali Imron, and K. A. I. Nekaris. "Wildlife Trade, Captive Breeding and the Imminent Extinction of a Songbird." *Global Ecology and Conservation* 15 (2018): https://doi.org/10.1016/j.gecco.2018.e00425.

Nijman, Vincent, and C. Shepherd. *Wildlife Trade from ASEAN to the EU: Issues with the Trade in Captive-Bred Reptiles from Indonesia.* Brussels: TRAFFIC, 2009.

Normile, Dennis. "Driven to Extinction." *Science* 319 (2008): 1606–1609.

O'Hanlon, Simon J., Adrien Rieux, Rhys A. Farrer, Gonçalo M. Rosa, Bruce Waldman, et al. "Recent Asian Origin of Chytrid Fungi Causing Global Amphibian Declines." *Science* 360 (2018): 621–627.

Okin, Gregory S. "Environmental Impacts of Food Consumption by Dogs and Cats." *PLOS ONE* 12 (2017): e0181301.

Olah, George, Stuart H. M. Butchart, Andy Symes, Iliana Medina Guzman, Ross Cunningham, et al. "Ecological and Socio-Economic Factors Affecting Extinction Risk in Parrots." *Biodiversity Conservation* 25 (2016): 205–223.

Owens, Brian. "The Big Cull." *Nature* 541 (2017): 148–150.

Palomino, Marco, Tim Taylor, Ayse Göker, John Isaacs, and Sara Warber. "The Online Dissemination of Nature–Health Concepts: Lessons from Sentiment Analysis of Social Media Relating to 'Nature-Deficit Disorder.'" *International Journal Environmental Research and Public Health* 13 (2016): https://doi.org/10.3390/ijerph13010142.

Parker, Gordon B., Aimee Gayed, Catherine A. Owen, Matthew P. Hyett, Therese M. Hilton, et al. "Survival Following an Acute Coronary Syndrome: A Pet Theory Put to the Test." *Acta Psychiatrica Scandinavica* 121 (2010): 65–70.

Pasmans, Frank, Serge Bogaerts, Johan Braeckman, Andrew A. Cunningham, Tom Hellebuyck, et al. "Future of Keeping Pet Reptiles and Amphibians: Towards Integrating Animal Welfare, Human Health and Environmental Sustainability." *Veterinary Record* (2017): https://doi.org/10.1136/vr.104 296.

Pauly, Daniel, and Dirk Zeller, eds. *Global Atlas of Marine Fisheries: A Critical Appraisal of Catches and Ecosystem Impacts.* Washington, DC: Island Press, 2016.

Pearce, Fred. *The New Wild: Why Invasive Species Will Be Nature's Salvation.* Boston: Beacon Press, 2016.

Pierotti, Raymond, and Brandy R. Fogg. *The First Domestication: How Wolves and Humans Coevolved.* New Haven, CT: Yale University Press, 2017.

Pikitch, Ellen, P. Dee Boersma, Ian L. Boyd, David O. Conover, Philippe Cury, et al. *Little Fish, Big Impact: Managing a Crucial Link in Ocean Food Webs.* Washington, DC: Lenfest Ocean Program, 2012.

Pimentel, David, Rodolfo Zuniga, and Doug Morrison. "Update on the Environmental and Economic Costs Associated with Alien-Invasive Species in the United States." *Ecological Economics* 52 (2005): 273–288.

Raghavan, Rajeev, Anvar Ali, Siby Philip, and Neelesh Dahanukar. "Effect of Unmanaged Harvests for the Aquarium Trade on the Population Status and Dynamics of Redline Torpedo Barb: A Threatened Aquatic Flagship." *Aquatic Conservation: Marine and Freshwater Ecosystems* 28 (2018): 567–574.

Rhyne, Andrew L., Michael F. Tlusty, Joseph T. Szczebak, and Robert J. Holmberg. "Expanding Our Understanding of the Trade in Marine Aquarium Animals." *PeerJ* 5 (2017): https://doi.org/10.7717/peerj.2949.

Ricciardi, Anthony, and Rachael Ryan. "The Exponential Growth of Invasive Species Denialism." *Biological Invasions* 20 (2018): 549–553.

Richgels, Katherine L. D., Robin E. Russell, Michael J. Adams, C. LeAnn White, and Evan H. Campbell. "Spatial Variation in Risk and Consequence of *Batrachochytrium salamandrivorans* Introduction in the USA." *Royal Society Open Science* 3 (2016): https://doi.org/10.1098/rsos.150616.

Riesen, Melissa. "The Pet Overpopulation Crisis: How Training the Public Can Make a Difference." *Journal of Applied Companion Animal Behavior* 1 (2007): 22–27.

Ripple, William J., James A. Estes, Robert L. Beschta, Christopher C. Wilmers, Euan G. Ritchie, et al. "Status and Ecological Effects of the World's Largest Carnivores." *Science* 343 (2014): https://doi.org/10.1126/science.1241484.

Robertson, Hugh A., Karen Baird, John E. Dowding, Graeme P. Elliott, Rodney A. Hitchmough, et al. *Conservation Status of New Zealand Birds, 2016.* Wellington: New Zealand Department of Conservation, 2016.

Roelke-Parker, Melody, Linda Munson, Craig Packer, Richard Kock, Sarah Cleaveland, et al. "A Canine Distemper Virus Epidemic in Serengeti Lions (*Panthera leo*)." *Nature* 379 (1996): 441–445.

Rosenberg, Kenneth V., Adriaan M. Dokter, Peter J. Blancher, John R. Sauer,

Adam C, Smith, et al. "Decline of the North American Avifauna." *Science* 366 (2019): 120–124.

Rowan, Andrew N. "Companion Animal Statistics in the USA." *Demography and Statistics for Companion Animal Populations* 7 (2018): https://animal studiesrepository.org/demscapop/7.

Ruiz-Izaguirre, Eliza, Arthur van Woersem, Karen H. A. M. Eilers, Sipke E. van Wieren, Guido Bosch, et al. "Roaming Characteristics and Feeding Practices of Village Dogs Scavenging Sea-Turtle Nests." *Animal Conservation* 18 (2015): 146–156.

Russell, James C., and Tim M. Blackburn. "The Rise of Invasive Species Denialism." *Trends in Ecology & Evolution* 32 (2017): 3–6.

Rust, Nicola A., Katherine M. Whitehouse-Tedd, and Douglas C. Macmillan. "Perceived Efficacy of Livestock-Guarding Dogs in South Africa: Implications for Cheetah Conservation." *Wildlife Society Bulletin* 37 (2013): 690–697.

Saul, Wolf-Christian, Helen E. Ro, Olaf Booy, Lucilla Carnevali, Hsuan-Ju Chen, et al. "Assessing Patterns in Introduction Pathways of Alien Species by Linking Major Invasion Data Bases." *Journal of Applied Ecology* 54 (2017): 657–669.

Saunders, Jessica, Layla Parast, Susan H. Babey, and Jeremy V. Miles. "Exploring the Differences between Pet and Non-Pet Owners: Implications for Human Animal Interaction Research and Policy." *PLOS ONE* 12 (2017): e0179494.

Scheele, Ben C., Frank Pasmans, Lee F. Skerratt, Lee Berger, An Martel, et al. "Amphibian Fungal Panzootic Causes Catastrophic and Ongoing Loss of Biodiversity." *Science* 363 (2019): 1459–1463.

Scott, J. Michael, Sheila Conant, and Charles van Riper III, eds. *Evolution, Ecology, Conservation, and Management of Hawaiian Birds: A Vanishing Avifauna.* Studies in Avian Biology 22. Chicago: Cooper Ornithological Society, 2001.

Seeterama, Nadia A., Victor Engel, and Pallab Mozumder. "Implications of a Valuation Study for Ecological and Social Indicators Associated with Everglades Restoration." *Science of the Total Environment* 627 (2018): 792–801.

Shapiro, Karen, Elizabeth VanWormer, Andrea Packham, Erin Dodd, Patricia A. Conrad, et al. "Type X Strains of *Toxoplasma gondii* Are Virulent for Southern Sea Otters (*Enhydra lutris nereis*) and Present in Felids from

Nearby Watersheds." *Proceedings of the Royal Society B* 286 (2019): https://doi.org/10.1098/rspb.2019.1334.

Shuttlewood, Cameron Z., Phillip J. Greenwell, and V. Tamara Montrose. "Pet Ownership, Attitude toward Pets, and Support for Wildlife Management Strategies." *Human Dimensions of Wildlife* 21 (2016): 180–188.

Simons, Lucas. *Changing the Food Game.* London: Routledge, 2015.

Skoglund, Pontus, Erik Ersmark, Eleftheria Palkopoulou, and Love Dalén. "Ancient Wolf Genome Reveals an Early Divergence of Domestic Dog Ancestors and Admixture into High-Latitude Breeds." *Current Biology* 25 (2015): 1515–1519.

Smil, Vaclav. "Harvesting the Biosphere: The Human Impact." *Population and Development Review* 37 (2011): 613–636.

Smith, Kristine M., Carlos Zambrana-Torrelio, Allison White, Marianne Asmussen, Catherine Machalaba, et al. "Summarizing US Wildlife Trade with an Eye toward Assessing the Risk of Infectious Disease Introduction." *EcoHealth* 14 (2017): 29–39.

Sneader, Walter. *Drug Discovery: A History.* Hoboken, NJ: John Wiley and Sons, 2005.

Spitzen-van der Sluijs, Annemarieke, Frank Spikmans, Wilbert Bosman, Mamix de Zeeuw, Tom van der Meij, et al. "Rapid Enigmatic Decline Drives the Fire Salamander (*Salamandra salamandra*) to the Edge of Extinction in the Netherlands." *Amphibia-Reptilia* 34 (2013): 233–239.

Stoeckel, Luke E., Lori S. Palley, Randy L. Gollub, Steven M. Niemi, and Anne Eden Evins. "Patterns of Brain Activation When Mothers View Their Own Child and Dog: An fMRI Study." *PLOS ONE* 9 (2014): e107205.

Stoll-Kleemann, Susan, and Tim O'Riordan. "The Sustainability Challenges." *Environment* 57 (2015): 34–48.

Stork, Nigel E. "How Many Species of Insects and Other Terrestrial Arthropods Are There on Earth?" *Annual Review of Entomology* 63 (2018): 31–45.

Stringham, Oliver C., and Julie L. Lockwood. "Pet Problems: Biological and Economic Factors That Influence the Release of Alien Reptiles and Amphibians by Pet Owners." *Journal of Applied Ecology* 55 (2018): 2632–2640.

Sydeman, William J., Sarah Ann Thompson, Tycho Anker-Nilssen, Mayumi Arimitsu, Ashley Bennison, et al. "Best Practices for Assessing Forage Fish Fisheries–Seabird Resource Competition." *Fisheries Research* 194 (2017) 209–221.

Tejeda, Victoria Bogdan. "Science and Sleuthing: Improving CITES Enforcement through Innovations in Wildlife Forensic Technology." *Environmental Law Reporter* 47 (2017): 10580–10590.

Tomita, Andrew, Alain M. Vandormael, Diego Cuadros, Enrico Di Minin, Vuokko Heikinheimo, et al. "Green Environment and Incident Depression in South Africa: A Geospatial Analysis and Mental Health Implications in a Resource-Limited Setting." *Lancet Planet Health* 1 (July 2017): 152–162.

Tompkins, Daniel M., Scott Carver, Menna E. Jones, Martin Krkosek, and Lee F. Skerratt. "Emerging Infectious Diseases of Wildlife: A Critical Perspective." *Trends in Parasitology* 31 (2015): 149–159.

Twardek, William M., Kathryn S. Peiman, Austin J. Gallagher, and Steven J. Cooke. "Fido, Fluffy, and Wildlife Conservation: The Environmental Consequences of Domesticated Animals." *Environmental Review* 25 (2017): 381–395.

Ulrich, Roger S. "Biophilia, Biophobia, and Natural Landscapes." In *The Biophilia Hypothesis*, edited by Stephen R. Kellert and Edward O. Wilson, 73–137. Washington, DC: Island Press, 1993.

United Nations. *The World's Cities in 2016: Data Booklet.* Geneva: United Nations, Department of Economic and Social Affairs, 2016, http://www.un.org/en/development/desa/population/publications/pdf/urbanization/the_worlds_cities_in_2016_data_booklet.pdf.

United Nations. *World's Population Increasingly Urban with More Than Half Living in Urban Areas.* Geneva: United Nations, Department of Economic and Social Affairs, 2014, http://www.un.org/en/development/desa/news/population/world-urbanization-prospects-2014.html.

Vale, Robert, and Brenda Vale. *Time to Eat the Dog: The Real Guide to Sustainable Living.* London: Thames and Hudson, 2009.

Vance, Erik. "The Axolotl Paradox." *Nature* 551 (2017): 286–289.

Vianaa, Mafalda, Sarah Cleaveland, Jason Matthiopoulos, Jo Halliday, Craig Packer, et al. "Dynamics of a Morbillivirus at the Domestic–Wildlife Interface: Canine Distemper Virus in Domestic Dogs and Lions." *PNAS* 112 (2015): 1464–1469.

Voss, S. Randal, M. Ryan Woodcock, and Luis Zambrano. "A Tale of Two Axolotls." *BioScience* 65 (2015): 1134–1140.

Waldron, Anthony, Daniel C. Miller, Dave Redding, Arne Mooers, Tyler S.

Kuhn, et al. "Reductions in Global Biodiversity Loss Predicted from Conservation Spending." *Nature* 551 (2017): 364–367.

Waldron, Anthony, Arne O. Mooers, Daniel C. Miller, Nate Nibbelink, David Redding, et al. "Targeting Global Conservation Funding to Limit Immediate Biodiversity Declines." *PNAS* 110 (2013): 12144–12148.

Wallach, Arian D., Marc Bekoff, Chelsea Batavia, Michael Paul Nelson, and Daniel Ramp. "Summoning Compassion to Address the Challenges of Conservation." *Conservation Biology* 32 (2018): 1255–1265.

Wang, Sifeng, Yin Ho, and L. M. Chu. "Diet and Feeding Behavior of the Critically Endangered Yellow-Crested Cockatoo (*Cacatua sulphurea*) in a Nonnative Urban Environment." *Wilson Journal of Ornithology* 130 (2018): 746–754.

Warwick, Clifford, Mike Jessop, Phillip Arena, A. Pliny, Emma Nicholas, et al. "Future of Keeping Pet Reptiles and Amphibians: Animal Welfare and Public Health Perspective." *Veterinary Record* (2017): https://doi.org/10.1136/vr.j4640.

Wasser, Samuel K., Heath Smith, Lindsay Madden, Nathaniel Marks, and Carly Vynne. "Scent-Matching Dogs Determine Number of Unique Individuals from Scat." *Journal of Wildlife Management* 73 (2009): 1233–1240.

Watson, James E. M., Oscar Venter, Jasmine Lee, Kendall R. Jones, John G. Robinson, et al. "Protect the Last of the Wild." *Nature* 563 (2018): 27–30.

Weise, Florian J., Varsha Vijay, Andrew P. Jacobson, Rebecca F. Schoonover, Rosemary J. Groom, et al. "The Distribution and Numbers of Cheetah (*Acinonyx jubatus*) in Southern Africa." *PeerJ* 5 (2017): https://doi.org/10.7717/peerj.4096.

Weiss, Emily, Shannon Gramann, C. Victor Spain, and Margaret Slater. "Goodbye to a Good Friend: An Exploration of the Re-Homing of Cats and Dogs in the U.S." *Open Journal of Animal Sciences* 5 (2015): 435–456.

Williams, Kathryn J. H., Michael A. Weston, Stacey Henry, and Grainne S. Maguire. "Birds and Beaches, Dogs and Leashes: Dog Owners' Sense of Obligation to Leash Dogs on Beaches in Victoria, Australia." *Human Dimensions of Wildlife* 14 (2009): 89–101.

Wilson, Edward O. *Biophilia*. Cambridge, MA: Harvard University Press, 1984.

Wilson, Edward O. "Biophilia and the Conservation Ethic." In *The Biophilia*

Hypothesis, edited by Stephen R. Kellert and Edward O. Wilson, 31–41. Washington, DC: Island Press, 1993.

Wilson, Edward O. *Naturalist,* 2nd ed. Washington, DC: Island Press, 2006.

Wodzicki, Kazimierz, and Shelley Wright. "Introduced Birds and Mammals in New Zealand and Their Effect on the Environment." *Tuatara* 7 (1984): 78–102.

Woinarski, John C. Z., Andrew A. Burbidge, and Peter L. Harrison. "Ongoing Unraveling of a Continental Fauna: Decline and Extinction of Australian Mammals since European Settlement." *PNAS* 112 (2015): 4531–4540.

World Wildlife Fund (WWF). *Living Planet Report—2018: Aiming Higher.* Gland, Switzerland: WWF, 2018.

Worm, Boris, Edward B. Barbier, Nicola Beaumont, Emmett Duffy, Carl Folke, et al. "Impacts of Biodiversity Loss on Ocean Ecosystem Services." *Science* 314 (2006): 787–790.

Worm, Boris, and Trevor A. Branch. "The Future of Fish." *Trends in Ecology and Evolution* 27 (2012): 594–599.

Worm, Boris, Ray Hilborn, Julia K. Baum, Trevor A. Branch, Jeremy S. Collie, et al. "Rebuilding Global Fisheries." *Science* 325 (2009): 578–585.

Wright, Timothy F., Catherine A. Toft, Ernesto Enkerlin-Hoeflich, Jaime Gonzalez-Elizondo, Mariana Albornoz, et al. "Nest Poaching in Neotropical Parrots." *Conservation Biology* 15 (2001): 710–720.

Yap, Tiffany A., Michelle S. Koo, Richard F. Ambrose, David B. Wake, and Vance T. Vredenburg. "Averting a North American Biodiversity Crisis: A Newly Described Pathogen Poses a Major Threat to Salamanders via Trade." *Science* 349 (2015): 481–482.

Index

Island Press | Board of Directors

Pamela Murphy
(Chair)

Rob Griffen
(Vice Chair)
Managing Director,
Hillbrook Capital

Deborah Wiley
(Secretary and Treasurer)
Chair, Wiley Foundation, Inc.

Decker Anstrom
Board of Directors,
Discovery Communications

Terry Gamble Boyer
Author

Margot Ernst

Alison Greenberg

Marsha Maytum
Principal,
Leddy Maytum Stacy Architects

David Miller
President,
Island Press

Alison Sant
Cofounder and Partner,
Studio for Urban Projects

Ron Sims
Former Deputy Secretary,
US Department of Housing
and Urban Development

Sandra E. Taylor
CEO,
Sustainable Business
International LLC

Anthony A. Williams
CEO and Executive Director,
Federal City Council

Sally Yozell
Senior Fellow and Director
of Environmental Security,
Stimson Center